CW01511510

The Italians creating our Italy

Richard Lonsdale

Stamfordham

First published in the United Kingdom in 2024

by Stamfordham.

ISBN: 978-1-0687676-0-9

Stamfordham

For Jackie, who taught me how to live.

Front cover images

Giovanni Maria Ragazzi
& Tatyana Tokar

Elena Gambino &
Fabrizio Lisciandrello

Maria Giovanna Cimino

Nadia Finelli

Andrea Favale

Giuseppe Vicari

Anna Finelli

Pasquale Sorrentino

Stefania Martinato

Lorenzo Scandellari

Contents

Acknowledgements

This book only exists because Jackie, and I, have a shared love of Italy. For her encouragement, support and indulgence, I am extremely grateful.

The following Italian friends have provided invaluable advice and companionship, in support of this project: Anna Tagliapietra, Roberto Manfren, Francesco D'Urso, Claudio Manucci, Fabio Dente, Debora Polito, Alfonso Mollo and Silvia Capelli. *Grazie mille, amici.*

I'm especially grateful to Jane Edwards and Jackie Lonsdale, for proofreading the manuscript.

Finally, I owe a huge debt to the individuals who are the heart and soul of this book. The next three pages provide details for each establishment featured, including the dates of the interviews and the names of the interviewees. This book is their story, not mine. They gave their time, they shared their thoughts and experiences, and it was a privilege to meet every one of them.

To these amazing people - thank you!

Richard Lonsdale
September 2024

Establishments

Map of locations

Introduction

Why are holidaymakers drawn to Italy, and why do so many return year after year?

Undoubtedly, Italy's cultural heritage is a major factor. Artistic treasures, beautiful buildings and ancient city centres attract people from across the world. The warm climate and the spectacular scenery provide more reasons to visit. Last, but not least, visitors know that they will enjoy the wonderful food, Italian wines, and Italian coffee.

Once we are in Italy, much of our enjoyment comes from the services we receive: in hotels, bars, restaurants and shops. Recalling a holiday, these establishments often feature prominently in our memories. The country we recall, our Italy, is shaped by the owners and managers of these businesses. Who are they? Where do these people come from, that have created *our Italy*?

I have travelled across the country, meeting some of these owners and managers, and recording their stories. By telling their stories here, I hope to give you a deeper understanding of this beautiful country.

However, I must begin with a confession.

I did not travel across Italy, meeting these people, so that I could write this book. I chose to write this book because it provided me with an excuse to travel across Italy, and meet these people.

Having a project like this has made it much easier for me to justify all the time I spend in Italy. When discussing my travel plans for the year ahead, I know what listeners are thinking, even if they are too polite to say it out loud: "Why are you always going to Italy? Surely nobody needs this many holidays, all in the same country?" By explaining that this travel is to enable the research for a book I am writing, I hopefully stop them viewing me as an unbalanced eccentric.

Moreover, once in Italy, being an author with a mission makes me more interesting to Italians than the average tourist. It's easier to engage with the local people, and to learn about them.

If you ask a busy restaurant owner or hotel manager if they have time for a chat, then they will look at you as if you have just arrived in a spacecraft from an alien world. However, if you explain that you'd like to publish their story in a book then, more often than not, they will find the time, somehow, to sit down and talk to you. And let me assure you that they are well worth talking to. These people are not ordinary Italians. They are *extraordinary* Italians, brimming with passion and energy, who devote long hours to doing something they love.

For centuries, Italy has provided a welcome to foreign travellers as a core part of its identity. Italians who cater for tourists are respected, and hospitality is a noble profession. A single statistic demonstrates this clearly: 360 of Italy's senior schools are *scuole alberghiere*, meaning they specialise in training students for hotel and restaurant work. It's unthinkable that a senior school in the UK might focus predominantly upon educating children in hospitality services.

To understand a country, you must understand its people. This book provides you with an opportunity to get under the skin of Italy, to see the country from the inside, from the perspective of Italians who play a key role in projecting Italy to the world. You will meet 30 business owners and managers, from across the country. You will learn what challenges they have faced, their hopes and dreams, and how they came to be doing what they do.

Their stories are often surprising. For example, in the first chapter you learn how the collapse of the Soviet Union, the downfall of Colonel Gaddafi, and the love between two people born on opposite sides of the world, together created a special little restaurant in Ferrara. Packed with passion, pain and drama, this tale delivers the happy ending we expect from a Hollywood script. But it really happened.

In the second chapter, you learn about two people who helped to re-establish a small industry that had disappeared for 180 years. The revival of this lost craft has brought pleasure to people worldwide, and changed shop windows across an entire city.

Every chapter brings you a person whose story is worth hearing. Every chapter will tell you something about Italy that you didn't know before.

In addition to learning their stories, you may choose to visit establishments mentioned in the book on your next trip to Italy. You can share in the happy ending of chapter one, by dining at that restaurant in Ferrara. If you happen to meet these people, after reading their story, then this adds a new dimension to your holiday, not experienced by the average tourist.

A question I am often asked is how I chose which establishments to feature in the book. Some places were recommended to me by Italian friends, some are places I visited on a previous holiday, and some I came across by searching on the internet for an interesting shop or restaurant. They are all places where I like what they offer to their customers, places I would happily recommend to a friend planning a holiday.

In some ways, this book is a travel guide. Like any other travel guide, it provides suggestions for places to visit.

Moreover, by visiting 20 different locations across the country, it might provide you with ideas for future trips to Italy, introducing new places that you would enjoy.

However, unlike a typical travel guide that focuses upon places, here we focus upon *people*. This is a more personal portrait of Italy.   You will see the country with a new perspective, through the eyes of Italians who devote their lives to welcoming visitors. Hopefully, it enables you to understand where they come from, and why they do what they do.

1 From Russia with love

It's late September. I am basking in the evening sunshine at Bologna airport's bus station, having just arrived from the UK. I reflect on how a few degrees of extra warmth can lift my mood significantly.

I have booked a hotel in the centre of Ferrara, planning to spend a few days here. A friend advised me to take a bus direct from the airport to Ferrara, rather than the more circuitous train journey via the centre of Bologna. However, the web site for this bus service stated that I should buy a ticket at least two days in advance, otherwise the bus might not turn up! Dutifully, I pre-booked my seat online.

Various buses arrive, but none claims to be heading for Ferrara. It's now getting close to the scheduled departure time, and I'm a little anxious. Then I notice a man in a suit, carrying a yellow sign, walking off to the far end of the bus station. Chasing after him, I manage to read the sign which is asking for *passengers to Ferrara*. It turns out that this gentleman is a taxi driver, sent to replace the bus to Ferrara because only four people have booked seats in advance.

Two of these four people don't turn up, which is good news for two young Italian girls who also want to take this "bus", but haven't pre-booked tickets. So, a few minutes behind schedule, we depart for Ferrara in a black Mercedes.

It seems the taxi driver is keen not to be late for his dinner. He zooms along the autostrada much faster than any bus - braking, swerving and weaving as required to overtake all slower vehicles. I'm confident that we will arrive either early or never.

To take my mind off this risk, that is beyond my control - the death rate on Italian roads is almost twice that in the UK - I start chatting to my neighbour in the car. He turns out to be a retired journalist and newspaper editor from Belgium, and he is happy to talk. Realising I am English, he immediately tells me that he used to work alongside Boris Johnson in Brussels.

"Boris was very helpful. He would ask European officials the questions that I wanted to ask, but I was afraid they sounded dumb. However, I couldn't believe the blatant lies he put into his reports. He just made it all up!"

I take a closer look at my companion. He has a round, friendly face with spectacles. In the half light, it's difficult to tell whether his hair is fair or grey. Although not obese, his corpulence is consistent with his homeland's reputation for beer and chocolate.

I ask what brings him to Ferrara. He is visiting his widowed Italian daughter-in-law and her three sons, who live near the city. Every year, he comes here for a few weeks to help her out. Tragically his son, the father of the boys, died in a motorcycle accident five years ago.

He asks why I am here, and I explain that it is primarily for a holiday but I am also doing research for a book. "Do you know any interesting restaurants or bars in Ferrara?" I ask.

"We don't eat out often, but we did go to a nice restaurant last year. I can't remember the name of it though."

Now we are arriving in the centre of Ferrara. The driver stops to turf us all out, near the famous castle. As bags are unloaded, the friendly Belgian comes over to speak to me.

"I messaged my daughter-in-law, and she gave me the name of that restaurant. It is *I Piaceri di Lucrezia*. I hope you have a nice time in Ferrara."

I thank him, we say goodbye and go our separate ways.

This is my first visit to Ferrara, but it won't be the last. It's a nice place. Like many small Italian cities, the centre is relatively free of traffic and prides itself on being bicycle-friendly. My hotel provides bicycles to guests during their stay, making it easy to explore the town.

The centre is well preserved, with many streets and buildings retaining their character from medieval times. During the Renaissance, the city expanded significantly to the north and west, as part of an ambitious plan by the rulers. These "newer" areas are recognisable today, because of their wide streets and grand palazzos. The old city, comprising both medieval and Renaissance areas, is surrounded by substantial perimeter walls, designed to defend inhabitants against external aggressors. You can now cycle most of the way around the top of these city walls, which are surprisingly wide.

During the Renaissance, the cities and kingdoms of northern Italy, the wealthiest region in Europe, were in an almost perpetual state of war with each other. They also competed in art, music, literature and architecture - not just militarily. Without such diversity and competition, across this patchwork of principalities in northern Italy, perhaps that great cultural revolution of the 14th and 15th centuries would not have happened.

For 350 years, Ferrara was ruled by the Este family. Medieval and Renaissance princes governed through the threat of violence. They provided order and stability, organised communal defence against external aggressors and, in return, ruthlessly exploited their own citizens.

Sometimes rulers would overstep the mark, perhaps taxing too heavily, and the citizens rebelled. One such rebellion so frightened the Este rulers that they constructed a grand castle, with a wide moat, which dominates the city centre to this day. It is ironic that this castle, constructed to protect the rulers from their own citizens, is more impressive and imposing than the city walls designed to protect the whole community.

On my first evening in Ferrara, I head straight to the restaurant recommended by the friendly Belgian: I Piaceri di Lucrezia. Located in a quiet street in the medieval quarter, it's a 15-minute walk from the main piazza and cathedral in the city centre. The hostess greets me with a warm smile, but she has bad news. They are full tonight. I book a table for another evening.

Returning two days later, I am pleasantly surprised to be recognised and shown straight to my table, near the back. I am the first diner to arrive. In the corner, on the other side of the room, I notice the chef preparing his kitchen. Seeing me, he wanders over and asks if I have any questions about the menu. A large middle-aged man, with short dark hair, beard and moustache, he is wearing a comically tall chef's hat.

It soon becomes clear that the chef is happy to stay and chat, and he is in no hurry to return to preparing the kitchen. With cheerful enthusiasm, he talks about the menu and asks me how I am today. He extracts a toy mouse from inside his hat, knowing that this always raises a smile.

The whole experience is similar to being greeted by an excited puppy, jumping up repeatedly, vigorously wagging its tail, and determined that you will become its friend. For chef Giovanni, it's absolutely vital that every customer enjoys their time in the restaurant. This is to be achieved by providing good food, good wine and, above all, good company. The amuse-bouche, in I Piaceri di Lucrezia, is a large serving of bonhomie.

After the meal, I talk to the hostess, Tatyana. She consults

Giovanni, and we agree that I will return at noon the following day, to hear their story.

The next day, I wait outside the restaurant, under a clear blue sky. Giovanni and Tatyana arrive in their van. They raise the shutters, unlock the restaurant and usher me inside. The restaurant is not open at lunchtime, only in the evening. Giovanni explains that he teaches at school during the day, for about 18 hours per week, in addition to his role at their restaurant. Tatyana, Giovanni's wife, owns and manages the restaurant business.

The tables are already set out for that night's dinner, but they clear one and we sit down. A bottle of prosecco appears and I am offered a glass. I decline, but, after we've been talking a while, I get caught up in the emotion of their story and decide that I do need a drink after all.

Tatyana was born near Khabarovsk in south east Russia, about 500 miles north of Vladivostok, by the Chinese border. Aged two, her family moved across the Soviet Union to Sumy in Ukraine, seeking a milder climate to improve the health of Tatyana's sick brother.

The collapse of the Soviet Union in 1991 brought turbulent times, and many people struggled to make ends meet. By 1998, Tatyana was in a critical situation. She found herself a single parent, in poverty, with a seven-year-old daughter. A friend of Tatyana's had already moved to Bologna, and found work there. Although she spoke no Italian, Tatyana decided to take the plunge and join this friend in Italy, leaving her young daughter in the care of her parents. Take a moment to imagine the angst, the fear and the courage, involved in this life-changing decision.

Tatyana arrived in Italy, without a work visa. However, she managed to find an unofficial job, as a maid in a Bologna hotel.

Tatyana was now living in a foreign land, with no family and few friends, and struggling to learn a new language. Inevitably, her mind was still in Ukraine, thinking about her family and when she might see her daughter again. At least now she could send money home, to ease their situation.

Then an unwelcome complication intruded upon her daily routine. She would arrive at the hotel, ready to start work at 8am every morning. However, an Italian man working on the reception desk, whose shift finished at 8am, would often wander over and start talking to her. This was irritating on several fronts. She didn't have time to talk. She wanted to start work! Also, still struggling with the language, Tatyana didn't understand much of what he was saying. Most worrying of all was that the hotel manager noticed what was happening, and he was not pleased. Tatyana really could not afford to lose this job.

The Italian on the reception desk was our friend Giovanni, of course.

Born in Ferrara, Giovanni is the oldest of three children, and both his parents were teachers. When Giovanni was ten, the family moved out of the city into the countryside. From the age of 14, he attended a Hotel School (*scuola alberghiera*) in Ferrara, requiring a daily commute in his parents' car. This school focused on the skills required in the hotel and restaurant trades. There are approximately 360 such Hotel Schools in Italy, reflecting the elevated status of the hospitality business for Italians, who take pride in looking after tourists.

"I was a volcano," is how Giovanni describes his younger self. By this, he means that he had far too much energy. He loved caving and parachuting, and became a lifeguard at the seaside. At school, Giovanni earned two qualifications in hospitality, that would later prove vital in shaping the rest of his life: a *hotel receptionist* certificate and a *restaurant chef* certificate. After leaving school, he spent a year in the Carabinieri, to fulfil his national service obligation. Compulsory national service in Italy ended only in 2005.

Then Giovanni took stock, and started to think about a career. He found work, as the night shift receptionist at a hotel in Bologna. Living in Ferrara, this required a daily commute by train, but at least the hotel was near the station.

One day, as his shift ended at 8am, Giovanni noticed a very pretty girl arriving to start her shift cleaning rooms. After a few days, he plucked up the courage to start chatting to her, although she didn't seem quite so keen to talk to him. In these few snatched conversations, Giovanni learnt a little of Tatyana's background, including her daughter and parents in Ukraine.

Giovanni already had experience of chatting up girls, especially when he was a lifeguard at the beach. But this woman was different. The girls on the beach were interested in a good night out, drinking and smoking. Contrasting this with Tatyana's experience, these beach girls now appeared immature and shallow. Although Tatyana was only one year older than Giovanni, he recalled that "she was a woman, and I was a boy."

Then the hotel manager intervened. He took Giovanni to one side, and told him in no uncertain terms that he had to stop distracting the maid from Ukraine while she was trying to work, or else he would lose his job. Giovanni's response was to arrive several hours early for his shift, so that he could meet Tatyana after she had finished work. They started to spend more time together. If you ever meet Giovanni, then you will understand why Tatyana found it difficult to say "no" when he asked her out.

The first present Giovanni bought her was Nivea hand

cream, to deal with the consequences of her work. Within a week of getting to know Tatyana, Giovanni had introduced her to his parents, making it clear that he was serious about this girl. Giovanni's parents are very traditional, and his mother wanted nothing but the best for him, ideally a princess. Her only experience of girls from the old Soviet Union, in Italy, was as prostitutes. She struggled to understand how a girl from Ukraine could be good enough for her boy.

Five months later, in August 1999, Giovanni proposed to Tatyana. That same month, the government learnt of her situation and she was forced to leave the country. She travelled back to Ukraine, and re-joined her family.

Giovanni knew exactly where he wanted to take his life, but it was all falling apart. The woman of his dreams was now more than 2,000 km away in a foreign land, unable to return to Italy. He couldn't even go to see her, because he didn't have a passport. But "volcano" Giovanni was never going to give up on his dream.

The first task was to get himself a passport. Then, in September, he flew to Ukraine to see Tatyana, and stay with the family: her daughter, parents, and two brothers. They reaffirmed their plan to marry. The next problem was that Giovanni required evidence that he wasn't already married, in order to wed legally in Ukraine. This is when Giovanni's parents put any private doubts to one side, and pulled out all the stops for their boy. They obtained official documentation, in Italian of course, confirming that Giovanni was unmarried. Then they travelled to the Ukrainian embassy in Rome, to get these documents translated and sent to Ukraine as evidence for the authorities in Sumy. The documents arrived on 12th November. Within 18 hours, Tatyana had organised their wedding and they married on 13th November. On 14th November, amidst floods of tears, Giovanni boarded a plane and flew back to Italy!

His employer, at the hotel in Bologna, was not happy with him disappearing for two months. However, they let him return to his old role as a receptionist. Now Giovanni began perhaps the biggest battle of all, taking on the bureaucracy of the Italian state. Nobody does red tape better than the Italians.

Meanwhile, all was not well in Ukraine. ·Local xenophobic thugs, hearing about Tatyana's marriage to an Italian, kidnapped and assaulted her in December 1999. They caused significant injuries, including a broken cheek bone, and Tatyana spent a week in hospital, recovering.

By March 2000, Giovanni had finally obtained authorisation to bring his new family to Italy. He flew to Ukraine, for a joyous reunion. When he returned to Italy, he was accompanied by Tatyana, her nine-year-old daughter Lena and, of course, the family cat. By this time Giovanni was an expert on bureaucracy and paperwork, so transporting the cat to a different country was no challenge at all.

The family settled down in a rented apartment in Ferrara, and Tatyana found work at the local NATO base, as a maid and sous-chef. In 2003, a general at the NATO base mentioned to Tatyana that they really needed a coffee bar. Tatyana suggested that she and her husband would be happy to run this coffee bar, if the base could provide suitable premises. Her offer was accepted. Giovanni gave up his job as hotel receptionist, and the couple went into business together, running the new coffee bar at the NATO base.

Although in his thirties, Giovanni still had too much energy! In 2006, he had the opportunity to take on additional work as a supply teacher. He has been teaching ever since, in addition to helping run a hospitality business with his wife.

In 2008, came another addition to family life. A second daughter, Giorgia Maria, was born.

Then, in 2011, the Arab Spring had a big impact on their lives. NATO involvement, in the civil war in Libya, brought a large number of additional military personnel to the base. The bars in Ferrara had never been so popular. The coffee bar at the NATO base was incredibly busy, and had to stay open all day, every day. Giovanni started cooking lots of food for the bar, but they were struggling to keep up with demand. Over an intense period of six months, business was so good that Tatyana and Giovanni managed to accumulate a nest egg. Although not a fortune, this was sufficient to enable them to start their own business outside the NATO base, if they so wished.

Giovanni's big passion had always been cooking. He could imagine nothing better than having his own restaurant, where he cooked wonderful food for appreciative customers, with Tatyana as the perfect partner. At last, here was an opportunity to fulfil his dream.

That summer, Giovanni attended master class training in Rome with the famous Italian chef Igles Corelli, who is from Ferrara. Igles gave him the recipe for his version of a traditional Ferrara pasta dish: *cappellacci di zucca*.

Meanwhile, Giovanni and Tatyana were searching Ferrara for a potential location for their new business. Lorenzo, Giovanni's younger brother, helped to run a boy scout group at a church in Ferrara. He was aware of premises, just 50m from this church, that were vacant and had an interesting history. For 100 years, this had been a famous gambling den, where people from across Emilia-Romagna would come to play games for money and drink the night away. From 1980 to 2010, it had a simpler life, as a bar without gambling. But in 2012, it had been vacant for two years.

Giovanni and Tatyana approached the owner, who agreed that they could rent the premises for their new business. Wary of overstretching themselves, they decided initially to just transfer the operation from the NATO base to Ferrara. In October 2012, *I Piaceri di Lucrezia* opened its doors as Ferrara's newest eatery.

The most obvious question to ask is "where did this name, meaning *Lucrezia's pleasure*, come from?" *Lucrezia* refers to the controversial Renaissance princess, and daughter of Pope Alexander VI, Lucrezia Borgia. Married three times, she spent her final 17 years in Ferrara with husband Alfonso I, ruler of the city. Both she and Alfonso were serial adulterers. Unsurprisingly, Giovanni's mother did not like the name he had chosen. She thought it unsavoury. Giovanni pointed out that, because the restaurant was not located in the busy heart of the city, where they could expect passing trade, it was necessary to have an interesting name to attract attention.

When talking about his restaurant, I notice that Giovanni keeps calling it a *bar*, using the English word "bar" rather than the Italian equivalent, *osteria*. Confused, I ask him whether they initially opened the business as a bar, and later converted it to be a restaurant.

"Oh no! We cannot call this a restaurant. Because we don't have five toilets, we don't meet the regulatory requirements for a restaurant. That's why we call it a bar."

"Can't you call it a trattoria, or an osteria?"

He looks thoughtful, then shakes his head. "No! You see, each of these has specific regulations, which we might not comply with. We call it a bar because there are no specific regulations for bars. For the same reason, you might see a dining establishment called a *polenteria*. There are rules for restaurants, trattorias and osterias, but *polenteria* is a newly invented word, aiming to describe a place that serves polenta. The government hasn't yet created lots of regulations governing such places."

Any Italian businessman will tell you that bureaucracy is the curse of Italy. The country only works because people find ways to avoid complicated regulations, for example by calling a restaurant a bar. Giovanni tells me about the mythical government department, UCAS: *Ufficio per Complicare gli Affari Semplici*, meaning *the office for complicating simple businesses*. This exists only in the imaginations of business owners, as a joke they share to relieve their frustration.

Initially, I Piaceri di Lucrezia catered primarily for students at the nearby architecture department of the University of Ferrara, providing drinks and sandwiches. However, as summer approached, they decided that this was the time to offer a more ambitious menu. In August, the traditional holiday season, it can seem like the whole of Italy has gone to the beach. Most restaurants in Ferrara would be closed in August 2013. So, where would all the foreign tourists eat? The answer, of course, is I Piaceri di Lucrezia.

As a result, that summer provided good business. More importantly, because of the internet, they established their reputation for the future. Favourable reviews on TripAdvisor etc. continued to attract customers, long after the end of the summer season. Ferrara dignitaries, including the president of the local chamber of commerce, began frequenting the restaurant.

In 2015, Giovanni cooked in front of a much larger audience, when he won the competitive Italian TV show for professional chefs: Cena di Mezzanotte. But it's pride in their family and their business that brings happiness to Giovanni & Tatyana. Older daughter Lena is now an aerospace engineer, working on the Leonardo Agusta helicopter. Younger daughter Giorgia, when not doing schoolwork, learns cooking from her parents and helps out at the restaurant.

In 2019, they created a covered garden at the rear. This significantly extended the season for outdoor dining, and helped their business to survive through the dark days of Covid.

Post-pandemic, life returned to a predictable daily routine. Giovanni teaches in the daytime, while Tatyana prepares the restaurant and cooks desserts. She is especially proud of her cheesecake recipe, perfected by trial and error over an extended period. Chef Igles Corelli, who visits the restaurant whenever he is back in his home town, is keen get his hands on this cheesecake recipe. He has offered Tatyana five of his own recipes in exchange, but she is still keeping it a secret.

Hopefully, one day you will have the opportunity to visit I Piaceri d Lucrezia in Ferrara, and try their signature dishes. I am confident you will have an enjoyable evening. And, while savouring *Cappellacci di Zucca alla moda di Corelli*, or Tatyana's cheesecake, just take a moment to think of the difficult road that's been travelled so that you can share in Lucrezia's pleasure.

2 Changing the faces of a city

Millions of words have been written about Venice, so many that the city itself has become a cliché. The majority of visitors have strong feelings, either loving it or hating it.

Those that dislike Venice talk about how it is packed with tourists, who outnumber residents and dominate the local economy. Most shops sell tourist trinkets, most jobs are in hospitality, and the city feels like a giant theme park. Moreover, the canals smell in summer and you cannot get a good meal without spending a fortune.

But anybody who takes time to explore, and gets to know the real Venice, can't help but succumb to its charms. Beauty is everywhere, in the buildings, the bridges and the shimmering canals. The city's alternative name, *La Serenissima*, is perfect. Away from tourist hotspots, like San Marco and Rialto, streets are tranquil.

This is a city without cars, bicycles, or even horses, enabling pedestrians to truly relax. The only wheels in Venice are tiny, supporting those extraordinary carts used by porters to carry goods along pavements and over bridges. This complete absence of traffic, combined with picturesque canals and beautiful buildings, makes this, for me, the most relaxing city on Earth.

There is no more pleasant way to get lost than by wandering through a maze of alleys in Venice. In the evening, after day trippers have left, Piazza San Marco becomes a magical place, where the grand cafés play live music for passers-by late into the night.

Because most people in Venice are on holiday, most people in Venice are happy. It is a feel-good city. I pity the cynics who cannot immerse themselves in the wonderful atmosphere of this place, perhaps because they feel it's beneath them. Next time you visit Venice, take time to watch the gondoliers gliding and guiding their clients. Just manoeuvring the gondola takes admirable skill, but you should also notice that they enjoy interacting with their passengers. This is a pleasant experience for all concerned, and that's true of most activities in *La Serenissima*.

If it were possible to measure the amount of enjoyment every person gets out of each day, then I think we would discover that Venice is the happiest city on earth.

It is very much a city of the world. Wander through Venice, and you hear dozens of languages. This is not just a modern phenomenon, since the city has been attracting international visitors for at least 800 years. Initially, as the primary trading hub linking the East with Europe, visitors came for business. On the Rialto, in the 13th century, you would find a unique range of exotic goods from across Asia, Africa and Europe. Spices, gems, dyes, ivory, feathers, textiles and much more were on offer, overloading the senses with exotic colours and smells. The Rialto was the most diverse and exciting marketplace in Europe. Later, as the city's pre-eminence in trade faded, it became better known as a centre for the arts and as a beautiful place to visit. Venice has been making its living from tourism for centuries.

Two things make Venice unique. Firstly, it is canals and not roads that permeate the city. People and goods move on water, or at a walking pace on pavements. Secondly, the city has hardly changed in the last 250 years. Most of the world's cities grew and transformed as a direct result of industrialisation, but the industrial revolution left Venice almost untouched. It is an oasis, preserving a tranquil, idealised vision of the past, for people to experience with modern comforts in the present.

My introduction to Venice came about 30 years ago, at the end of a walking holiday in the Dolomites. My friend and I had a few hours to spend sightseeing in the city, before our flight back to the UK. I was awestruck. I hadn't realised just how different it would be, from any place I'd previously experienced. For many, including me, this city is addictive, and I've lost count of how many times I have returned.

Much later, in the process of learning Italian online, I acquired Venetian friends who were born in the city but now live on the mainland. After telling them of my intention to write this book, they advised me to visit a shop call Ca' Macana, in Dorsoduro.

That is why, on this warm, sunny October morning, I am wandering through Venetian alleys, on my way to Ca' Macana. The shop sells Venetian masks, and also runs workshops for people who wish to learn how to make the masks themselves. As I enter the shop, I see a few customers browsing, a lady serving at the till, and a middle-aged man unpacking boxes. When he has finished unpacking, I approach this man and ask if he is the owner.

"Yes, I am the owner" he says, with a welcoming smile.

I explain that I am an author, doing research for my next book, and ask whether he might consider being interviewed so that I can hear his story. If he says "yes," then I plan to ask if we can set the date and time for an interview.

To my surprise, he says "yes of course, shall we do it now?"

"That would be great."

"Let's go to a café", he suggests.

Close by, across a bridge, is Campo San Barnaba where we

choose a café, sit outside and order two freshly squeezed orange juice (spremuta). Mario introduces himself, and starts telling me how he and his friend, Carlos, started their mask business 40 years earlier. What strikes me most about Mario is how relaxed he is, even though we have only just met. This is a man comfortable with himself and, I sense, the life he has led.

Mario was born and brought up in Genoa, and then studied urban planning at university in Venice. On this course, he met fellow student Carlos, taking the same examinations, who turned out to be from Argentina.

Carlos had left Argentina because he was in fear for his life! Between 1974 and 1983, the right-wing military junta conducted a dirty war against political dissidents and anybody associated with socialism, including students, journalists, artists, writers and trade unionists. This involved death squads kidnapping, torturing and killing the government's opponents, without trial. It is estimated that between 9,000 and 30,000 Argentinians disappeared, or were killed, during this dirty war. Carlos was a left-wing activist, and several of his friends had mysteriously disappeared. He decided to leave before he met the same fate.

As they got to know each other, Mario and Carlos discovered they had much in common. They both liked living in Venice, and neither of them wanted a career in urban planning! Indeed, since the urban plan for Venice is effectively to "preserve the city and change as little as possible", they would likely have had to leave town if they wished to find work in their university degree subject.

While students, they began looking into the history of Venice, in particular the wearing of masks. Venetians have worn masks since at least the 13th century. Historians speculate that masks might partly have been a response to the rigid class structure of the Venetian republic, enabling citizens to mingle anonymously without fear of censure.

Masks were used especially at the annual Carnevale celebrations, in February. The first Carnevale was held in 1162, to celebrate the Republic's victory in a local war. It became an annual event thereafter, a joyous celebration immediately before the privations of Lent. However, Venetians did not only wear masks at Carnevale. Mask wearing was permitted in specified periods, totalling up to six months of the year.

The Venetian Republic ended in 1797, when Napoleon took possession of the city, subsequently handing it over to the Austrian Empire. These new rulers banned the Carnevale and mask wearing, and both traditions disappeared for 180 years. Always fearful of revolt, the anonymity provided by mask wearing was perhaps perceived as a threat by the Austrian rulers.

In 1979 the Carnevale was revived, generating a renewed interest in Venetian masks. In the early 1980s, Mario and Carlos began experimenting in how to make masks and, once happy with their technique, they started selling them outdoors in the evening. They were still studying for their degrees, so this had to be a spare time activity. Mario recalls how, while selling at the Rialto or in Piazza San Marco, they would quickly gather their wares and run if the police appeared. They had no licence to trade on the streets.

While selling, out in the open, they were approached by the owners of local souvenir shops, asking if they could supply them with masks. Demand from these shops grew and grew. Clearly, tourists couldn't get enough of them. In many ways, a Venetian mask is an excellent souvenir. I remember, on one of my early visits to Venice, searching for gifts to take home to my two young daughters. The masks were perfect because they were inexpensive, attractive, a bit of fun and uniquely Venetian.

In the early 1980s, Mario and Carlos both got married. When Mario was still a student, in 1978, a group of friends from Genoa visited him. With them was a girl called Antonella, whom Mario didn't know, although he quickly decided that he would like to get to know her. Their relationship developed from there.

Carlos had first met Carolina in Argentina, where she attended the academy of fine arts and studied architecture. Carolina also left Argentina, to escape potential persecution, and initially went to Sweden. Later she came to Venice, where she reunited with Carlos.

Finishing their studies in 1984, Mario and Carlos decided that their future lay in the mask business. They continued selling on the streets, and to local souvenir merchants, but they really wanted premises for their own shop. Eventually they had some money saved and, on a corner next to Ponte San Barnaba, quite near the current Ca' Macana in Dorsoduro, they found an empty building to rent. However, this structure required a great deal of work to make it fit for the business. Initially, there wasn't even an electricity supply. Mario recalls how the two men, together with their pregnant wives, all worked by candlelight to get the shop ready. Ca' Macana opened for business in 1986.

I ask Mario for the origin of the name Ca' Macana. He explains how it is constructed from their names and their wives' names: CArlos, MArio, CArolina and ANtonella, with the final "AN" reversed to make it sound better. *Ca'* means *house* in the Venetian dialect.

As well as selling masks in their own shop, Mario and Carlos continued to supply other shops in Venice. They were pleasantly surprised to see their new business growing, slowly but surely. Their families also grew! Mario's son Davide and Carlos's daughter Tania were both born in 1986, an eventful year for the two couples. In 1988, Carlos's son Filippo arrived and, in 1991, Mario and his wife were blessed with a daughter Eloisa.

Throughout the 1990s, business was good. In addition to producing masks for other vendors, and selling through their own shop, they made masks for various films, including Eyes Wide Shut (1999). Carlos was fascinated by the potential in theatre and cinema. He wanted to be more involved in the design and production of props and scenery, for stage shows and movies. Mario, however, was more interested in the original, core mask business.

Eventually, they decided that splitting the business would be the best way to accommodate these differences. However, having established a good reputation for their brand, Ca' Macana, both partners wanted to retain this name. They devised a pragmatic solution: Carlos opened a new shop *Ca' Macana (Atelier)* across the city in Cannaregio, while Mario continued with *Ca' Macana (Original)* in Dorsoduro. Thus Ca' Macana became two separate enterprises, with a common name reflecting their shared origins. Carlos and Mario managed their separation amicably and, as a result, they remain good friends to this day.

Mario explains how, following the split, Carlos has taken on major projects in interesting areas. "Carlos worked on the Brazilian pavilion at this year's Biennale", he cites as an example. Having visited the Biennale yesterday, and enjoyed this particular exhibit, I am fascinated to discover that Mario's ex-partner played a key role. Brazilian artist Jonathas de Andrade commissioned Carlos to construct some amazing pieces for his exhibition, entitled *With the heart coming out of the mouth.* It features over-sized models of bits of the human body, inspired by idioms such as "in one ear and out the other" and "the eye of the storm". Visitors enter through a giant ear, and leave through another giant ear on the far side. In between, they encounter larger than life representations of other body parts, including a severed tongue, a single index finger, and an eyeball that sparkles, all constructed by Carlos and his team.

Mario has also taken his business in new directions. Around the time of the split, Mario and Antonella started running hands-on workshops to teach customers how to make Venetian masks. These have proved very popular.

Nowadays, Mario has stepped back from the business. His son Davide has taken over, as principal owner and manager of the Dorsoduro shop, although Mario still helps out in the background. Perhaps I am fortunate to find him in the shop today.

Sadly, our pleasant time in Campo San Barnaba is coming to an end. I have no more questions for Mario, so we shake hands and say our goodbyes. Wandering back through the alleys, towards my apartment, I can't help noticing just how many shop windows display masks. 50 years ago, there would have been none to see anywhere. It takes surprisingly few people to change the look of a city.

3 Crossing the lagoon

We are renting an apartment, in the Castello district of Venice, for ten days. It is on the top floor of an old palazzo, and there is no lift so we get plenty of exercise. On the Rio de San Severo canal, our neighbourhood is extremely quiet, but Campo Santa Maria Formosa provides lively bars and restaurants within easy reach. After one week, my wife will return to the UK – Jackie has to work – but I will stay on to visit the Biennale.

Near our apartment is a restaurant, with good online reviews, so we decide to dine there one evening. We turn up at 7.30pm on Monday, without a reservation, but the restaurant is full. I ask whether we can book a table for later in the week but the cheerful lady, who is clearly in charge, informs me that they don't take reservations! They are closed on Tuesday, so we arrive at 6.30pm, opening time, on Wednesday evening, determined to get a table. This time we are successful.

Osteria Alla Staffa is small, with seating for about 20 people inside and 6 outside. Their reputation is such that they have no trouble filling the restaurant every evening, which is why they don't take bookings. Why risk having an empty table from a no-show?

Our cheerful lady provides cheerful service, and she is very efficient. Moreover, the food is lovely. Jackie points out that their kitchen, at the end of the dining area, is tiny. The chef must be very organised.

As we leave, I ask the cheerful lady if I might speak to the owner. She says that he normally only attends at lunchtime. The next day I turn up, as they are opening for lunch, and see a tall man inside. He introduces himself as Sebastiano, the owner, and he is happy to tell me his story. We arrange to meet, one morning early next week.

The day before I am due to meet Sebastiano, the weather is glorious. There is a perfectly clear blue sky, with no clouds and no wind. On this pleasantly warm October day, my plan is to go for a bike ride. I take the vaporetto across the lagoon to the Lido di Venezia, and hire a bicycle for the day.

Although only a few hundred metres from Venice proper, across a short stretch of water, the Lido is another world. This is an affluent beach resort. Clean, modern buildings line the wide roads, where cars proceed sedately. Whilst Venice feels almost claustrophobic, with narrow alleys and tall buildings, the Lido welcomes you with big skies and open spaces.

I seek advice at the bicycle rental shop on where to cycle. The friendly young man, having supplied my bicycle, also gives me a map and explains how I can use ferries to extend today's ride. The Venetian lagoon is protected from the Adriatic by two long, thin islands: the Lido and Pellestrina. Here, separated from Venice by a short stretch of water, we are near the north end of the Lido. At the south end of the Lido, a car ferry shuttles back and forth, taking people and vehicles to and from the north end of Pellestrina. Moreover, near the far (south) end of Pellestrina, is another ferry that takes you to the small town of Chioggia, on the mainland. Depending upon how energetic I feel, I could potentially cycle to Chioggia and back in the day.

After thanking the young man, I head south along the main road on the west side of the Lido. The weather is absolutely perfect, with no clouds and no wind. The surface of the lagoon forms a blue mirror, sat beneath a few inches of wispy mist.

An uneventful, pleasant ride brings me to Alberoni Rocchetta where, after a short wait, I catch the car ferry to Pellestrina. There is one other cyclist on the ferry, clearly a local and not a tourist. After we disembark, I follow him down the road. Making a big effort, I catch him and ask if there is a café en route. He says "yes", and tells me that he will point out when we get there. Ten minutes later, we reach the café and I stop for a coffee, while he continues. Sadly, I am disappointed by this café, having been spoiled in Venice. Here, there are no other customers to watch, no pastries and the environment is quite basic.

Continuing my ride, to the other end of Pellestrina, I start to get a feel for the place. It seems to be a quiet backwater, with few sources of employment. Some make a living from growing food: market gardening. Along the shoreline, occasional boats and nets, plus huts sat on stilts in the lagoon, all demonstrate that fishing is important here. Then I come across a boatyard, where vaporetti (water buses) from Venice are maintained and repaired.

Just off shore, there is also a strange metal ship, rectangular rather than streamlined, with a central gap running full length from bow to stern. It occurs to me that this may have been used to help construct the MOSE flood defence barriers. MOSE stands for MOdulo Sperimentale Elettromeccanico, meaning Experimental Electromechanical Module, and aptly alludes to Moses parting the Red Sea.

Following the 1966 great flood in Venice, much thought went into how the city might be protected. Every year, mostly in autumn and winter, high tides and storms produce the acqua alta, flooding parts of the city. At high tide, water from the Adriatic enters the lagoon through just three narrow passages: north of the Lido; between the Lido and Pellestrina; and south of Pellestrina. By building movable barriers on the sea bed at these inlets, and raising them only at exceptionally high tides, the most severe floods would be prevented. After decades of campaigning, and despite surprisingly vociferous opposition, approval and funding was given and construction started in 2009. The MOSE project has suffered delays, and been the centre of a major corruption scandal, but it finally began operations in 2022 and has so far proved successful in preventing the worst floods.

At the southern end of Pellestrina, I cycle beyond the ferry terminal to explore the final section of the island. I soon come across a remarkable sea wall, the Murazzi, constructed more than two hundred years ago to prevent erosion on the banks of the lagoon. For more than a kilometre, the Adriatic and the lagoon are separated by a sliver of land, just a few metres wide, topped by this finely built two-metre stone wall. Because the water is low, I am able to cycle along a well-made path of concrete flags at the base of the wall, just a few centimetres above the lagoon. It's an unnerving experience. After a few hundred metres, I see the ferry in the distance coming from Chioggia. Wishing to catch this boat, I turn around and dash back to the ferry terminal.

Like the ferry from the Lido, it is surprisingly busy. Multiple cars and trucks have appeared, apparently out of nowhere, to make the trip to the mainland. As we leave, I gaze across to the sea wall and see somebody cycling along the top of it! Given that it's only about 60cm wide on top, this would be a bit too exciting for me.

Quickly we arrive at Chioggia, which is like a miniature version of Venice, but with cars. The bright sunshine shows the colourful houses and the shimmering canals at their best. I wander around Chioggia, which seems especially busy after the tranquillity of Pellestrina, finally settling down in a pizzcria for lunch.

The return journey to the Lido is uneventful, except that my legs are really quite tired for the final few kilometres. I am grateful to return the bicycle, and then sit on a bench waiting for the boat back to Venice.

The next morning, I arrive at Osteria Alla Staffa to see Sebastiano. His chef Carim arrives first, and opens up the restaurant. He assures me that Sebastiano won't be long, and starts work preparing the kitchen for lunch.

Ten minutes later Sebastiano arrives, breathlessly clutching a bag containing the bread he has just bought for today's diners. He is tall and wiry, with an energy that he struggles to contain. It is difficult to imagine Sebastiano sitting still for more than a few seconds. However, after talking briefly with Carim, Sebastiano joins me at one of the tables and we start our conversation.

He begins by explaining that his surname, Vianello, is Venetian. In particular, it is common on the island of Pellestrina, where he is from.

"I was cycling on Pellestrina yesterday!" I exclaim.

"Really!", says Sebastiano. "You were very lucky with the weather. Normally in October it is misty and cold. This warm, sunny weather is strange."

I start by asking Sebastiano if he is sole proprietor of the restaurant. He confirms that he is, but goes on to emphasise that the other people working here are his colleagues and not his employees. They work as a team of equals.

Although brought up on Pellestrina, Sebastiano, along with his twin brother, Nicolò, was born in a hospital on the Lido. They arrived into a family steeped in the bar & restaurant business, for at least the previous three generations.

Sebastiano and Nicolò attended school on Pellestrina until the age of 14 when, being unsure of their future direction, their mother enrolled them into the Enrico Fermi technical high school in Venice. Sebastiano began the daily commute across the lagoon which has been a feature of most of his life.

After leaving school, Sebastiano found his first job at Gran Caffè Chioggia, one of the historical cafés in Piazza San Marco. Here, he spent one year training to become a bar manager. He loved the work, which came naturally to him given his family background.

Sebastiano's great-grandfather ran an osteria on Pellestrina, later managed by Sebastiano's grandfather Aldo who also opened the first discotheque in the whole of Veneto in 1970. Youngsters came from far and wide to visit Aldo's disco. Sebastiano's father took over Ostaria La Rosa from Aldo. The restaurant is named after Sebastiano's grandmother, Rosa, and uses a more ancient spelling of the word osteria.

I ask Sebastiano why he did not follow the family tradition, running the restaurant in Pellestrina. He explains that this would have required that the business be expanded, to take more customers. He proposed this to his family but, at that time, they didn't feel able to make the investment required for the renovation works. However, about ten years later, after Sebastiano had established himself in Venice, his family did expand their business to create the restaurant they have today.

Sebastiano explains that life on the island of Pellestrina has changed in recent years. Today, the island is visited by more tourists, and the number of visitors grows year-on-year. His parents' restaurant is fully booked every day through the summer season.

After one year at Gran Caffè Chioggia, Sebastiano was

called up for ten months' national service in the army. Coming out of the army in June 2003, Sebastiano felt lost. He travelled for a while, but that did not provide the answer. He returned to Pellestrina. What should he do with his life? Should he try to work in the family business? There was much discussion with the family, including his idea to expand their restaurant.

Eventually, Sebastiano realised that he needed to find his own way. There was no reason why he couldn't go it alone. He didn't have to work with his father or uncles. It was agreed with the family that Sebastiano would start his own business on Pellestrina.

In October 2003, at the tender age of 22, Sebastiano opened a bar/trattoria. Slowly, he developed his offerings, starting with drinks, panini and bruschetta, and later adding pasta dishes.

On a small island like Pellestrina, Sebastiano inevitably knew most of his customers. One winter's evening, in 2005, he started chatting with a girl who had been a friend since school days. But this time something sparked. Pretty soon, Sebastiano and Sara were a couple.

Meanwhile, after eight years with the bar, Sebastiano was becoming restless. The natural next step would be to open a restaurant but, for this, he would have to leave the island. There were too few customers on Pellestrina, at that time, to support anything more ambitious.

Sebastiano's friend, Alberto, managed a restaurant on the Lido di Venezia. Alberto suggested that Sebastiano join him to develop and run this business together. Keen to grasp such an opportunity, Sebastiano left his bar on Pellestrina and went to work with Alberto.

They immediately modernised the outdoor terrace, providing new tables and chairs. However, the biggest change was the injection of energy and ideas from Sebastiano. Prior to Sebastiano's arrival, Alberto's restaurant saw a trickle of 20 to 30 customers per day. Once Sebastiano had settled in, this grew to a river, with up to 300 customers per day!

Alberto was able to pay off his debts. However, Sebastiano felt that he was not receiving a fair share of the profits from the revitalised business. After two years, he and Alberto fell out and Sebastiano left.

Sebastiano and Sara married in 2012, just one week before he split with Alberto. Straight after your wedding is not the ideal time to become unemployed.

"Almost as soon as I was married, I came over to Venice searching, like a mad man, for my new restaurant!"

It took several months to find the right place – a worrying time for the newly married couple.

At that time, Osteria Alla Staffa was managed by ambitious young restaurateurs, Alberto & Dario Spezzamonte, who wanted to expand. Sebastiano, still early in his career, was looking for a small place that he could manage on his own. The Spezzamontes agreed to sell their business to Sebastiano, enabling them to move to a bigger restaurant, called Estro: Vino e Cucina, near the Scuola Grande di San Rocco.

I ask Sebastiano if he knows the origin of the name, Osteria alla Staffa. Staffa literally means stirrup. He explains that the building was once a stable. Horses kept here were required for moving timber, stored in a nearby Calle, Barbaria de le Tole. That timber was used for building the Venetian republic's boats, in the Arsenale. Horse riding in Venice was banned in the 16th century, but horses would have been used to haul goods for a long time after that.

Before he could start his new restaurant, Sebastiano needed

to put a team in place, including a new chef. At the restaurant on the Lido, Sebastiano had befriended a chef called Carim. He successfully persuaded Carim to join him at Osteria Alla Staffa, which reopened under new management in August 2013.

His painful experience at the restaurant on the Lido reinforced, for Sebastiano, how important it is that all team members feel valued. He goes out of his way to treat the staff at Osteria Alla Staffa as partners in their joint venture.

Since taking over Osteria Alla Staffa, there have been some changes in family life. Sebastiano now has two sons, Samuel aged 7 and Mattia aged 5. In 2020 Sebastiano's father died. His uncle and aunt now manage Ostaria La Rosa on Pellestrina.

Carim and Sebastiano have worked together successfully for 11 years. However, Carim now wishes to see more of the world, and to improve his English. Next year, he plans to move with his family to the UK, and Sebastiano must find a replacement.

Sebastiano still lives on Pellestrina, and he has a friend and neighbour who commutes with him to work as a chef at another restaurant in Venice. Sebastiano has started persuading this friend that he belongs in the kitchen at Osteria Alla Staffa, and is hopeful that he will win him over. However, this friend has been working in the same Venetian establishment for 30 years, so this is not an easy decision!

Many workers in Venice commute daily from outside the old city. Venice now has more beds for tourists than beds for residents, and this competition for accommodation from tourism makes residential housing much more expensive, no doubt contributing to the decline in population from 175,000, in 1951, to 50,000 today.

However, I suspect Sebastiano's roots in Pellestrina are the main reason he is happy to commute. Family bonds are strong in Italy, where young people often stay near their parents, even when they find work and start their own family. Sebastiano's twin brother Nicolò, now married with two children, also lives nearby, on the Lido di Venezia. He is manager of the fruit and vegetable department in the local Coop.

I cast my mind back to yesterday afternoon, when I took the vaporetto from the Lido to Venice. The city was a mirage, floating between lagoon and cloudless sky. As we got closer, individual buildings became real, but no less beautiful. I felt excitement at the thought that soon I would be walking amongst them, experiencing the vitality of daily life in the city.

Sebastiano experiences this journey almost every day, although each time it is different. There might be a thick fog, with nothing visible and all sound muffled by the humidity. There might be a cold wind whipping up waves on the lagoon, making for a choppy crossing. Crossing the lagoon is a sensory experience, determined by the weather, and unlike the daily commute in a train or bus, where you are separated from the elements.

Anybody born on an island must ultimately decide whether to spend their life there, or seek adventure in the rest of the world. Sebastiano has found an elegant compromise, remaining with his roots on Pellestrina whilst also pursuing his dream career in Venice, where the rest of the world comes to him.

4 From sparkling blue to ethereal grey

Prior to my conversation with Ivana, I'd never thought about how Venice and the Amalfi coast demonstrate the diversity of Italy. Both are popular coastal tourist destinations, not reliant upon beaches and bathing, but they are completely different.

Nature's drama dominates on the Amalfi coast. Venice is a beautiful human creation, in an unpromising location. Towns and villages cling to steep hillsides around Amalfi, with cliffs plunging hundreds of feet to the sea. Venice is the world's flattest city, just a few feet above sea level. Southern Italy has dazzling sunshine, a dry landscape, and wide blue expanses of sky and sea. Venice has mist and drizzle in the winter, and views that are intimate rather than extensive.

These contrasts define the backdrop to Ivana's life. Now living in Venice, she was born and raised near Amalfi.

Amalfi is one of four maritime republics celebrated on the flag of the Italian navy. In the Middle Ages, the cities of Venice, Genoa, Pisa and Amalfi each had substantial fleets that supported trade networks across the Mediterranean. Amalfi, the first of these republics to create a colony in Constantinople, established maritime laws that were adopted internationally. In the 12th century however, the Amalfi republic suffered military defeats and forever lost its independence. Today, Venice, Genoa and Pisa are all substantial cities, while Amalfi is just a small town, with a population of 5,000.

But it's not history that draws visitors to the Amalfi coast. It's the scenery, the climate and picturesque towns and villages. Jackie and I first went there for our honeymoon in 2007, staying in Ravello.

We rented an apartment, unforgettable for two reasons.

Italians seem to prefer hard beds, and this apartment excelled in that respect. It was like sleeping, or rather not sleeping, on a concrete floor. But it was the jaw dropping view from our balcony that can never be forgotten. We looked across to a rugged hillside, tumbling down to the small coastal town of Maiori, and the Gulf of Salerno. One thousand feet below, tiny white boats, leaving delicate trails behind them, crawled across a deep shiny blue that stretched to infinity. Nothing could be more relaxing than sitting and looking at that view. The highlight of each day was breakfast on the balcony.

Ravello is especially pleasant to walk around in the evening, when the heat of the day has eased. Built on a hillside, the town is a maze of narrow alleys, with steps everywhere. To reach the centre from our apartment meant climbing up 250 steps. There is no obesity epidemic in Ravello.

The town has one level expanse: the main square, Piazza Duomo. In the morning, you can sip coffee at one of the cafés and forget all your worries. You might see a wedding party gather on the steps of the Duomo, waiting to welcome the bride and follow her into the church. In the evening, local families bring children to the piazza, to play on bicycles and scooters, amongst the tourists enjoying their aperitifs. It's a happy place.

However, the towns of the Amalfi coast are connected by a coast road that no sane person would describe as a happy place. This narrow road twists and turns across the hillside, with cliffs above and below. The same view, that brings relaxation on the balcony of our apartment, brings sheer terror when you are driving along this road.

On our honeymoon, we wanted to visit Positano, further along the coast. Wisely, we decided to take the bus rather than use our hire car. The first bus took us to Amalfi, where we had to catch a second bus to Positano. It wasn't at all clear when the Positano bus was due to leave, so I asked the driver of another bus: "When does the bus to Positano depart?"

"ANY minute! ANY minute!" he said with a smile.

Of course, he had no idea when that bus would leave. He was telling me that, eventually, a bus would leave for Positano, and I shouldn't worry about it. Whether I spend my time here enjoying the sunshine, or in Positano enjoying the sunshine, what's the difference? We northern Europeans should learn to enjoy life, to live in the present, and lose our obsession with timetables.

The skill of Amalfi coast bus drivers has to be seen to be believed. The road is rarely straight and rarely level, but they barrel down it, missing walls and vehicles by inches. However, when one bus meets another bus at a bend, they must both stop. One of them reverses to the nearest straight section, so that they can pass. That's fine, as long as they haven't acquired a queue of traffic behind them, making reversing impossible.

Inevitably, our bus met another bus at a bend, and both buses had a queue of traffic behind. Everything stopped. A man on a scooter tried to overtake our bus, then screeched to a halt because there was no way through. He got off his scooter, walked to the back of the queue of cars behind us, and directed them all to reverse down the road. Eventually, our bus was able to start reversing and, as soon as a small gap appeared, scooter man was on his way!

There is pleasure in the unexpected, whether it's a beautifully dressed wedding party, children playing in the piazza, or the traffic jam unlocked by an impatient man on a scooter. Italy is not just beautiful scenery, sunshine and good food. Italy is theatre.

After ten days in Ravello, we knew we had to see more of this country. We have returned to Italy every year since. Although we always seek out new areas, there are also places that we love to revisit, and chief among these is Venice.

It was on our third trip to Venice, that we came across Ristorante Acqua Pazza in Campo Sant' Angelo. Acqua Pazza, meaning crazy water, is a traditional fish recipe from Cetara on the Amalfi coast.

Outdoor dining in a typical Venetian campo tends to be quite informal, but this was different. The tables were laid with high quality white tablecloths. The waiters were dressed in smart uniforms. There was an efficient, professional atmosphere. Intriguingly, the restaurant was managed by a family from the Amalfi coast. How did that happen? How did people from the other end of Italy come to be running a restaurant in Venice?

Eight years later, I am returning to seek answers to these questions. We arrive at the restaurant, having booked a table for 8pm. Although this is October, it's warm enough to sit outside. The restaurant is very busy, and we are given one of the last tables. We order, we eat and, as usual, the food is excellent. I notice that there is a tall, youngish man helping to clear the tables who, unlike the other staff, is not wearing a uniform. Jackie speculates that he might be a member of the family that owns the restaurant so, on my way to the bathroom, I stop to speak to him. He is indeed a member of the family running this business. After I explain that I'd like to discover the story behind the restaurant, to include in a book, he suggests that I return the next day at 9.30am when his mother will be here.

I arrive the following morning, to see the tables still set out, tablecloths bright in the sunshine. But now only one table is occupied. A middle-aged lady sits with her telephone, reading some papers. She looks up, calls me over and introduces herself as Ivana Mostaccioli, mother of Rocco whom I spoke to last night. I sit down, and we start talking.

Although we have only just met, the conversation is friendly and relaxed. Ivana is a natural raconteur, and I often find myself laughing. She explains that the story of this restaurant is really the story of her husband, Antonio.

"Antonio was born in Amalfi, and I was born in a little place called Scala."

"Oh yes, I know Scala."

"How can you possibly know Scala, it's tiny!"

"I had my moony honey in Ravello, and Scala is near Ravello." This helps you understand how bad my Italian is. I am trying to say honeymoon. Ivana is too polite to correct me, and she continues their story.

Antonio's father was a policeman, a member of the Carabinieri. He wanted his son to also become a government employee. However, much to his father's displeasure, from the very beginning Antonio was fascinated by the restaurant business. His uncle Franco was a successful chef in Rome, and he would teach Antonio cooking whenever he visited the family in Amalfi.

Ivana explains that tourism and hospitality were very different in the 1970s & 1980s, compared with the mass tourism of today. In those days, tourism on the Amalfi coast was restricted to wealthy foreigners, mostly Americans, staying in upmarket hotels. Refined dining was to be found only in these hotels. Outside the big hotels, there were no upmarket restaurants. Local people would eat in trattorias and osterias, where the food was much simpler.

After leaving school, Antonio found work as a waiter at the

Hotel Luna in Amalfi, where manager Roberto Barbaro became a key friend and mentor. Antonio learnt about service and worked his way up the restaurant promotion ladder. Roberto taught him the importance of ambience: how the look and feel of a restaurant, and the style of the service, create the customer's experience and determine whether they return.

It's now becoming clear to me why Ristorante Acqua Pazza feels so different to most Venetian restaurants. I imagine the dining room of a grand hotel in the last century, catering to wealthy guests, where elegance, refinement and impeccable service are every bit as important as the quality of the food. This is Antonio's inheritance, reflected in his restaurant in Venice. That same legacy is evident elsewhere in Venice of course, in the dining rooms of grand hotels, and the cafés of Piazza San Marco, but most Venetian restaurants are less formal.

As a hotel employee, Antonio became restless. He wanted to run his own restaurant. His father still disapproved of Antonio's chosen career, but his mother was supportive and encouraging. Antonio found a small restaurant for sale in Atrani, the next village along the coast from Amalfi. Borrowing a significant amount of money, and quitting his job in the hotel, he took the plunge.

Ivana describes the scene when Antonio took his mother along, to proudly show her his new acquisition: "'Madonna!' his mamma exclaimed. It was little more than a cave, with room to seat four people in a line, provided the last of them sat in the W.C. It was not possible to employ a fat chef, because he would not fit in the kitchen."

The local mayor gave Antonio permission to have tables outside, in Piazza Umberto I. Unfortunately, this space was shared with the neighbouring café, whose owner wasn't happy.

He insisted that Antonio not be allowed to serve coffee, liqueurs or desserts! Despite this little feud, the restaurant thrived. From day one it was full.

As a young man, Antonio didn't only live for work. He liked cars, he liked girls, and he visited the local discotheques. It was there that he met Ivana, and they began dating.

Meanwhile, with only 30 covers, the restaurant was too small for Antonio who had bigger ambitions. Antonio decided that it would be difficult to start a larger restaurant here on the Amalfi coast, and he should look further afield.

Antonio and Ivana were planning to marry, so they started discussing this possible move away from Amalfi. There was a history of Amalfitani relocating to northern Italy, especially Lombardy and Veneto, to find work. However, Antonio and Ivana wanted to start a family, and she refused to bring up children in a big city like Milan. As a compromise, they agreed that Bologna should be big enough to support the kind of restaurant Antonio wanted, yet small enough to be family-friendly. In 1989, Antonio sold the restaurant in Atrani, found suitable premises, and started his new, much larger restaurant in the centre of Bologna, near the famous Two Towers.

Early in 1990, Antonio and Ivana were married. At the end of that year, their son Rocco was born, with daughter Anna arriving in 1992. Within a short period, the new restaurant in Bologna was thriving. Antonio typically catered for 300 covers per day. Now they had a young family, and a successful business. Ivana was looking forward to building a happy, settled life in Bologna.

However, Antonio was still restless. Coming from the Amalfi coast, his passion was seafood. He designed a menu with amazing seafood dishes, but the local Bolognese still ordered their traditional pasta in meat sauce. He felt that he wasn't fulfilling his original dream.

One of Antonio's regular customers, Roberto Jovino, was a Venetian businessman who also had commercial interests in Bologna. He often visited Bologna, and he loved Antonio's restaurant. He started talking to Antonio about a building he had just bought in Venice, that would be the perfect location for a new restaurant. Roberto wanted Antonio to be his partner in this venture. At first, Antonio was reluctant to make another move, but Roberto was persistent and persuasive. Eventually, he convinced Antonio to at least come and view the premises. Antonio travelled to Venice, and fell in love with the location, in Campo Sant' Angelo. He was now convinced that his future lay in Venice. All he had to do was persuade Ivana.

However, Ivana absolutely refused to move to Venice, a city she disliked: "I thought Venice was decadent and depressing." But Antonio's mind was made up. He sold the Bologna restaurant to his staff, went into partnership with Roberto and relocated to Venice, leaving his family in Bologna! Ristorante Acqua Pazza opened for business on 24th July 1998.

"The children and I remained in Bologna for two years. In my head, we were divorced!" recalls Ivana. Eventually, there was a reconciliation. Ivana and the children moved to Venice.

With both children at school, Ivana was looking for a way to be more active and fulfilled. Her father had been a baker, running his own bread shop, with Ivana helping out as a small child. He provided a stool for her to stand on, so that she could reach the counter.

Ivana understood the commitment, hard work and rewards associated with running your own business. In 2000, she took on her own restaurant, in nearby Campo Santo Stefano.

"Did Antonio help you?" I ask.

"Antonio helped by giving me a kick up the backside." Initially, Ivana was terrified at the prospect of running her own business: "like driving a lorry full of explosives". Antonio knew she could do it, and wouldn't let her back out.

Antonio also provided helpful advice, on how to run a restaurant, but he seems to have enjoyed packaging this mysteriously.

"There is just one rule for running a restaurant. That rule is: 'there are no rules.'"

"You must remember all your clients, and you must forget all your clients." Ivana explains what he meant by this. "Remember every client by giving everybody good service, and not favouring your friends. However, if a man turns up with his wife one evening and another lady the next evening, you must forget this completely."

Over time, Antonio's business activities, in partnership with Roberto, broadened to include a bar, another restaurant and four holiday apartments. As the business and the children grew, there were always too few hours in the day. But a busy life, doing what you love, is surely a happy life.

Then, in 2006, their lives changed completely. Antonio was struck down by a debilitating heart condition, that left him incapacitated. They had to retrench. All family business activities were sold, except for Acqua Pazza which Ivana would manage. Later, in 2014, they bought Roberto's share of the Acqua Pazza business, and now they just rent the premises from him.

From 2006 to 2008 was an incredibly tough period for Ivana, who had never felt so alone. "It had been very difficult for us to make friends in Venice. This is not because the Venetians are unfriendly – in fact, they have tremendous respect for Antonio – but because we were working every hour of every day. We had nothing else in our lives. There was no time for friends! In those days, I wanted so much to return to my family in the south."

But Ivana and the family remained in Venice to rebuild their lives. "Now," she says, "I am happy to stay here. I love Venice."

Around this time, the children were becoming adults. Rocco wanted to work in the restaurant, but Ivana was keen for him to explore alternative careers.

"Rocco is a big fish," explains Ivana. "You cannot catch a big fish using brute force. You must let out the line, and have patience."

She tried to persuade him to go to university, but he resisted: "That would be a waste of time. I would rather take a three-year holiday!" Ivana let Rocco work in the restaurant for a year, expecting him to realise how hard it was and decide to do something else. But Rocco never changed his mind. He still works there.

Anna obtained a degree in anthropology, at the University of Bologna, but she also gravitated back to the restaurant business in Venice. Between them, Anna and Rocco now manage Acqua Pazza, with Ivana helping in the background.

In fact, the loyalty and longevity of the Acqua Pazza team is quite remarkable. Six of the waiters and kitchen staff have worked there for 20 years.

Ivana reflects on her experience in the restaurant business. "You must have strong values." (The word she uses is moralità, literally morality, but I think strong values is a better translation.) "You need an honest relationship with your suppliers, an honest relationship with your staff, and an honest relationship with your customers. In Venice, the same customers return year after year. There is no greater pleasure than recognising the face of a customer who visited 5 years ago."

"'Oh good, we've found you. You're still here!' they say."

I'll echo that.

5 Third time lucky

Although I have used Naples airport, stayed on the Amalfi coast, and visited Pompei and Vesuvius, I have never ventured into the city of Naples. To be honest, I have always been a little scared by its reputation.

In 2007, Jackie and I were struggling to find a parking spot near Pompei. We finally found somewhere on the street, got out of our hire car and were approached by a young man, wearing jeans and T-shirt, carrying a stack of tickets. He announced that the parking charge was 5 euros, and held out a slip of paper for us to purchase. We were naïve enough to think he just might be a real parking official, and also nervous that, even if he wasn't, it might not be a good idea to refuse to pay, given the ease with which he could damage the car. So, we paid up and took the ticket.

When we got inside the archaeological site, we asked one of the staff whether our "parking official" was legitimate.

"This is Naples," he said cheerfully, "anything can happen in Naples."

More frightening was a story I heard from a friend in Rome, who describes Naples as "a place apart, unlike anywhere else in Italy." His Neapolitan wife was driving through Naples, with her jacket on the passenger seat, and she stopped in a queue of traffic. Suddenly, the passenger side window was smashed and her jacket stolen!

Anyway, I have now plucked up the courage and booked a few days in the centre of Naples. Something that helps significantly is knowing that I will see Fabio, a friend I met on a language exchange website. Fabio is a native of Naples, who has done well for himself. Firstly, he is a judge. It's hard to think of a more respectable job. Secondly, he has a beautiful wife and two sweet daughters.

The taxi drops me on Via Toledo and I follow the map a short distance into the back streets, to find my hotel and check-in. It's now 8pm and I am hungry, so I go out again with the intention of tasting my first ever authentic Neapolitan pizza. There are several very old pizzerias in Naples, all claiming to have played a key role in the creation of the world's favourite food. It's all good marketing, useful for attracting the tourists. Declaring itself the oldest pizzeria in Naples, Antica Pizzeria Port'Alba was founded in 1738, although I doubt they served pizza in those days. I can assure you that they serve pizza now, and damned good pizza at that. Feeling mellow, after enjoying a good meal and red wine, I wander back to the hotel to retire for the night.

The next morning, I find an up-market place for breakfast: Caffè Ceraldi. Here I can relax, with a cappuccino and a pastry, reflecting on my first impressions of the city. The main streets are busy, with people and traffic. It feels much more crowded than a typical European city. It also feels darker – literally. The city is paved with large black basalt blocks, a gift from Vesuvius. These are hard wearing and smooth, but they also absorb the light. The dirty narrow back streets of the Spanish Quarter, near my hotel, are hemmed in by tall buildings. They seem dark, even on the brightest day.

However, here in Caffè Ceraldi all is bright lights and smiles. The décor is traditional but fresh, and the staff cheerfully busy. Every few minutes, a dumb waiter brings a tray of pastries and tartlets up from the kitchen below. These are set out behind the glass counter and, remarkably quickly, they disappear. A constant stream of people enters the café, grabs a coffee and a bite while standing at the counter, and then leaves. I comment to one of the waiters that he never stops moving, and ask how long his shift is. "Nine hours," he says, "which keeps me slim." I decide there is no need to seek anywhere else for breakfast, during my stay in Naples.

Exchanging messages with Fabio, I am delighted to learn that he can spend time with me today and tomorrow. In the afternoon we take the funicular up to Vomero, where he was born and brought up. Here, Castel Sant'Elmo provides a stunning view of the city. Then we pop into a local café, where the drinks are fine but the staff are grumpy and bicker with each other. Fabio comments on this, and we agree that it is usually the personality and attitude of the manager that determines the atmosphere.

The next afternoon, Fabio picks me up in his car and we visit the main art gallery in Naples at Capodimonte, an old royal palace on a hill overlooking the city. We race through the gallery to see as much as we can, before it closes for the day. Then we wander across the beautiful park surrounding the palace, to reach a viewpoint from which we watch the sun go down on Capri and Naples, spread out below. Fabio leads me back through the park for a drink in a delightful tea room open until 8pm: Delizie Reali Stufa dei Fiori. Notwithstanding its long, complicated name, the tea room feels like a little bit of England.

On the drive back into the city, we are waiting at traffic lights and Fabio starts musing about how Naples has changed.

"I can't believe what I see nowadays. Nobody drives through a red light anymore!" he laments. "In the old days, people ignored traffic lights."

He hasn't finished.

"I remember going to the football stadium 30 years ago, to

watch Napoli play. In those times, when we were allowed to stand, 100,000 people would attend a big match. There was no queue. Everybody pushed and jostled for position, to get in. Nowadays people ask where the end of the line is, and politely wait their turn. It's terrible!"

Of course, my friend Fabio - the judge - is joking, but he is only half-joking. To understand where this comes from, we need a brief history lesson.

The country that we call Italy was created by a complex series of events between 1860 and 1870. Before 1860, the Italian peninsula comprised many separate states, including: the independent kingdom of Piedmont-Sardinia; the north east, including Veneto, governed by Austria; the papal states in the centre, ruled by the Pope in Rome; and the southern third of the peninsula, plus Sicily, all ruled from Naples by a Bourbon king. Naples was the largest city in Italy, and capital of the richest and most populous state.

In 1860, the soldier-adventurer Garibaldi landed on Sicily with just 1,000 armed men, and raised support from across the island to defeat local Bourbon forces and take over. Soon thereafter, he crossed over to the mainland and, with the support of Piedmont-Sardina, defeated the Bourbons there also. The former Bourbon state thus became part of the kingdom of Piedmont-Sardinia, with the two together declared to be a new country: Italy. This takeover was legitimised by a plebiscite of the people in October 1860 when, apparently, over 99% of voters chose to become part of Italy! To celebrate this fraud, the beautiful square outside the main Bourbon palace in Naples was renamed Piazza del Plebiscito.

Later in the decade, the rest of the Italian peninsula was acquired to complete this new European country. The belief in

Naples is that the riches of the Bourbon kingdom were stolen, and used to pay off the debts of the rest of Italy. Further resentment was created in the south by stories spun in the north, about how the old Bourbon kingdom was corrupt and exploitative, and that the cultural legacy of the south was much poorer than that of the north, birthplace of the Renaissance.

Over 160 years later, this resentment persists in Naples. Once a proud capital city, it is keen to display its artistic treasures from the past. In the centuries before unification, Naples produced spectacular art, and beautiful buildings. You can see the evidence in Cappella Sansevero, the Palazzo Reale, or the art gallery at Capodimonte. Moreover, although presiding over a highly unequal society, Bourbon rulers were often more enlightened and progressive than their northern neighbours.

This legacy of injustice has motivated Neapolitans to rebel against any law made in Rome, imbuing their culture with a general disdain for rules and regulations. Yet, ironically, Naples has the oldest secular university in the world, founded in 1224, with a strong reputation in the study of law!

As we near Via Toledo, where Fabio will drop me off, we start talking about my book. He recommends that I visit a small family restaurant close to his office, called Trattoria Da Ettore.

"Ettore, who started the restaurant, is actually the grandfather of the current owner," says Fabio. "Mention my name. They know me well in there."

With that, we say our goodbyes and I return to my hotel.

At 8pm the next evening, I arrive at Trattoria Da Ettore just as it opens. It's a small place – just eight tables – and only three tables are occupied, each by a single tourist. The waiter gives the impression of being quite serious, perhaps even a bit gruff. Later, a local family of four arrives and they are clearly old friends, since he greets them warmly and they chat for a while. Judging by online reviews, the restaurant is usually much busier than this. The pasta meal I order is lovely and, afterwards, I chat to the waiter who takes me to see the manager. Raffaele, who is middle aged, warm and friendly, is interested in my project and happy to help. We agree that I will return another day, for a longer conversation.

I come back two days later, on a bright sunny morning. Raffaele introduces me to his wife Maddalena, who works in the kitchen, and his brother Ettore, the waiter I saw on the first night. All three are preparing for that day's lunch, but Raffaele ducks out so that he can sit and talk to me for an hour.

I start learning about Raffaele's family, and the history of the trattoria. Raffaele's great grandfather Carlo was from Turin. He came to Naples towards the end of the 19th century, to be a tram driver. Carlo's son Ettore was born in Naples and, as a young man, he found work in a bread shop. After gaining experience in the trade, he eventually came to manage his own bread shop in Via Gennaro Serra. Ettore and his wife Linda worked hard, and expanded their business to include two or three additional grocery shops/cafés. Then, in 1940, Ettore opened a trattoria, in a former dairy across the street from his original bread shop. Trattoria Da Ettore was born.

Raffaele is unable to recall the name of the first chef in the trattoria but, in 1955, a new chef Tonino arrived who nobody could ever forget. Larger than life, Tonino would tell jokes to the customers, whenever he left the kitchen. He numbered the tables 41 to 48, telling everybody that tables 1 to 40 were in a grand room upstairs that, oddly, nobody ever got to see. Further entertainment was provided to customers on some evenings, when Ettore came along to sing at the restaurant.

Nearby, at the end of Via Gennaro Serra, is the Politeama theatre, built in 1870. Many of Ettore's customers had connections with this theatre. For example, Italian conductor Beppe Vessicchio often dined at Ettore's, in the days before he became famous. Sometimes, Ettore offered a free meal to an actor, or ballerina, who was short of money. Today, the walls of the Trattoria are adorned with photographs of show business personalities, who ate here between performances at the theatre. Perhaps the most well-known is Totò, the comedian.

One of Ettore's sons, Giuseppe, together with his wife Angela, managed the family grocery shop around the corner. Giuseppe and Angela had three children: Linda, Ettore and Raffaele. After leaving school, in the 1980s, Ettore went to work at the trattoria as a waiter. Almost 40 years later, he is still here.

Meanwhile, Tonino wasn't getting any younger and in 1990, when he turned 80, he finally recognised that it was time to retire. Giuseppe and Angela decided that they would close the grocery business and take over in the kitchen at the trattoria.

Raffaele attended a technical school in Naples, the Casanova Liceo, and trained to be a dental technician. His parents encouraged him to seek opportunities outside the restaurant business, which they knew could be a demanding career choice. It took five years for Raffaele to complete his studies and qualify. However, he realised that working alone in a laboratory wasn't right for him. He missed contact with people.

Raffaele changed direction, and enlisted in the navy for a minimum of three years. He trained as a sonar operator on minesweepers, and was looking forward to a maritime career. In order to qualify for a military pension, it was necessary to serve for at least 30 years, with 18 of those years on board ship.

For the second time, Raffaele realised that he was heading down a road that didn't suit him. In particular, living on board ship was uncomfortable and lonely, being isolated from family and friends. Raffaele just didn't love the work enough to make those sacrifices worthwhile.

Aged 24, he left the navy and came to work in the trattoria. In the kitchen, he learnt to cook by watching his parents. At last, on his third attempt, Raffaele found something that he really enjoyed, and it turned out to have been right on his doorstep!

Seven years after starting at the trattoria, in 2005, Raffaele first met Maddalena, in the gym. They started going out together, getting married in 2008 and setting up home in the Spanish Quarter.

At this point Maddalena wanders over to join our conversation, giving me the opportunity to find out more about her. She has an engaging manner, with a broad smile.

Maddalena trained as a graphic designer in her final years at school, then studied natural sciences at university in Naples. Until aged 20, Maddalena had no interest whatsoever in food. She just didn't enjoy eating! Then her attitude changed, and she started cooking and exploring different foods. After university, Maddalena found work as the secretary for a paediatrician. During this period, she met Raffaele.

In 2014, more change was underway at the trattoria. Angela was unwell, and decided to retire. The next year, Giuseppe also stopped work, leaving Raffaele solely responsible for the kitchen. In that same year, Maddalena's employer retired, so she was looking for a new role. Given her interest in food, it seemed only natural, even inevitable, that Maddalena should join Raffaele in the kitchen at Trattoria Da Ettore.

The menu at the trattoria consists of traditional Neapolitan dishes that change with the seasons, reflecting the availability of local ingredients, but are consistent from year to year. Some dishes, such as Pasta alla Genovese, require many hours to prepare.

In 2019, Raffaele and Maddalena had a baby boy, Noah. Being familiar with the menu at the trattoria, Noah sometimes asks for Spaghetti alla Vongole (spaghetti with clams) for lunch at his nursery!

I ask Raffaele about his customers, whether they are mostly locals or tourists. He tells me that, until about seven years ago, they were almost all Neapolitans. However, the last seven years has seen a huge increase in the number of tourists visiting Naples, and also his restaurant.

I recall talking to Fabio about this. Naples' reputation has undoubtedly changed. For example, the Spanish Quarter used to be almost a no-go area for foreign tourists, considered too dangerous. However, in recent times more and more tourists have used social media to publicise that it's an interesting place to visit, that the locals are generally friendly and there's no good reason to avoid it. Property prices are rising in the centre of Naples, and some of Fabio's friends are buying places in the Spanish Quarter in the expectation of making a good profit. We both think this area will become gentrified in the next 20 years.

Raffaele, Maddalena and I are now drawing our conversation to a close. They must soon return to the kitchen, to complete preparations for the lunchtime guests. I thank them, we say our goodbyes, and I step out into Via Gennaro Serra, a typical Neapolitan street. The pavement is narrow. You must have your wits about you as you walk, to avoid dogshit on the pavement and the cars and scooters that race past just inches away.

I head to Gran Caffè Gambrinus, near Piazza del Plebiscito. Whilst enjoying a spremuta, sat outside in the sunshine, I reflect upon what I learnt today.

It took three attempts for Raffaele to find his vocation, but he seems happy now. I can't help feeling that his home city, in contrast, has lost its way, dwelling too much on the injustices of the past. Yet it is obvious that Naples is changing - quite significantly in recent years. Hopefully, like Raffaele, it will find its place in the world and learn to look to the future as well as treasure its past.

6 The first hundred years

"In life there is a treasure more precious even than gold, do you want to know what it is? It is peace and harmony."

These wise words, attributed to Giuseppe Di Porzio, are inscribed on the opening page of a small booklet I was given by Giuseppe's son, Massimo. Written by Giuseppe's daughter, Ermelinda, the booklet presents the history of their family restaurant, Umberto, in Naples.

I visited Umberto earlier this week, for an enjoyable lunch. The waiters were friendly and welcoming, as was the food. I spoke to manager Massimo, who gave me the booklet, and we agreed a time for me to return and learn more. Umberto has been here over 100 years, and I want to understand what it takes to keep a family business going for such a long period.

The booklet explains how it all began.

The restaurant is named after Massimo's grandfather, Umberto, who was born in Posillipo. Today, Posillipo is an affluent area to the west of Naples, with good sea food restaurants and several small beaches. It is a popular destination for Neapolitans, relaxing at the weekend. However, in the early 1900s Posillipo was very different, supporting a predominantly agricultural population living in small farmhouses. Umberto Di Porzio was born in one of these houses, in 1889. From an early age, Umberto learnt the ways of farming, like previous generations in his family. As a young man, he took it upon himself to supply produce from the family farm to shops in the Chiaia district of Naples. This involved driving a horse-driven buggy four kilometres along a twisting road, constructed 100 years earlier on the orders of Joachim Murat, appointed King of Naples by Napoleon. Although tiring, the journey provided breath-taking views, over the bay of Naples, and a quiet time for thinking which Umberto put to good use.

He was intrigued by city living, so very different to the farming life he was born into. Umberto also realised that the city would continue to expand, eventually sweeping away Posillipo's rural lifestyle. If he wanted to provide for his children in the long term, then he must find a way to benefit from these changes.

At this time, the First World War was raging. Umberto had lost two fingers from his right hand in a hunting accident, which excused him from military service. Despite the widespread privation resulting from the war, he suggested to his wife Ermelinda that they start a business in Naples. By getting established before the end of the war, they would benefit from the good times that would surely arrive once peace returned.

The natural place to base their business was Chiaia, a wealthy and green suburb by the sea. In June 1916, Umberto and Ermelinda purchased premises and opened a small trattoria, Da Umberto, in Via Alabardieri, raising their five children in a new home above the restaurant.

The workload was divided in accordance with their individual strengths. Ermelinda was expert in the preparation of traditional local dishes, so she worked in the kitchen. Umberto provided overall management of the business, and welcomed customers front of house. Perhaps "welcomed" is not the right word, because Umberto had a reputation for being gruff, almost rude, with customers. This was his natural manner, bringing the same blunt approach to every customer, from the poorest beggar to the richest noble. Unknown to Ermelinda however, Umberto would secretly give discounts to the poorest customers. His hard headed wife, with a constant eye on the finances, would never have permitted this had she known.

Ingredients for the menu were provided by Umberto's father Vitale, still cultivating the family holding, and by other Posillipo farmers and fishermen. Ermelinda and Umberto served dishes typically enjoyed by the common people. However, on feast days they would present sumptuous recipes copied from the royal court and the houses of the nobility.

Cooking their signature dish, a traditional, dark meat sauce, generated a delectable aroma that never failed to capture the attention of passers-by. To this sauce would be added chops and meatballs. Other dishes for which Ermelinda was famous included Pasta e Fagioli (pasta with beans), a mouth-watering Genovese sauce, and exquisite soups including Maritata.

Genovese is a meat sauce made using caramelised onions, found in Naples but not in Genoa! It is thought to have been introduced to Naples by Swiss soldiers, many years ago, during the Spanish occupation. The name is derived from Geneva, changed to Genevoise and finally, in the Neapolitan dialect, it became Genovese. It appears there is no connection to Genoa.

Maritata soup, or wedding soup, is a peasants' dish made from meat and vegetables. Tradition requires three different types of meat and seven different local leafy vegetables.

The restaurant thrived, attracting customers of every class, all enjoying the honest, traditional food and the familiar atmosphere. It became clear that they needed to expand their premises. In 1926 Da Umberto closed for a brief period of reconstruction work, reopening with the new name Ristorante Pizzeria Umberto, and significantly more space for diners. This configuration of the restaurant has survived little-changed to the modern day.

One of Umberto's regular customers, often dining alone, was the brilliant mathematician Renato Caccioppoli, famous for his publications on functions of complex variables. A native of Naples, and a professor at the university, Renato lived nearby in Palazzo Cellammare. He was also an excellent pianist, and known for being nonconformist. For example, Renato experimented by living as a vagrant for a period, until he was arrested for begging. He also gave speeches against Hitler and Mussolini in 1938, while Mussolini was visiting Naples. Further anti-fascist pronouncements led to his imprisonment, and he was only released when his aunt, a professor of Chemistry at the university, convinced authorities that he was of unsound mind. After the war, Professor Caccioppoli suffered bouts of depression, became an alcoholic, and finally committed suicide in 1959.

Caccioppoli's story recalls for me those words from Giuseppe Di Porzio, that peace and harmony are more precious than gold.

The Second World War brought hard times for everybody in Naples. Food was scarce, and the government imposed strict regulations that restaurants must not provide a meal to anybody unable to hand over the relevant ration card stamps. Nevertheless, Umberto kept his restaurant open throughout the war, and proudly stated that he had never refused a meal to those in need.

After the war, in Chiaia and Posillipo, people were keen to return to normal life and build a future for their children. There were big changes at the restaurant. Ermelinda retired from the kitchen, giving way to professional cooks. Then, in 1951, with the three daughters married, management of the restaurant passed from Umberto to his two sons, Giuseppe and Mario.

The post-war decades saw an economic boom in Italy, as the country embraced new technologies and working methods. Following the death of Umberto in 1959, Giuseppe and Mario, with help from their sisters, modernised the management and menu of the restaurant, to adapt as Italy went through dramatic changes. For a brief period, the restaurant was even renamed Umberto's, influenced by the post-war presence of American soldiers in the city.

The menu was modified to include international dishes. Umberto's daughter Bianca was now working in the kitchen and, together with chef Ciro Bellocchio, they introduced more modern dishes, including prawn cocktail and banana flambé. The novel showmanship of preparing a flambé at the table, with the flash of burning alcohol, elicited gasps and applause from diners.

The family decided to expand the business, opening a second restaurant by the seaside, on Via Francesco Caracciolo. They chose a 1930s building owned by the local council, with stunning views across the bay of Naples. The menu offered a range of grilled meats, grilled fish, mussels and clams. At this time only the wealthy could afford regular seaside holidays, but there was still a queue outside the restaurant every evening, such was its popularity. Sadly, this venture came to an end when the council decided to demolish the building and not replace it.

One by one, the children of Umberto stepped away from the family business to pursue other opportunities, leaving just Flora, married to Guido, and younger brother Giuseppe, married to Maria. In the 1970s, Flora and Guido decided to step back and leave the business to Giuseppe and Maria, because Giuseppe's children were showing a real interest in the restaurant and represented a long-term future.

Giuseppe and Maria first met in the bar owned by Maria's mother, not far from Ristorante Umberto in Via Alabardieri, and they fell in love immediately. Giuseppe was serious, careful and sometimes quite gruff because, deep down, he was a shy person. With a strong desire to maintain order and control, he took naturally to managing the restaurant. Maria was very different. Ever cheerful, with a ready smile, she was always happy to stop and chat.

The combination of these contrasting personalities meant that the business was efficiently managed and welcoming to diners. The couple were popular, and many customers became good friends. There was also an amicable, professional atmosphere within the team at the restaurant. Staff at Umberto tended to stay for a long time, and their strong relationship with Giuseppe and Maria meant that this tradition continued.

Giuseppe's and Maria's four children, Ermelinda, Lorella, Roberta and Massimo, divided their time between schoolwork and helping at the restaurant. Their parents believed it important that they become familiar with the business at an early age.

Chef Gennaro Pace offered traditional local fare, including pasta dishes, stuffed peppers, parmigiana di melenzane, and a range of fried foods. In this period, Umberto also established a reputation for excellent pizza.

Meanwhile, Chiaia was changing. In the 1970s, poorer residents still lived in *bassi*: tiny, ground floor homes of one or two rooms, whose living space spilled into the street. Over time, these poorer residents moved out, or died out, and their homes became incorporated into shops and bars. Major offices, for Gas and Telecoms companies, also used to be in Chiaia, but they relocated to other areas. By the 1990s, the area had developed into an up-market shopping and nightlife centre for the city of

Naples.

Giuseppe and Maria handed over management of the restaurant to their children, in the late 1990s. Ermelinda pursued a career as an architect, but Massimo, Lorella and Roberta, together brought Umberto into the new millennium.

Having finished reading Ermelinda's booklet, it's now time for me to return to Umberto and talk to Massimo.

Leaving early, I take a circuitous route to the restaurant. It is a cool crisp March day, and Galleria Umberto I, the beautiful 19th century shopping arcade, sparkles in bright sunshine. The wide-open traffic-free space of Piazza del Plebiscito has a scattering of tourists. One group is playing the popular local game whereby a blindfolded person must walk across the piazza and pass between a pair of equestrian statues on the far side. I have been told that this is much more difficult than it appears, and the success rate is low.

At last, I arrive at Umberto, and pass hesitantly through the door. Tall and slim, Massimo greets me with a handshake and a warm smile. Although towering above me, with a strong, deep voice, his gentle manner is disarming. We sit down at a quiet table towards the back of the restaurant, where we can talk undisturbed.

I begin by asking Massimo about his sisters.

First-born Ermelinda studied Architecture at university, and developed a successful career as an architect. She is employed as an architect by the Comune, the local government for the city of Naples. Ermelinda has occasionally been involved in the restaurant business, leading design work for redecoration and renovation projects, and documenting the story of Umberto's first hundred years in the booklet I was given.

Lorella studied Mathematics at university in Naples. She

started work in the restaurant in the early 1980s. Lorella works full time at Umberto, as the expert sommelier responsible for choosing and procuring their wines. Lorella and Massimo, between them, take turns leading the front of house team, welcoming customers.

Roberta started to study architecture, then joined the team at Umberto a few years later. Today she divides her time between the restaurant and her bed and breakfast business, called In Centro, founded in 2018 and located on Via Toledo. At Umberto, Roberta has particular responsibility for craft beers and choosing the dishes for the seasonal menu.

Massimo himself obtained a degree in International Economics, at the Parthenope University in Naples, and then did a year's national service in the navy based in Rome. He very much enjoyed the navy, and wanted to spend time travelling the world. From a young age, Giuseppe's children were all involved in the restaurant business so, for Massimo, his period in the navy felt like a holiday! However, in 1996 his father Giuseppe hurt his leg in a car accident, and was immobilised for six months. Massimo was required to help manage the restaurant. Like his sisters, Lorella and Roberta, once he became involved in the business as an adult, he never left.

In the wider team at the restaurant, there is a tendency for people to stay a long time. Their expert pizza-makers, Gaetano and Vincenzo, have worked at Umberto for 40 years! Chef Guido Manco started in the kitchen aged 16 and is still there at the age of 38. Even the waiters, Stefano and Gennaro, have been at Umberto for more than 20 years. When I ate here the other evening, I sensed a harmonious atmosphere front of house, as if everybody knew what they were doing and felt trusted to get on with it.

As a prime representative of Umberto, in 1997 Massimo became vice president of Verace Pizza Napoletana, the society formed in 1984 to promote and protect, in Italy and worldwide, the true Neapolitan pizza. Hundreds of restaurants, across the world, belong to this association. They are committed to preserving traditional recipes, and providing authentic Neapolitan pizza to their customers.

Since 2020, Massimo has also been President of the Campania region for FIPE Confcommercio, a national organisation of 335,000 businesses, representing restaurants, bars and other retail establishments. FIPE aims to spread business best practice, with a focus on the Italian lifestyle. Tourism is important for many of FIPE's members.

"How many of Umberto's customers are tourists, as opposed to local people?" I ask Massimo.

"During the week, I would say that about 50% of our customers are tourists, but at weekends most diners are local. Ten years ago, there would have been very few tourists. There has been a significant increase in recent years."

We move on to discuss Massimo's family, and I ask how he met his wife.

"My wife, Jane, is Australian!" he says. "We met because she worked as an English teacher, and helped me with my English. At that time, she was seeing another Italian, from Rome, although that didn't last."

Much later, when Jane was planning to leave Italy and return to Melbourne, she telephoned Massimo to book a table at the restaurant, for her and her sister who was visiting Naples. After dining, the sisters mentioned to Massimo that they were going to a nearby bar for a drink. Coincidentally, this was the bar once owned by Massimo's grandmother, and the building in which

Massimo himself was born.

When the restaurant quietened down, Massimo went to the bar to look for Jane and her sister, but it was extremely crowded and he couldn't see them. Eventually, he gave up and was just leaving when Jane appeared in front of him. On the spur of the moment, and in the building where he was born, Massimo kissed her! I used to think that romances started like this only in the movies, but now I know better.

"If you had been just a few seconds earlier, or later, then your life now might be completely different," I suggest, and he agrees.

Fairly quickly, Jane decided not to return to Australia but to stay in Naples. She and Massimo married in July 2003. Their wedding took place on one of the hottest days of the year, and Jane's parents came over to attend the ceremony. Her parents regularly revisit Naples, typically twice per year, but they never again came in July. The unbearable heat and humidity of that wedding day was emblazoned in their memories.

Massimo and Jane have two boys, Jamie and Leonardo. Jamie, driven by an interest in food, is studying Mediterranean Gastronomical Science at Portici university, on the outskirts of Naples. Leonardo is still at school.

I ask Massimo about other members of the next generation, his nieces and nephews.

Ermelinda's son, Alessandro Teo, graduated in law, then studied at cooking school in Parma. After working for three years in Umberto's kitchen, he moved to Milan and opened his own restaurant there in 2016, called Monzu. Alessandro's brother Riccardo has followed in his mother's footsteps, as an architect.

Lorella's son, Lucca, graduated in engineering in Naples,

and has gone into business with Roberta's son, Lorenzo, who obtained an economics degree from Naples University, and a master's in marketing at Bocconi University in Milan. Together, they have started a home-delivery food business Da Kitchen. In the north of Italy, home-delivery and take-away food outlets are common, but this is one of the first such enterprises in Naples.

Roberta's daughter, Giulia, chose a very different path and studied medicine. While studying, she also worked front of house in the restaurant. Now qualified, she practises in Rome.

It is clear that the grandchildren of Giuseppe and Maria are following a variety of paths, but there is also significant interest in food and hospitality in that generation. It shouldn't be difficult to find family members willing to take Umberto into the future, once it is time for Massimo and his sisters to relinquish the reins.

Massimo talks about what is required to maintain a family business for over 100 years.

"The critical time is the handover, from one generation to the next. This can be tricky."

The obvious way in which a handover can fail is if there is nobody in the next generation willing to take on the enterprise. A different type of challenge arises when there are multiple family members able and willing to take the business forward, forcing difficult choices. Ideally, a solution will be found that provides all members of the next generation with an acceptable future. Umberto has twice faced this second type of challenge, and navigated those difficulties successfully, thanks to consideration and compromise from family members. It is easy to see how conflict and in-fighting over the succession could sink a business, if key players have differing priorities.

Massimo, who has visited his wife's family in Australia, talks about the differences between restaurant businesses in the two countries.

"Over there, it is more about money. A restaurant exists in order to turn a profit. First and foremost, it is an investment, and everything else is of secondary importance. In Italy, usually, it is about family. Our priority is to preserve the enterprise for the family. Of course, we have to think about money in order to make that happen, but it is not our first thought."

I imagine that, as a business becomes more venerable, the weight of expectations upon the owners becomes greater. Massimo, Lorella and Roberta must feel a great responsibility not to let their legacy, now a distinguished Neapolitan landmark, disappear into obscurity after all these years. They and their children must always look ahead, to the second century of Ristorante Umberto.

7 Space to breathe

It's another beautiful spring day in Palermo. I walk to the shore near Porta Felice, a ceremonial city gate in the form of two imposing 16th century towers, and watch morning joggers in Parco della Salute. The air is fresh, and the clean open spaces of the park lead my eyes out to sea, where container ships dot the horizon. Glancing at the phone, I see that Palazzo Chiaramonte will soon be open.

Upon entering this grand, elegant 700-year-old Palazzo, I am shown to the ticket office where two young women stand behind the counter. One of them explains that a guided tour starts at 9am.

"Oh good! Can I join that?"

"You have to," she replies, "you can only visit the palazzo with a guide."

Since it is now five minutes past nine, I quickly ask where the tour starts.

"Oh, over there . . . " she waves vaguely. She is in no hurry to give me my ticket, and I am anxious that I will miss this tour and have to wait a long time for the next one. Finally, I receive a ticket.

"Shall we go?" says the second lady.

"Oh! Are you the guide?"

"Yes, that's right. There's only you on the tour."

Although very young – she looks like she has just left school – my guide knows her stuff. She speaks Italian throughout, but her speech is unhurried and crystal clear, so that I understand almost every word, and have the opportunity to seek clarification when I don't. The most interesting part of the tour is the old cells, where prisoners of the Spanish Inquisition were kept. These inmates left graffiti on the walls, telling their personal stories, and one of them was an Englishman from Plymouth. The girl tells me how the Inquisition rang a bell, before they came to take a prisoner away for interrogation and torture, knowing the anxiety this would create in the mind of every prisoner, each wondering if it was to be their turn.

After leaving the Palazzo, I admire the enormous, tangled fig trees in nearby Giardino Garibaldi. One of these was planted in 1864, to celebrate Italian unification.

Walking back to my apartment, I cross an area of open ground, by Via Castrofilippo. The remains of apparently ancient walls, just a few centimetres tall, appear here and there amongst the grass. On a stone block, I spy a plaque and, expecting it to tell me about some ancient Roman or medieval ruins, I approach so that I can read the words.

In Italian, the plaque states: "To the memory of Giovanni Falcone, who was born in this place on the 20th May 1939, with gratitude and admiration. 23rd May 1995. The city of Palermo."

It is impossible to understand today's Sicily, if you don't know the story of Giovanni Falcone and his friend, and colleague, Paolo Borsellino. They grew up in this neighbourhood of Palermo, knowing each other as schoolboys and later meeting again at Palermo University, where they both studied law. Many of their childhood acquaintances later joined the Mafia, but Falcone and Borsellino dedicated their lives, literally, to the fight against organised crime.

Falcone and Borsellino both became prosecuting magistrates and judges in Sicily. In their early years, many officials in Sicily denied the existence of the Mafia, claiming that it was a Hollywood invention and a story spun by northern Italians as part of their prejudice against the south. However, by 1986 the duo had amassed sufficient evidence to prosecute 475 accused mafiosi, in the famous Maxi Trial. 338 of these defendants were convicted. For the first time, the existence of the Sicilian Mafia was confirmed judicially.

Falcone and Borsellino continued to pursue Mafia operatives, becoming assassination targets as a result.

On 23rd May 1992, as Giovanni Falcone was driven from the airport to his home along the A29 autostrada, a huge bomb exploded on the road beneath the car, killing him, his wife Francesca and three police officers. Their funerals, at the church of San Domenico, were attended by thousands and broadcast live on national TV, with regular programs suspended. Italy's national parliament declared a day of mourning. Then, less than two months later, on 19th July near his mother's house, Paolo Borsellino was killed by a car bomb, together with five police officers.

The backlash against the Mafia was vigorous. Totò Riina, the boss who ordered the killings, was arrested in January 1993 and jailed until his death in 2017. Falcone and Borsellino became revered martyrs, with Palermo's airport named after them.

More importantly, the attitude of the Sicilian population towards the Mafia changed completely and permanently. In 2004, five graduates, who wanted to open a bar in Palermo, decided they did not want to pay the *pizzo*, protection money for the local Mafia. They started the Addiopizzo (goodbye to extortion) campaign, with the message: "A people that pays the pizzo is a people without dignity." Shopkeepers were encouraged to display signs stating they do not pay the pizzo, and consumers were urged to only shop at establishments displaying these signs, with the slogan "Pago chi non paga" (I pay those who don't pay). Crucially, local law enforcement looked after establishments joining the campaign.

Of course, organised crime still has a strong presence in Sicily. It takes a long time to change a culture so deeply ingrained. But it is no exaggeration to say that, in Sicily, the deaths of Falcone and Borsellino changed everything.

All of this passes through my mind, as I stand in the place where Falcone was born. His house, like the others in this neighbourhood, was demolished in the 1950s.

The next morning, I walk to Piazza Aragona to visit a small shop selling handmade items such as wallets, bags and sandals. Before travelling to Palermo, I had arranged to meet the young owners, Elena Gambino and Fabrizio Lisciandrello, and hear their story. It is predominantly young Sicilians who have led the anti-Mafia movement in Sicily, so it's young people I want to meet and understand.

The shop is called Ciatu (pronounced shatu), which means breath in the local dialect. To me this conveys the desire of the youth of Sicily to breathe, free from their suffocating heritage of the Mafia, the pizzo and poverty.

As I enter, I am struck by the lovely aroma of new leather: wallets and purses arranged on shelves on the left, bags hanging from hooks on the right. At the back of the shop is a counter and a workbench, where Fabrizio sits. Although he opened up only a few minutes ago, he is already working on something, bent over in concentration. It looks like a wallet.

I notice that "Pago chi non paga" and "Addiopizzo" signs are displayed prominently.

Looking up, Fabrizio greets me cheerfully, and explains that Elena will arrive soon. Although I'm a stranger, there's warmth and friendliness in Fabrizio's welcome. But he's also a little tentative, not knowing what to expect from our encounter. We chat for a few minutes then, as promised, Elena arrives and I start asking questions. Both of them continue working at the bench while we talk. The shop is very small, so they can easily manufacture the products they sell, while looking out for customers who arrive and need serving, as well as answering my questions.

Fabrizio was born in Palermo. His father was a lawyer, and his mother a social worker, but they separated when Fabrizio was young, so that he grew up with his mother and sister. Fabrizio attended a Liceo Classico school, where the focus is on humanities subjects, including Latin and Ancient Greek. After finishing school, Fabrizio attended university in Palermo, wishing to become an instructor in Capoeira, the Brazilian martial art. Capoeira originated hundreds of years ago, developed by African slaves in Brazil as a way of affirming their identity. At university, Fabrizio also studied physiotherapy and massage. However, he found university quite boring and soon decided that it wasn't for him. Wanting something more immediately practical, he decided not to continue his studies there.

Leaving university, he was drawn into the life of a craftsman by his mother's partner Giovanni, who taught Fabrizio how to work leather. Together, they set up a small workshop at Giovanni's house, made products and sold them in local markets. Fabrizio emphasises that, due to his inexperience, the products he made in those days were much more rudimentary than those on offer in their shop today.

One day, at a market in 2012, Fabrizio saw a girl he thought he recognised at another stall, selling similar products but made from recycled inner tubes.

"Hi! You're Lidia, aren't you?"

"No!" she replied, but with a smile.

Inevitably, Fabrizio now felt embarrassed and awkward, but he continued the conversation, not least because this girl was exceptionally pretty.

He discovered that her name was Elena, also from Palermo, and that she was born into a family of independent artisans. Her grandfather made baskets and her grandmother embroidered, both as their main source of income. Her aunt was a seamstress and her uncle made shoes. Even Elena's mother knitted as a hobby.

Elena attended a Liceo Scientifico senior school, then studied Physics for a year at the University of Palermo, after which she switched to Psychology. Elena completed her university studies, but didn't graduate. After university, Elena did one year of voluntary service as a child-minding assistant, looking after children under five, as part of Italy's national Servizio Civile program. Then she found work, responsible for looking after children at a nursery. Typically, Elena and another experienced child-minder, helped by a more junior volunteer, would mind up to ten children. She truly loved this work, but it was tiring, with long hours, and the funding was sporadic. Pay checks were often delayed by up to three months.

After seven years the funding dried up completely, the nursery was closed, and Elena found herself without a job. Although very fond of her family, Elena preferred to live in her own apartment in Palermo, determined to have her independence. To pay the bills, she started babysitting, with friends recommending her to families seeking childcare. Her business grew by word of mouth.

However, Elena wasn't enjoying this as much as she had

hoped.

One day, her moped had a puncture and she took it to be repaired. While waiting for a new inner tube, she saw somebody cutting up an old inner tube and asked what they were doing. In this way, Elena discovered the potential for making new products out of old inner tubes. Liking the idea of recycling, she taught herself this new skill, and sold the resulting products at local markets. Astonishingly, Elena learnt without a teacher. Perhaps her family background, an upbringing watching people fabricate diverse items with their hands, gave her a natural ability to learn a new craft. Initially her products were relatively primitive but, over time, her abilities and her output improved.

Two years later, she met Fabrizio at one of these markets, and that accelerated the learning for both of them. With a common interest in their work, they began meeting up and sharing ideas. Each learned new techniques from the other. In parallel, romance blossomed and, after 6 months, they moved in together.

At this point, Fabrizio and Elena tell me about a third person who plays a key role in their story. In 1968, aged 18, Pietro Muratore won a competition and, as a result, went to work in Florence at the National Central Library. He later transferred to Palermo, establishing himself as a distinguished state archivist. However, Pietro did not fit the traditional caricature of an Italian state employee. He did not want to just keep his head down, doing the minimum necessary to earn a comfortable pension.

Fabrizio relates that, in his youth, Pietro also involved himself in numerous enterprises, including owning a supermarket and becoming a pizza maker. Moreover, paradoxically, this budding entrepreneur also describes himself as a communist! His sympathies are overwhelmingly for the less fortunate in society. Throughout his adult life, Pietro has been a passionate campaigner for worthy causes.

It may be difficult for citizens of the UK or USA to comprehend how a communist can also be an entrepreneur. But in southern Italy, this is a natural response to inequality and poverty, when the government is sclerotic, and organised crime is pervasive. For many, there are only two ways to find a decent living: you leave your homeland, or you start your own business.

In 2010, the aftermath of the financial crisis, youth unemployment in southern Italy was astonishingly high. Pietro came across many talented youngsters, with the ability to create beautiful hand-crafted products, but unable to make a living in Sicily. Only those who left were able to use their skills profitably. He was determined to do something to help.

A major barrier was that opening a shop immediately required the full payment of local and national taxes, bringing an unacceptable financial and administrative burden for a fledgling business. Pietro analysed the legal position and realised that, by setting up a non-profit umbrella organisation, and having artisans working within that organisation, he could protect them from the full burden, their finances being administered within the co-operative. Thus, in 2010, together with two or three partners, Pietro created the Associazione Liberi Artigiani-Artisti Balarm (Association of Free Artisans-Artists Balarm), known as ALAB, which is perhaps the only organisation of its type in Europe.

ALAB's mission is summarised beautifully on its website: "We promote craftsmanship as a way to develop innovation, economy and culture, through our presence in the streets and the schools, by educating a younger public and inspiring people who seek to do something practical for a living."

ALAB organises markets where crafts people can sell their products. Initially, this was its main function. Pietro used his connections to obtain permission from local government, to operate a market in Via Roma for example. Quickly, however, support was extended to enable artisans to open their own shops, as members of ALAB. Members are subject to strict rules, for example it is forbidden to use industrial machinery since everything must be handmade.

Elena joined ALAB in 2011, and Fabrizio in 2012 when there were about 30 members. Today the association supports more than 250 activities, mostly in Sicily, although there are members elsewhere, in Turin and France for example.

Although they initially used craft markets, some organised by ALAB, to sell their products, in September 2013 Fabrizio and Elena opened their shop Ciatu, within the ALAB association. They found premises for Ciatu in Piazza Aragona which, in those days, was a mixture of empty premises and old shops. Many businesses had closed during the nineties. "Dusty" is how Fabrizio describes it: "old people, with old ideas." After Ciatu opened, over time, more new businesses appeared.

In those days, the piazza was used as a car park by commuters working in Palermo. The square was jam packed with cars, from early in the morning until evening, such that it was difficult to see and approach the shops around the perimeter. Store owners, led by Fabrizio and Elena, organised a vigorous campaign to have parking banned in the piazza, achieving success in 2016. This was a significant step forward, enabling their business to breathe at last!

For the first four years of Ciatu, Elena continued babysitting because this provided an important source of income for the couple. She worked in the shop weekday mornings, and at weekends, in addition to her childminding assignments. Fabrizio also worked seven days per week, in the store. Because they both see their craft as a pleasure, this doesn't feel onerous to either of them.

For the first two years, they shared the premises at Ciatu with two other artisans, Marco and Enza, who made bags and other accessories. In 2015, Marco and Enza moved out, having acquired their own premises across the street, a shop now called LaboRiuso. Ciatu was the first ALAB presence in Piazza Aragona, but now the square supports four ALAB activities, plus a fifth which became sufficiently successful to leave the ALAB umbrella and become an independent business.

Initially, all Ciatu's customers were tourists. However, as their reputation became established, more and more locals began frequenting the shop. They now depend on tourism for only 50% of their income. Elena talks about how the attitudes of Sicilians have changed in recent years, attaching more value to handmade, durable products, and appreciating how recycling benefits the environment. All this has helped to increase local demand for Ciatu's products.

In 2020, Elena once more found herself childminding, but now it was because she had her own baby daughter, Emma!

By 2020, Ciatu was almost doing well enough for the owners to consider leaving ALAB and creating an independent business. But then Covid arrived, and the lockdowns drastically reduced their revenues for 2020 and 2021. Many members of ALAB closed completely as a result of the pandemic. Ciatu has survived – just – but now they must slowly recover, perhaps over several years, before they can once again consider becoming independent.

Whilst discussing the impact of the pandemic upon ALAB, we also start talking about local politics, in which Elena and Fabrizio take a keen interest. Fabrizio tells me that Leoluca Orlando, mayor of Palermo until 2022, has done much for the city, especially by investing in its cultural heritage.

I nod in agreement, and tell them about my first day in Palermo, when I visited the recently restored Palazzo Reale. This 900-year-old building was spectacular: sparkling and gleaming, as if finished just the day before. Moreover, it was a pleasure to visit, well signposted with professional, friendly staff. At many Italian monuments, staff are unhelpful, surly and thin on the ground.

Fabrizio recommends that I also visit Teatro Massimo, the largest theatre in Italy.

I come to the end of my time at Ciatu. We say our goodbyes, and I start the long walk back to my apartment near the cathedral. I reflect on how much Palermo has changed since the 1950s, when many of the schoolfriends of Falcone and Borsellino were drawn into the Mafia, because there were no better options available.

Elena and Fabrizio represent a completely different generation, able to live a life of real value, contributing positively to the world around them. They are intelligent, they love their work, and they care passionately about the future of their community. It seems to me that, slowly but surely, the people of Palermo are creating space to breathe.

8 Sunday family lunch

As a young boy, in the early 1960s, I lived with my parents and maternal grandparents in a Liverpool council house. Every Sunday afternoon, sometimes joined by my uncle and aunty, we enjoyed a traditional roast dinner.

At noon, the men walked down to a local pub, The Allerton, for several beers. The women peeled potatoes, prepared vegetables and cooked dinner. The men returned around 2.30pm, whereupon my grandfather invariably picked me up, and entertained me. His rough, stubbly chin, and the sweet smell of alcohol on his breath, are unforgettable early memories.

We all sat at the table, and the women served dinner. Once the meal was over, the men fell asleep on the settee, while the women cleared the table and washed the dishes, to the accompaniment of rhythmic snoring, percolating through from the lounge. In case you are wondering, my grandmother worked full time, Monday to Friday, but nobody questioned the division of labour on Sundays. This was a different age.

It is another Sunday afternoon, 60 years later, and I am sitting outside a restaurant in Palermo, enjoying the sunshine and recalling those days in Liverpool. Today, for the first time, I am going to experience an Italian Sunday family lunch, organised by my Sicilian friend Debora, who I met on a language exchange website. I am meeting her and her family at this restaurant, Il Culinario.

Throughout Italy, families still get together on Sunday for a substantial lunch, either at home or in a restaurant. The tradition is stronger in the south but, since family and food are top priorities for every Italian, it is hard to see the ritual disappearing, even in a modern metropolis like Milan.

With smiles and waves, Debora and her family arrive and I am introduced. Her partner Gianni is tall and distinguished, sporting a beard that matches his silver hair. He greets me with a warm handshake. Debora's parents, Franco and Enza, are equally friendly while her five-year-old son, Taka, is quiet and understandably shy. We are shown to a table outside, under a canopy since it is a fresh spring day. The waitress brings menus, but they sit unopened on the table.

"The owner will be here soon," explains Franco, implying that this makes the menus superfluous.

Since I am the novelty at the table, the conversation revolves around what I have been doing since I arrived in Palermo, and what I think of the city. After five to ten minutes, proprietor Giuseppe arrives, beaming from ear to ear. He is sporting a flat cap, familiar to me as the standard attire for working class men in the UK in the first half of the 20th century. Yet this cap is completely different, because it is sparkling with an intricate multi-coloured pattern. I comment on the cap, which they assure me is traditional Sicilian headgear. In the south of Italy, they employ bright cheerful colours with abandon, something that we northern Europeans avoid in our dour, grey climate.

It is clear that Giuseppe and Franco are old friends. Giuseppe is really pleased that we are here, and we are equally happy! A long conversation begins regarding what is on the menu today, and what foods I, as the guest, like and dislike. Eventually, Giuseppe has the complete order for the whole table, for three courses, all in his head, beneath the multi-coloured cap and behind the broad smile. I am not sure what I am getting, but I know I will enjoy it.

As the conversation progresses, I learn more about my companions and am surprised to discover that most of them have spent years in an English-speaking country. I already knew that Debora had the travel bug when she was young, working in London for a few months and then Australia for several years. Her partner Gianni, a professional photographer, lived and worked in London for nine years. Eventually, like Debora, he returned home to Sicily.

"It is not so easy to find work here, but that's more than compensated for by the climate, and the low cost of living," says Gianni.

Debora's mother Enza was brought up in New York city. When she was a teenager, her father decided to take the family back to Sicily, where Enza has remained ever since. She tells this story with regret, imagining a different life that, perhaps, would have been much better, had she remained in the United States. Although it is never stated, I get the impression that Debora still has wanderlust, and Gianni also muses about the world outside Sicily. But they clearly both adore little Taka, now attending school, and he will anchor them here for the foreseeable future.

Only Franco seems unambiguously comfortable with his lot. Like me, he enjoys good food and fine wine. He is here with his family, at his friend's restaurant, on a sunny day, with the promise of an excellent lunch. What more could you possibly want from life?

Giuseppe returns and introduces his father Silvio. Franco explains to them that I am doing research for a book, and I might be interested in the story of how Il Culinario was born. The restaurant is very busy and, at this point, they are called away.

After all these years of viewing Italian menus, broken down into antipasti, primi piatti, secondi and dolci, today is the first time I plan to consume all four courses. A selection of antipasti arrives, of which the meatballs in tomato sauce is my favourite. This is followed by pasta with sardines, then grilled seabass, and finally a chocolate and almond cake with ricotta, all accompanied by a lovely white wine selected by Franco. We talk, eat and drink for three hours, and I cannot imagine a more pleasant way to spend Sunday afternoon. It's all over too soon, and I wish my hosts goodbye with a tinge of sadness.

The next morning, with the sun shining for me again, I return to Il Culinario and ask to see Giuseppe. He is not surprised when I ask if he can tell me the story behind his restaurant. We sit down at a table inside, and Giuseppe asks his son to join us.

"Richard, this is Silvio, who will one day take over the restaurant." Following the Italian tradition, Giuseppe's first son is named after his grandfather.

Like Giuseppe, son Silvio always wanted to work in the restaurant trade. He attended a school specialising in languages, and is now studying online for three years with the eCampus University.

"Tomorrow, I have my first exam . . . it's in English!" says Silvio.

As it happens, Silvio is not the only one being examined tomorrow. Giuseppe tells me that Il Culinario has been selected to compete in a national, televised cooking competition: Il Migliore Chef Italia. Tomorrow evening, the recipe they have created for the occasion, called Etna because it resembles an erupting volcano, will be judged to decide whether they progress to the next stage. Giuseppe explains how the dish is constructed.

"The cone of the volcano is swordfish, surrounded by cuttlefish representing old, frozen lava, while sea urchins on bruschetta form the hot, erupting lava."

In his late forties, Guiseppe Vicari is blessed with a cheerful face and abundant smiles. The family name comes from the small village of Vicari, 50km from Palermo.

We begin by discussing Giuseppe's father Silvio, who first introduced the family to the hospitality business. Silvio senior was the seventh child of Giuseppe senior. Giuseppe made his living in a variety of ways, including as a fisherman and as a plumber. After leaving school, Silvio found work as a waiter at a high-end restaurant called Harry's Bar in Palermo. This establishment was owned by an aristocrat, a marquis, and patronised mostly by wealthy Palermitani. The head chef was a member of the Cavalieri di Cucina (Knights of Gastronomy), a small, select group of the most honoured chefs in Italy, and the maître d' also had a strong reputation. Here Silvio learnt his trade, from the best in the business. He also met and married Mariella, who worked in a jeweller's shop. Together, they started a family.

After Silvio had worked there for 13 years, Harry's Bar closed down. However, four members of the Harry's Bar team then founded their own restaurant in Via Brunelleschi, called Friend's Bar. Silvio accepted a position as maître d' at this new restaurant. From the age of 11, Silvio's son Giuseppe also helped out in Friend's Bar, learning about the business from a young age. Giuseppe never doubted that this was how he wanted to spend his life. He went to a school specialising in the hotel and restaurant business, in Palermo.

In 2001, at the age of 26, Giuseppe started his own place, Villafranca Pub, in Via Principe di Villafranca, open only in the evenings. His father continued working at Friend's Bar, feeling he should remain loyal to his colleagues there, but Giuseppe's mother Mariella came to work at Villafranca. Giuseppe's friend, Salvo, from school days, also worked at the bar with him.

One day, not long after the bar opened, a striking young lady walked into Villafranca with her friends, and Giuseppe was transfixed. "I will marry her," he said to his friend Salvo. When the opportunity arose, Giuseppe started a conversation with this girl, Claudia. They hit it off, but Giuseppe wasn't sure whether she was only interested in him because, as owner of the bar, she assumed he was well off. As a test of her true feelings, Giuseppe invited her out to lunch at a grotty restaurant, his logic being that, if she accepted, that would prove she really liked him! However, Claudia said she was too busy. Poor Giuseppe had painted himself into a corner.

Three months passed. Then, fortunately for our hero, Claudia's sister, Veronica, came into Villafranca one evening, and Giuseppe asked her about Claudia. Veronica returned another evening, this time bringing her sister, and Giuseppe was able to ask Claudia out again. This time, the path of true love was followed without a hitch, and the couple became engaged, and then married. Towards the end of 2002, they had their first child, son Silvio. Later, the young boy acquired a little sister, Zaira.

In 2008, Giuseppe's sister Roberta was about to get married and their mother was planning the wedding. For Mariella, the combination of planning the wedding and long hours at the bar left her with little time for sleep. She really wanted to do both, but it was clearly impossible. Concerned for his mother's well-being, Giuseppe decided to sell the bar, as the only way to stop her working there! The bar had other minor problems at this time, for example complaints from neighbours about the music, so Giuseppe felt it was time for a change. His friend Salvo took advantage of this opportunity to travel the world, working as he went.

In that period, there was a shortage of well-qualified managers for Palermo's bars and restaurants, so Giuseppe had no difficulty finding work. Because the name of the establishment resonated, being the same as Silvio's first restaurant, Giuseppe chose to work at a place called Harry's Bar, in Via Marchese di Villabianca.

Meanwhile, father Silvio's business, Friend's Bar, was struggling. They were not changing with the times and, as a result, not attracting younger customers. As their loyal customers grew older, and died off, their income diminished until, in 2009, it was unsustainable and Friend's Bar closed. For Giuseppe, this represented a golden opportunity. With sister Roberta happily married, now both his parents were available to join with him in starting a new business.

They found small premises, previously functioning as a bread shop, near the spectacular Massimo Theatre, in an area frequented by tourists. Here, they opened their new restaurant in 2009. To distinguish themselves from other tourist-focused establishments in the area, they planned a menu of authentic Sicilian cuisine. Silvio chose Il Culinario (The Culinary) as the name for the new restaurant, to emphasise their focus on good quality food. Giuseppe managed the bar and helped in various areas, with Silvio responsible front of house and Mariella as head chef.

Giuseppe was delighted. Now he had the business he'd always wanted, and was working with family and friends. Although they could only accommodate ten tables, the business was a success from the beginning. Initially, only 20% of their custom came from tourists but, over time, this increased to about 70%.

In 2014 a new chef, Antonio Cavaretta, started. Also, Salvo returned from his travels, to join the team as a waiter. In that same year, they expanded by opening a second restaurant. However, the extra workload from managing two sites proved too much for the family so, in 2017, they closed the second site to concentrate only on Il Culinario.

In the spring of 2020, dark times came to Italy with the arrival of Covid, and all restaurant businesses were heavily restricted. Even when permitted to admit diners, there had to be significant spacing between occupied tables. With their premises so small, this was a big problem for Il Culinario.

Giuseppe seized on the opportunity to move to bigger premises. They found a suitable building in Via Principe di Belmonte, still only a ten-minute walk from the Massimo theatre, and relocated in the spring of 2020 during lockdown restrictions. When opened up fully to customers, they were now able to seat 100 people.

In 2020, both Silvio and Mariella retired and ceased full time work, to avoid the risk of Covid infection. The pandemic continued to present problems throughout 2020 and 2021. In 2021, the restaurant was effectively closed for six months, able only to earn revenue from take-aways and home delivery. Most of the team was put into furlough. Giuseppe bought a scooter for delivering food to customers. He, his wife, plus one other person, prepared and delivered all the food, to people in local hotels, and in their homes.

About 250m down the road, at number 87, was an empty building, previously occupied by another restaurant that closed in 2020. Almost every day, Giuseppe passed this place on his scooter, delivering food, and he became more and more convinced that it would be a better location for Il Culinario. It is slightly more spacious and, more importantly, it is much closer to the busy heart of pedestrianised Via Principe di Belmonte, Palermo's living room, where hundreds of Sicilians enjoy their evening passeggiata. Above all, for Giuseppe the new location just felt right.

"This was a decision of the heart."

Giuseppe rented the new premises in the spring of 2022, and spent three months cleaning and preparing them. Then Il Culinario relocated again, in the pitiless heat of a Sicilian July. They closed the restaurant for one day, while a team of 15 people moved everything 250 metres down the street, using only handcarts. Fortunately, the air conditioning was on in both buildings, providing a brief respite between journeys, but it was still a day that nobody would ever forget.

In the new building, they have 18 tables inside and 20 tables outside. Of the 20 outside, 10 are under cover and these can be used for most of the year. Not long after the move, the restaurant opened up to diners again.

Although nominally retired, Silvio still turns up to speak to customers, and he also produces a lovely mandarincello - like limoncello, but made with mandarins rather than lemons. Mariella still cooks desserts for the restaurant, and helps in other ways whenever they are especially busy. It's hard to stay away from the business that has come to define their family.

Giuseppe tells me that his friend Franco was keen to revisit Il Culinario, sometime after the prolonged closure. He phoned Giuseppe to make a reservation for four. They arrived at the allotted time, sat down, ordered their food, and started drinking the water. Then Franco noticed that he didn't recognise any of the staff in the restaurant. Puzzled, he telephoned Giuseppe to ask if they had relocated.

"Yes! I thought you knew." said Giuseppe.

Franco had gone to a new restaurant, recently opened at their old premises. Since they had already ordered, Giuseppe suggested to Franco that they stay there and finish their meal, then relocate to Il Culinario for a chat over digestivi.

Looking around, I notice that the restaurant's interior is beautifully presented. There are lovely frescoes, branches with leaves and strings of garlic reach down from the ceiling, and one wall presents row upon row of wine bottles.

"Did you do all of this?" I ask.

"Much of it, yes. Some of the original decor remains, but we personalised the space by making many changes ourselves. We have created a different atmosphere from that we inherited."

"Because our food is, as far as possible, natural, we have tried to bring a touch of nature to the dining area", adds young Silvio.

Silvio helps out at the restaurant, preparing for the day when he will take over from his father. During his career, Giuseppe has worked extensively in all areas of the business: cooking in the kitchen, serving customers at the bar and in the dining room, managing suppliers, financial control, and overall management. He believes that this long, broad apprenticeship is necessary to produce a top-class restaurant manager, and Silvio is happy to follow that path.

I am struck by how Giuseppe and Silvio both always knew that they wanted this life, a commitment that can be all-consuming. Family rhythms revolve around the restaurant, and its customers. Their life embodies that great Italian commitment to family and food, but with an ironic twist.

Because of the restaurant, they themselves can never sit down to enjoy a traditional Sunday family lunch.

9 Shy achievers

There are two cities, Rome and London, where I can always find new and interesting things to see. Both cities grew as the capitals of great empires, concentrating wealth, trade and ideas from diverse cultures. Both have an impressive heritage from those days of empire, for the modern visitor to enjoy.

Today's Rome is actually the product of two empires: the Roman empire and its spiritual offspring, the Roman Catholic Church. The Church, in particular, has brought durable wealth to the city, creating an astounding architectural and artistic heritage. No matter how many times you visit Rome, you will always find a new church, museum or palazzo worth visiting.

Some places are so good, that I can return again and again without becoming jaded. Such is the Borghese Gallery and Museum, where I find myself today, amongst a jaw-dropping array of sculptures and paintings, collected by Cardinal Scipione Borghese in the early 17th century. As the Pope's nephew, and one of the most powerful men in Italy, Cardinal Borghese used his position to purchase and commission the most dazzling masterpieces of his day. Once the Cardinal decided he wanted a piece, the owner had no option but to sell it at a reasonable price, or present it as a "gift". In those days, Romans lived in a mafia state, with the Pope as Godfather.

Painters Caravaggio, Raphael and Titian were all favourites of Scipione Borghese, and he was an especially devoted patron of Gian Lorenzo Bernini. For me, Bernini is the greatest sculptor who ever lived. In the Borghese Gallery you will find the Bernini masterpieces *David* and *Apollo and Daphne*, plus two astonishing portrait busts of the Cardinal himself. In Bernini's hands, marble becomes living flesh.

Leaving the gallery, I am welcomed by spring sunshine and enjoy a leafy stroll to the Pincio gardens. This area is awash with happy memories. I recall renting a bench seat bicycle, to pedal around the gardens with my daughters. Afterwards, we watched the sunset from the terrace overlooking Piazza del Popolo, with a distant view of the dome of St. Peter's, before descending to the Piazza to enjoy the party atmosphere, mingling with young locals eating ice creams and watching street performers. Another evening, I was here at sunset, alone but part of a large crowd enjoying live music from a band, there to celebrate World Earth Day. Several table football games were also provided, for anybody not interested in the music.

After enjoying an aperitif at a bar near Piazza del Popolo, I wander down Via Margutta. This quiet back street has always been a home for creative types, from Fortuny to Stravinsky, Picasso and Fellini. Fans of the wonderful 1953 movie Roman Holiday, starring Audrey Hepburn and Gregory Peck, can try to find the apartment of Gregory Peck's character, at number 51 (not easy). I am content to enjoy the beauty and tranquillity of Via Margutta, that contrasts with the noise and dirt in much of Rome. A couple of art galleries are still open, so I pop in to look around.

By now it's 7pm, and I have a dinner reservation at my favourite Roman restaurant, back at the top of Via Margutta. Although I have visited Babette several times over the years, I don't know how it was founded, or where the name came from. I remember reading somewhere that Babette was owned by two sisters so, before travelling to Rome, I contacted them by email and asked if we could meet so that I could hear their story. Happily, for me, they agreed and I have an appointment tomorrow morning. First though, I want to enjoy dinner there this evening.

It's almost empty when I walk in, 7pm being early for dinner in Rome. I'm welcomed by a very friendly lady, who is also quiet and self-effacing. I recognise her from my last visit, and assume that she is one of the Sallorenzo sisters, who own the restaurant. It's too cold to eat outside in the courtyard, so I'm shown to a table in one of the elegant, traditional interior rooms. I spend an hour over dinner, and the restaurant is quite busy by the time I leave. As always, the dishes, and especially the wines, are excellent and not too expensive. Walking back to my apartment through the cold night air, the memory of the meal provides a warm glow.

The next morning is fresh and sunny, as I return to Babette to meet the Sallorenzo sisters. The same friendly lady greets me, with the same broad smile. As I suspected, she turns out to be Flora, one of the owners. Flora explains that her sister Silvia is in the kitchen, but she will be available soon. After a few minutes, Silvia arrives, wearing a traditional chef's outfit minus the hat. Flora disappears, and Silvia takes me to a table in the courtyard. She explains that she must return to the kitchen in an hour, to start preparing lunch.

Silvia seems more serious and business-like than her sister, yet equally undemonstrative. I ask if I can take her picture, just as a memory aid for myself, but she refuses. I joke that I also hate having my picture taken, but Silvia shows little sign of relaxing. She wants to get on with the job, so she can return to the kitchen.

I ask where the sisters were born, to discover they are originally from Rome, with Flora two years older than Silvia. The girls attended a Liceo Classico, the traditional high school in Italy where it was compulsory to study Latin and Ancient

Greek.

Silvia wanted to study medicine, and she enrolled at university. However, keen to see more of the world before attending university, she worked for one year as an air hostess, visiting Rio de Janeiro, Tokyo and other exotic locations. She looks back with great fondness on that year, when she was young and impressionable. Then, having experienced the world of work, Silvia couldn't face dedicating herself to perhaps ten years of study before becoming a physician. She decided not to go to university after all, and found a job in advertising.

Flora meanwhile did not take a gap year, but studied literature at university. She left before completing her degree and, at about the same time as Silvia, also started in advertising, working for a different company.

Then Silvia met and married a businessman, moving to Florence where he ran his own travel agency. While in Florence, she was asked to translate medical journals from English to Italian. Although Silvia insists that her English was not especially good, she very much enjoyed this work, rekindling her passion for medicine.

Flora also married and, soon, both sisters had children, Silvia a daughter and Flora two sons. Initially they stopped working, but then they decided to work together. Drawing on their experience of publishing, from their various roles in advertising, they started producing guides, e.g. for American Express, and periodicals, including a knitting magazine.

After five years, Silvia returned to Rome. The sisters continued working together, and eventually they decided to start an ambitious new magazine called Audrey, covering fashion, culture and cuisine, with Silvia as Editor and Flora responsible for graphics. Each edition was enormous, comprising several hundred glossy pages, with high-quality images and articles in Italian, French and English. By covering the cultural scene in Milan, Paris and New York, they could reach a truly international market. Indeed, they employed more American than Italian writers.

Silvia shows me one of these issues, and I'm impressed by the quality, and also the weight of the magazine. With publication initially every three months, and later every two months, the pace was punishing. Their first few years were exceptionally challenging. Pulling together the material, ensuring the quality of each edition, and working with three publishers, in New York, Paris and London, all combined to become a gargantuan task, beset by problems. And once the mountain had been climbed, and that edition published, they immediately had to start work on the next.

After ten years in production, they decided they had done enough, and the magazine closed in 2001.

Throughout the 1980s and 1990s, while travelling the world because of work, Silvia enjoyed many opportunities to eat good food. Silvia had learned to cook at an early age, influenced by her mother who liked to eat well. Many of Silvia's happiest memories were associated with food. Towards the end of the 1990s, Silvia's interest in cooking grew and in the year 2000, before the magazine closed, the sisters became involved in a food catering business.

I express surprise at their willingness to take on such a demanding new activity, while still working on the magazine.

"It was a little tiring," admits Silvia with a smile.

Sometime after the magazine closed, capitalising on their catering experience, they took management of the restaurant at Circolo Ippico Acqua Santa, a private equestrian club on Via

Appia in the outskirts of Rome. Here they had their own chef. The club provided an ideal training ground, where they learnt how to run a kitchen, and how to serve a large number of customers.

Finally, they felt ready for what Silvia calls "our great adventure". Wishing to open a restaurant in the city, they found the perfect location in Via Margutta, previously occupied by a pizzeria. Here there was plenty of indoor space for diners – two good sized rooms – plus a shaded, quiet courtyard for the warmer months. They secured the premises and, after making minor changes to the interior, in 2006 Silvia and Flora opened Babette.

At this point, Silvia reflects that, as with their magazine, they wanted to create something exclusive and refined. Making money was never the priority. At Babette, serving good quality food, and providing a welcoming environment, are what matter.

"My joy, my happiness, comes from seeing the pleasure of our guests, here at Babette," says Silvia, adding that she wants visitors to feel like friends who have been invited to her home for dinner.

Collaborating with a local gallery, the sisters display works by up-and-coming artists, on the walls of the restaurant. These paintings and photographs, which change regularly, provide visual interest for the diners, and a platform for the artists.

Silvia starts talking about the menu at Babette. Inspired by the diversity of dishes she came across when travelling, Silvia is always looking to experiment, incorporating ideas from far and wide. At the same time, the recipes are inevitably influenced by Italian cuisine, "our great tradition" as Silvia calls it. The menu changes continually, incorporating seasonal, fresh produce of the highest quality.

I am struck by how the sisters never want to stand still, regularly changing the menu, and even the art on the walls. Perhaps they have unconsciously transferred the discipline of issuing a magazine, with brand new content every few months, to their restaurant business. It's clear that, for Silvia and Flora, work brings joy.

The name of the restaurant comes from the 1987 Danish film Babette's Feast, portraying two sisters in a puritanical 19th century rural community. The sisters lead a spartan life, following their strict protestant work ethic. A mysterious French refugee, Babette, comes to stay with them. Years later, to show her gratitude, Babette cooks a meal of the highest Parisian cuisine, for the sisters and their friends in the village.

Having met Silvia and Flora, I understand how they feel kinship with these fictional sisters, and how Babette's top-quality food inspires them. Silvia and Flora live to work, rather than work to live, and their pursuit of quality, whether in publishing or catering, comes above all else. I ask Silvia if she could imagine herself one day retiring from the restaurant business. She looks horrified at the mere thought.

As executive chef, Silvia runs the team in the kitchen, while Flora is in charge front of house. Now grown up, their children are also involved in the business.

Noon approaches, and Silvia must return to the kitchen. I thank her for her time, and emphasise that Babette is my favourite restaurant in Rome.

"Oh, there are much better," she says dismissively.

Objectively, she's correct. There are 20 Michelin starred restaurants in Rome and, if money is no object, you can find spectacular food and flawless service elsewhere. But there is no other restaurant that evokes such warm memories for me, and thus has a place in my heart.

As she gets up to leave, Silvia hesitates and appears to be having second thoughts about having spoken to me.

"It is the restaurant, and the customer experience, that matters – not our story. We wish to remain low-profile."

As a repressed, shy northern European, I understand Silvia's desire to avoid the limelight. We generally expect Italian restaurateurs to be loud and flamboyant, parading their passion. Yet here we have a successful restaurant, in the heart of southern Europe, which is managed by puritanical sisters, like the Scandinavians in Babette's Feast, who prize quiet control over showmanship.

10 The fire inside

It's a beautiful, fresh morning in Rome. I check out of my rented apartment, and walk towards Spagna station. At the foot of the Spanish Steps, within a cordoned off area, there is a film crew, watched by a small crowd pressed against the barrier ropes. I have time to linger, and discover what happens. The answer is very little. Eventually the director calls for silence, and they do a take, which involves an actor dressed as a priest walking past a group of nuns, to whom he nods in recognition. Ten minutes later, during which time nothing appears to have changed, the whole procedure is repeated. I wait another ten minutes, but everybody appears to be standing around, just waiting. . .

Feeling pleased that I don't work in the film business, I leave and take the metro to Termini, arriving in plenty of time for the 10am Frecciarossa to Lecce.

My memories of train travel in Italy, from ten-plus years ago, are not good. I recall dirty stations and shabby, unreliable trains. Cancellations, delays and strikes were routine. But I have never previously used the Frecciarossa (literally *red arrow*) high speed train service. Today, I am taking a single train directly from Rome to Lecce, in Puglia, the boot of Italy, covering a distance of almost 600km in under six hours.

So far, I'm impressed. The train is clean, the seats are comfortable and roomy, and I automatically have an assigned seat with my ticket. I have a window seat at a table, with another two seats opposite. An elderly gentleman, with dishevelled white hair, is already seated diagonally opposite me, watching something on his iPad. Then a portly middle-aged business man arrives, with a smart suit and briefcase. He leans over the elderly gentleman and shows him his ticket.

"This is my seat," says the businessman.

"Well, you can have my seat instead." He points to the seat opposite.

"But I booked this seat."

"What does it matter? That seat is just as good."

The white-haired man stares at his iPad, avoiding eye contact. The businessman shows no sign of backing down.

Up to now I have been feeling mellow, and I wish to stay in a tranquil mood for the journey. I try to defuse the situation before it escalates into an ugly conflict, by leaning across the table and looking the elderly man in the eye.

"Please. Is it difficult?"

It's interesting how, now outnumbered two to one, the man opposite feels forced to concede, by social pressure alone. Reluctantly, he gathers his stuff and moves to the seat next to me, making way for the businessman.

Our train departs promptly at 10am, and I gaze out of the window as we pass through the suburbs of Rome. The businessman has pulled out his laptop, and he is studiously typing. The dishevelled gentleman, next to me, is using earbuds and is fascinated by whatever he is watching on his iPad. I can't help but lean over and take a peek, to see videos of scantily clad teenage girls dancing to pop music. Every now and then, this music blares out loudly and fills the carriage, although the elderly gentleman seems totally unaware that this is happening. The businessman glares at him, eyes filled with hatred. After 20 minutes or so, of intermittent bursts of loud music, the businessman gathers his belongings and moves to the other end of the carriage.

Strangely, we have no more occurrences of the loud music.

Now that the train has picked up speed, the countryside through the window looks like a speeded-up movie. As we approach Caserta, my neighbour removes his earbuds and starts to pack away his things. I chat to him briefly, discovering that he is returning home, after visiting his son in the Veneto.

After Caserta, the journey passes quickly. Before long we are pulling into Bari, and I see the businessman preparing to alight. He nods and smiles in my direction, as he leaves the train. The journey from Bari to Lecce proceeds at a much slower pace. Clearly the railway lines this far south have not been upgraded for the high-speed service. At last, we arrive in Lecce and I descend from the train.

I take a taxi from the station to the rental apartment, where I contact a friend of the owner, who lets me in. Leaving my bag, I immediately exit the apartment and walk across the centre of Lecce to find a craft shop I have previously researched on the internet. By now it's 6pm, but this shop stays open until 8pm.

This is my first time in Lecce and, as I'd hoped, the city is spectacular. Soft, creamy limestone has been carved to create wonderful Baroque churches and palazzi. There is little traffic in the centre, as in most small Italian cities, so walking is a pleasure.

Lecce has been called The Florence of the South, but this is nonsense! Whoever suggested a similarity clearly had not visited both cities. The buildings in Lecce, with their characteristic local stone, look completely different from those in Florence. Lecce's centre is quiet. Florence, a world-renowned centre for art, is a much bigger, busier city.

If I were forced to choose a city in the north, that is similar to Lecce, then that would have to be Venice. Lecce is more like Venice, without the canals, because both places have a peaceful beauty untouched by modernity.

My stroll across Lecce is stunning, but brief. Within a few minutes, just off a small triangular piazza, I enter a narrow alley called Via Giacomo Matteotti. Opposite a jewellery store, and adjacent to a shop selling vinyl records, at last I can see Il Mercante d'Arte (The Art Merchant).

I climb some tiled steps, pass through the open door and enter what feels like a cave. A cave that might easily belong to Aladdin. There is an astonishing diversity of craft products, arranged on glass shelves, displayed in wooden box-frames, and hanging on strings. There are Venetian face masks, Murano glass, items of jewellery, papier-mâché sculptures, ceramic ornaments and more. I see several examples of a strange ceramic object, called a Pumo. Apparently, *pumo* is the Puglian dialect word for apple, although the Pumo is shaped more like a flower bud. These good luck charms can be found all over Puglia, and elsewhere in southern Italy.

A middle-aged, fair-haired lady is sitting at the counter. She looks up and smiles. After a brief look around, I introduce myself and explain that I am writing a book and would like to know the story of the shop's owner. She confirms that she is the owner, introducing herself as Nadia Carrafa. Nadia is happy to tell me her story but, when we start discussing her availability over the next few days, it becomes clear that she doesn't really have time to spare.

"Why don't we talk now?" says Nadia, "Here in the shop."

I feel unprepared, not having brought my notebook, but Nadia provides paper and lends me a pen. I sit down across the counter from her, and ask my first question, learning that Nadia was born in Lecce, in the early 1960s. From the age of 14, she attended an Istituto Tecnico Economico, a high school specialising in business and economics training.

After finishing school, Nadia found work in a photography shop. She started taking and exhibiting photographs, as a hobby. Clearly blessed with talent, she won several awards for her pictures. Later, Nadia opened her own photography shop, called Foto Arte, on the outskirts of Lecce, which she managed for five years. Wedding photography provided an important income stream, and it also provided Nadia with a husband! Marcello, the brother of the groom at one of these weddings, became Nadia's boyfriend. Marcello came from the coastal city of Taranto, about 90km from Lecce, and was an officer in the Italian navy. After two years together, they married.

The couple had three children, two boys and a girl, the first arriving 18 months after they wed. With Marcello often far away because of work, Nadia had to close the photography shop. However, her creative spirit refused to be caged. When the children were young, Nadia trained for two years, to become a qualified art restorer in 2001. She brings out her graduation certificate to show me, proudly explaining that this is equivalent to a university degree, which students today may take up to five years to earn.

Nadia also trained for three years (2003-2005) in the Leccese art of Cartapesta (papier-mâché), at the local E. Maccagnani art school, named after the famous artist Eugenio Maccagnani, born in Lecce in 1852. The school also hosts regular exhibitions, of paintings and other art work. Nadia, with her sister Ornella, and a friend, once presented an exhibition of their own works at the school.

Cartapesta has a long history in Lecce. In the 17th century, the Counter-Reformation created a need for more monuments and churches, to impress worshippers and counter the lure of

Lutheranism. Under pressure to produce sacred works, but unable to deploy expensive materials like stone and bronze, craftsmen in Lecce experimented with the plasticisation of paper. Many early practitioners of Cartapesta were barbers, practising in their back-rooms between haircuts. These skills, acquired in the 17th and 18th centuries, have been passed down from generation to generation for 300 years, and Lecce remains the primary centre for papier-mâché art in Puglia. Many shops display colourful miniature sculptures, normally with a religious theme, that exhibit astonishingly fine detail. There is even a Cartapesta museum in Lecce.

Every December, the Lecce Christmas market includes a puppets festival, where local craftsmen display Cartapesta puppets and nativity figures. Nadia has participated in this for several years.

In 2005, Nadia started work as a restorer. I am asking what type of restoration work, when we are interrupted by Italian tourists entering the shop, and asking the way to Piazza del Duomo. Nadia explains how to get there, but they promptly set off in the wrong direction and she has to chase after them. Back inside, she continues.

"I was assistant to an experienced restorer. She and I worked for private clients, and also museums."

Following a couple of years as an art restorer, everything changed for Nadia. In 2007, the navy transferred Marcello to a land-based role, at the Venice Arsenale. After years of Marcello being away, including a worrying period of active service in the Persian Gulf, at last they had the chance to be together as a family. Nadia and the children moved to Venice, to be with him. At that time the oldest boy was 15, and Nadia's daughter just 7.

The navy provided them with accommodation in an old

convent, attached to the church of San Daniele in Castello. This church was demolished in 1839, at which time the other buildings were converted to naval barracks. Being very close to the Arsenale, Marcello had just a short walk to work each day.

During 2007 and 2008, their time in Venice, Nadia was primarily a mother, but she also painted masks as a hobby. A friend had a small shop, where masks painted by Nadia were sold.

Nadia provided lessons in Cartapesta to other wives at the Officers Club, advertising these through a circular distributed to the families of servicemen. Amongst these military families, there was a lively cultural exchange. Nadia herself learnt how to make jewellery, from other officers' wives.

"What did you think of Venice?" I ask.

"Beautiful. Marvellous!" She smiles, with twinkling eyes, and affection in her voice.

"Do you prefer Venice to Lecce?"

Nadia looks uncertain.

"Hmmm. I had a good time there. I cried when I left Lecce, and I also cried when I left Venice. It's a special place to live."

At the end of 2008, because the children were not really happy in Venice, Nadia returned with them to Lecce. They went back to the family home, in a small village a few miles outside the city, where Nadia resumed contact with her friends and wider family. Marcello continued living and working in Venice, for another two years. After his Venice posting, Marcello did not return to the sea. He took land-based roles, initially in Taranto, closer to home, and then in Rome.

Back in Lecce, Nadia continued her creative output, predominantly working from home, with her sister Ornella. They produced more exhibitions of their work, especially for the

Christmas festivities.

In 2013, with the children older and more self-sufficient, Nadia opened her shop Il Mercante d'Arte. I ask whether it was difficult to find the initial investment, for starting the business. Nadia explains that she kept costs low, for example by constructing and painting the shop furniture herself.

"Initially, I focused on Venetian masks, Murano glass and jewellery. I made the jewellery myself."

Having seen many shops succeeding with these items in Venice, it's natural that Nadia saw this as a safe set of products to start with. Soon however, she added her Cartapesta statues to the product set. The shop has now operated successfully for ten years.

Marcello retired from the navy in 2019. I ask if he ever helps out with Nadia's business.

"No! He occasionally comes into Lecce, to join me for a coffee, but he has his own things to get on with, in the house and with the children."

This prompts me to ask what the children are up to now.

"My oldest boy Alessandro is a dentist, in Lecce. He's a very good dentist."

Nadia beams with pride.

"My second boy Riccardo trained as a chef and, aged 18, went to work in London. So, he speaks good English. However, after two years he returned to Lecce, deciding that a chef's life was not for him. Restaurant work is stressful and tiring. Then he did a degree in Business Economics, at an online university. He graduated just a couple of weeks ago. And tomorrow evening, we go to my daughter's graduation party!"

"Tell me about your daughter."

"Federica is 23 years old, and she is an Instagram influencer.

That's her hobby, but she is sponsored by various Italian businesses, enabling her to travel. She is studying sociology, criminals and deviance at university, and she has just completed the first three years, to obtain a standard degree. She is about to start a further two years of specialist studies. Federica wants to work in prisons."

"By the way, when Marcello and I married, I kept my surname Carrafa. However, the children take their father's surname, Leone. Since last year, babies born in Italy are automatically given the surnames of both parents, unless the parents agree on them taking the surname of just one parent."

Changing the subject, I ask how many days Nadia works in the shop.

"Always! Every day! Well, I open up late in the mornings, and the shop is closed at 8pm. Also, during January to March, and in November, the shop is often closed, because few people come in. I am very busy in the summer."

Whenever the shop is quiet, Nadia works on her next creation, be it Cartapesta or jewellery, behind the counter.

"You must really like this work?"

"Yes, I do! I've been here ten years. Many times, I thought about closing, but I am still here. I love it. But I don't know for how much longer. . ."

My Neapolitan friend Fabio once told me that the people of the Salento region, which includes Lecce, have a very different character from people in Bari and the rest of Puglia: "In Bari, they are like Neapolitans. They don't like rules. But in Lecce, they are virtually northerners, thinking for example that work is more important than food!"

As I leave the shop, and stroll through the beautiful streets of Lecce to my apartment, I reflect on Nadia's life. Her passion for making beautiful objects was always irresistible. Whatever else was happening, she had to be learning a new skill or creating something beautiful. Even if, one day, Il Mercante d'Arte closes, then I am sure Nadia will continue to be a prolific artist. The fire inside will not die. As long as she breathes, she has no choice.

11 The businessman

It's Friday, my first full day in Lecce. The sun is shining, but it's not hot. After breakfast at a nearby café, I walk across town to where I can hire a bicycle for the day. Most small Italian cities are bike friendly and, while walking around a city centre can be tiring, and hard on the feet, cycling is pleasant and relaxing.

Starting with the Bello Luogo (beautiful place) park, I tour the city on the bike, stopping for lunch at a restaurant called La Cucina di Mamma Elvira. Sat outside, enjoying the sunshine and the food, I can't help but overhear two Americans chatting at the next table. When the waitress appears, the man speaks to her in what sounds like perfect Italian. Curiosity gets the better of me, so I strike up a conversation with them.

They are from northern California. He works for a company that imports Italian food, and they are here combining his business trip with a holiday. He speaks good Italian because his parents are first generation Italian immigrants. Americans, who take the trouble to learn Italian, usually do so because they are of Italian descent and wish to reconnect with their roots. This man, however, learnt Italian as a child. His wife confesses that she totally relies on him when in Italy, and has no desire to learn the language.

Before leaving, I ask to speak to the restaurant owner. He is happy to tell me his story, and we agree to meet on Monday morning.

Having returned the hired bike, back in my apartment I look at the website for Mamma Elvira. It turns out that where I ate lunch is just one of five different establishments in Lecce, all in the Mamma Elvira group. One of these, Corte dei Pandolfi, is described as an Oyster House, and specialises in seafood. So, in the evening I go there for dinner. It's much smaller than La Cucina di Mamma Elvira, and fairly quiet, but I enjoy the quality food, the quality wine, and a brief conversation with the young Argentinian waitress.

Afterwards, I stroll to Piazzetta Santa Chiara, pleasantly green, with fragrant pittosporum trees and bars with outdoor seating. The April sunshine has left some warmth in the air, so I sit outside enjoying a drink and the orange-blossom-like perfume from those pittosporum. Soon, a small band sets up their instruments at the bar and starts playing. It feels like summer has come early.

The weekend passes in a blur of sightseeing. On Monday morning, I return to La Cucina di Mamma Elvira to see the owner, Andrea Favale. Andrea is a big man, with an open, friendly manner. But he is also calm and considered, and certainly no loud extrovert. We start talking in Italian, but his English is so good, and my Italian so poor, that we soon switch to English.

I begin by asking about Andrea's parents. Both are from Puglia, and now retired. His father was an industrial chemist, and Andrea followed him into this field. Andrea's mother was a schoolteacher. Born in Lecce, Andrea was their first child, followed four years later by his sister Chiara.

Andrea attended school in Lecce, including the Liceo Classico, and then studied industrial chemistry at the University of Bologna. This involved learning chemistry itself, plus chemical engineering, the management of industrial processing plants. Andrea graduated in 1997, and then studied for another year to gain a master's degree, which was effectively a science-focused MBA. This year included a four-month assignment, working for EniChem in Ravenna.

Every now and then, as we talk, a team member approaches Andrea to ask him a question. He deals with them efficiently, and quickly returns to our conversation.

After university, Andrea returned to Lecce and started working with his father, in his chemical analysis business. They advised their clients, who ranged from small local restaurants to big food processing factories, on safety and environmental issues, including health and safety regulations for consumers and workers.

After 18 months working with his father, in 1999, Andrea went travelling for a couple of months, visiting London and the United States. As a result, he decided to move to London, to seek work there. Initially, he hoped to apply his expertise in industrial chemistry. He sought work as a consultant, and approached major chemical companies, but he was unable to find a position.

To get by, Andrea worked in a pub for six months. His patience paid off, because he was then able to find work with a startup business. This new business provided a financial analysis of all major European business acquisitions, defined as those valued over five million euros. With the dotcom boom in 2000, there was great demand for this information and the business grew rapidly. Andrea was employee number 13. By the time he left, seven years later, the business employed 600 people.

With the company growing rapidly, Andrea's role typically changed every six months. Initially he worked on research, gathering the information that was their raw material. Later, he became product manager for the tools that presented this information to their customers. Sitting between the sales team and product development, he would manage the roadmap for product requirements.

Later, he created his own product within the business, called Wealth Monitor. Using data from big merger and acquisition transactions, called liquidity events, this tool identified who was making money, or about to make money. They then interviewed these people, to gather information about them and their companies, and stored all of this in a database. Private banks, luxury market businesses such as Rolex and American Express, auction houses like Sotheby's and Christie's, these were all happy to pay for this information, which gave them leads for new customers.

In 2006, while Andrea was running his Wealth Monitor business in London, serving the European market, his company was acquired by the Financial Times group. The new owners wanted to take the Wealth Monitor business to the USA, but Andrea advised against this for several reasons. Unlike European private banks, US private banks already knew about most high worth individuals, and so would be less motivated to pay for what Wealth Monitor could provide. Moreover, US privacy laws would require changes to the product, and US customers would expect additional information, not currently available in Wealth Monitor, which it might be difficult to provide.

Andrea recommended instead that Wealth Monitor be taken to the English-speaking Asian market, including Hong Kong and Singapore. However, the new owners already had an office in New York, and insisted that was where they wanted to expand initially. Andrea was moved to New York, continuing to run the European business from his new location, while also building the US business.

By now, the company was getting bigger and more bureaucratic. In 2007, when his managers asked him to plan his and his team's holidays for the next six months, Andrea realised that he was no longer enjoying his work. He resigned.

I ask Andrea whether he had shares in the company.

"When I first joined, I didn't really understand the nature of their business. So, when they offered me more stock options, I said 'no, I'd prefer a higher salary.' However, I did have some stock options, and so benefitted a little when the company was sold."

"I have wonderful memories from those times, and I made great friends, so I have no regrets. The owners in particular were tremendous mentors and good people."

Seeking a role with more freedom, he joined another startup business in Cambridge, in broadly the same sector: research and business intelligence. They focused on venture capital markets, where the merger and acquisition deals were smaller. American entrepreneur Doug Richard, known for his appearances on the Dragons' Den TV programme, was the main shareholder and Chairman.

Andrea explains that, fundamentally, this new business was unsustainable. Initially, they staged extravagant events, and the high-profile shareholders brought in a lot of business. But, as this tailed off, it became clear that the company was struggling. Andrea started as Chief Operating Officer, responsible for the core product, and a Chief Executive Officer (CEO) was appointed, to run the company and raise further investment. When the original CEO got fired, Andrea was put in charge. After a year of trying to restructure the business, but still struggling, they gave up and sold all the assets in 2009.

"Although that was a very difficult experience for me, I

learnt a lot. Every day was a challenge, trying to work out how to make payroll, how to keep going."

"That must have been a stressful period for you?"

"Yes, very", says Andrea.

"Did you have trouble sleeping? Did you work ridiculously long hours?"

"Too many hours? No. I think the most I worked was when I was working for my father. I don't think I've ever worked that much since!"

"I was used to working very long hours, so that was OK, but yes, this period in Cambridge was definitely the most stressful time. Because, you know, I was laying off very good people. It was difficult, from a personal point of view."

"What did you do next?"

Andrea returned to London and, with friends, got involved in a few startup businesses, but none of them came to anything. In 2010, Andrea returned to Lecce.

"My idea was to take a long holiday, and spend some time with the family. My sister had just had a daughter. I wanted to have a long break, and then leave Lecce again, although I wasn't sure where I would go. Maybe to the United States, maybe to Brazil. I wasn't quite sure."

In the end, Andrea stayed. He started a small business from home, selling preserved food products, such as dried tomatoes and artichokes.

At this moment, an older couple enters the restaurant.

"Those are my parents," says Andrea, and he introduces them. "This is Mamma Elvira."

Now I realise where the name of the business comes from.

They stay to chat for a short while and, after they depart, Andrea tells me that his mother has Alzheimer's disease.

"Did your mother cook?"

"Yes, she was a very good cook, but not professionally. She comes from a wealthy family, where they had lots of servants and their own cooks. From them she learnt to cook. Because it was a big family – she was one of six sisters and one brother - she would often cook for large gatherings. Sadly, now she can't cook anymore, so my father does all the cooking."

"On the other hand, my father comes from a very poor family. His father was a small farmer."

"Did your mother's parents disapprove of the match, when your mother wanted to marry your father?"

"Actually, no, because my mother's parents passed away before they met. Moreover, my grandfather, my mother's father, lost most of his wealth, by donating to the church, and making bad investments. All that my parents inherited from them was old furniture. The money was all gone."

"Are you married Andrea?"

"Yes, although I married late. Soon after I returned to Lecce, in 2011, a friend introduced me to Serena, who is also from Lecce. We have been together ever since. We married in 2019, and we have a young boy, five years old."

We return to discussing what happened after Andrea started his food business. He found a small place, near Basilica di Santa Croce in Lecce, that he took over to provide a shop front and operational centre for his business. Soon though, in April 2011, he made it into a wine bar, which quickly became popular.

"At the beginning, my place was really a food shop that also served wine. It was not a place where you would go to spend the evening. But soon it changed into a proper wine bar. In fact, maybe we were too successful."

"What do you mean?"

"Well, we were open every day, from 8am to late at night, and we were very well known in Lecce. On Friday, Saturday and Sunday, the bar was always packed, even if every other place in the street was empty, we were packed. The other bar owners, they all hated me!"

He smiles.

Mamma Elvira Enoteca is still open, serving customers, in the same location.

"I'd say we were successful for three reasons. Firstly, we had multilingual staff. We could speak English, French, Spanish, Dutch, Japanese etc., so we attracted tourists, we attracted international clientele."

"So even then, there was a lot of tourism in Lecce?"

"It was starting. But also, for some reason there happened to be a lot of English teachers in Lecce at that time. So, we called them, and organised English-speaking aperitif events, which lots of locals joined just so that they could practise their English."

Andrea explains that they also innovated as regards their food and drink offerings.

"We served coffee in little stove-top espresso pots, rather than using a big, high-pressure machine. We also introduced Puccia. Do you know what Puccia is?"

"Is it like a local sandwich?"

"Yes. In Lecce, 40 years ago, the bakeries all sold this light, aerated Puglian bread called Puccia. The kids loved it, because you could fill it with anything to make a satisfying sandwich. Yet I noticed that all the Lecce bars were selling Piadini."

Piadini are basically sandwiches made with flatbread.

"Aren't they from the north?"

"Yes! I thought: 'What the hell are they doing selling Piadini here in Lecce?' So, I took a good Puccia, and filled it with high-quality ingredients: burratina, capocollo, sun dried tomatoes, all the good stuff. Now every single place in Lecce does this, but I think I was the first. By using high-quality ingredients, I think we were pioneers here."

"We also had a very wide selection of wine, and we served every wine by the glass. We still do. In the bar, and the restaurant here, we have more than 500 different wines, and we serve every one of them by the glass."

In July 2015, in partnership with his cousin, Andrea opened a restaurant called Camillo, after their common great grandfather. Initially, the restaurant struggled, so Andrea had a talk with his cousin: "Either you take it on completely, or I will take it on, but I don't think we can continue as a partnership."

His cousin didn't want to run it alone, so Andrea took over the whole restaurant in December 2015. He changed everything: the chef, the menu and even the name, to La Cucina di Mamma Elvira. They served typical local cuisine, with the best ingredients, at low prices.

However, throughout 2016, the restaurant still struggled, partly because it is hidden away and therefore attracts little passing trade. Eventually, by 2017 they had established a good reputation and the business took off. Andrea's new chef from 2016 is still the main chef at the restaurant. During the tourist season, from April to October, it is always full and turns away more customers than they seat in the evenings.

Then, in 2019, Andrea and his wife took over a bed and breakfast business, just around the corner from La Cucina di Mamma Elvira.

"So, your wife is also involved in the business!"

"Yes, she is a very good manager."

"Is that why you married her?"

Andrea laughs.

With five double bedrooms and four apartments, able to accommodate 22 people in total, Casa Mamma Elvira represented a substantial addition to the business. They refurbished the premises but, just as the 2020 season was starting, Covid arrived. Inevitably, they struggled for the next two years.

At about the same time, Andrea became involved in a second restaurant venture. Corte dei Pandolfi was founded by another of Andrea's cousins, in the year 2000. It was later owned by others but, in 2019, Andrea decided to take it on. After closing for refurbishment, the restaurant reopened in 2020, and then had to close again nine days later because of Covid.

At this point, I interrupt Andrea to tell him about my visit to Corte dei Pandolfi, and how impressed I was by the team.

"Juana in particular was friendly, happy to chat at length to a customer, but also very professional. She was always surveying the room, to spot when she was needed at another table, at which point she would politely move on."

"Yes, I have been lucky with most of my team. However, the last four years at that restaurant have been difficult, and not just because of Covid. I'm now looking for a new manager. The previous manager was friendly with customers, but not good at running the operation behind the scenes."

Despite the pandemic hitting just as Andrea was significantly expanding his business, this has not stopped him from making further investments. The ground floor of Casa Mamma Elvira has two large rooms, which have been converted into another restaurant, with its own kitchen. In the high season, this is often used as an overflow for La Cucina, where they offer the same menu and service with seating for another 100 people, doubling the total number of covers. The spaces are also used for hosting special events, such as business meetings, birthday parties and weddings. La Cucina de Coste - meaning *next door* in the Leccese dialect - opened just recently, in April 2023.

I ask Andrea whether his separate businesses promote each other, e.g. with bed and breakfast customers more likely to eat at his restaurants.

"To some extent, yes. However, our restaurants tend to be a bit expensive for many of our bed and breakfast customers. Recommendations from luxury hotels drive much of the tourist business at the restaurants."

"How much of your restaurant business is from locals, as opposed to tourists?"

"In the winter, almost all clients are local. During the summer season, I'd say 90% of our customers are tourists. However, we do get local families coming also. Because we are very flexible regarding the menu etc., they feel like they are at home. In August, when most Italians go on holiday, we have no local diners, although we see Italian tourists from elsewhere in the country. However, overall, I'd say that 75% of our customers from June to October are non-Italian. This could be a problem."

"Why?"

"Well, tourists want an authentic Italian restaurant, so we want to attract more locals. But the locals won't keep coming back unless we provide surprises, such as new dishes on the menu. I'm so busy now that I have little time to think about changes to the menu, so I need other people in the team to either create new dishes or flesh out any ideas I might have."

"Has Lecce tourism changed a lot in recent years?"

"Yes, tourism has grown significantly in the last ten years, and the season is now longer. We used to have a mix of high and low spending tourists but, post-Covid, I've noticed that we see more high-end tourists and less 'mass tourism'. Part of this might be recent investments in luxury accommodation, in Puglia."

I comment that major restoration projects, improving Lecce's spectacular Baroque heritage, will also have helped. By investing simultaneously in all aspects of the tourist ecosystem, the core attractions, accommodation, restaurants, bars and shops, it's possible to drive spectacular growth in a city's tourism. Visitors attract more visitors, especially through social media, and momentum builds quickly.

I also speculate that perhaps the increased expense of air travel – almost every flight I take nowadays seems to be full – is filtering out those tourists with less money.

"Yes, all prices have gone up. I've found that my prices have to be higher, so that we can get through the winter. I try to keep most staff on through the winter. La Cucina does quite well off-season, but Corte dei Pandolfi and the Enoteca mostly serve only summer tourists. I currently have 45 staff, but I will need more to get through this summer."

I ask Andrea what he feels are his main challenges, running the business.

"The main challenges are related to staff. Especially now, it's really hard to find good people, that help you grow the business. When I worked in a pub in London, in 1999, the technology we had there for running the back office was better than I am able to use today, here in Lecce, almost 25 years later. It's very difficult to find staff able to use the tools I would really like to deploy, to make the operation more efficient. One of my goals for 2023 is to digitise the business, as much as possible. The staff rota, bookings for the tables and rooms, I want all this online, but I'm finding that really hard to achieve."

We discuss how running a business involves day to day challenges, and near constant firefighting, but it's important to step back every now and then, to see the big picture and appreciate the long-term achievements.

"Something happened recently that made me very proud. I happened to be walking near Santa Croce, and I overhead a local girl who was showing her friends around Lecce. She said to them, 'This is Santa Croce, the Basilica, and over there is Mamma Elvira.' I thought, 'OK. We must have done something right.' That is one of the highlights, one of the bright spots in my twelve years of suffering."

He smiles as he says "suffering", of course.

Acknowledging how all-consuming the work can be, I tell Andrea that, in researching this book, I have found it almost impossible to interview a bar owner. Typically, a bar is open from early morning, when it operates as a café, to late at night. To keep staff costs down, the owner will work every hour possible, leaving no time for anything else. Even their family, let alone some pesky English author, is unable to get time from them.

"This is why I am trying so hard to delegate now. It's vital that I am not the bottle neck, so that I can make the changes we need to grow the business, and I also see my family. I want to spend much more time with my son."

Our conversation draws to a close, and we exchange farewells.

Reflecting afterwards upon what drives Andrea, I sense he gets great satisfaction just from running a business well, from understanding his customers and their needs, and working out how to develop the business to be successful. Although he is interested in food and wine, that's not the great passion driving him. And he's certainly not doing this just for the money.

I'm sure Andrea thinks about what might have happened, had he left Lecce again in 2011 and gone to Brazil or America. It's easy to imagine an outcome where, with luck, he became a very rich man. But would he be happy? Happier than he is now in Lecce?

I doubt it.

12 The antique dealer

It's Sunday evening and, unusually on this trip, I am not alone. Sitting outside, at a bar in Piazzetta Santa Chiara, I am chatting to a fellow tourist, whom I first met the previous day. Ivonne was born in East Germany, before the wall came down. She currently works at a hotel in Berlin and, like me, she is holidaying alone in Lecce.

As we talk, a young man approaches our table and shows a small plastic card to Ivonne.

"Is this you?" he asks, in English with an Italian accent.

Ivonne looks closely at the card and can't quite believe what she is seeing. It is an ID card, with her name and photograph on it. Mouth open wide, she unzips a pocket in her jacket, looking for something. Failing to find it, she tries another pocket, but still no success. It's as if she is an innocent audience member, up on the stage as the subject for a magician's trick.

The young Italian smiles and shows her a wallet in his other hand.

"I think this is yours."

"Thank you! Thank you! But where did you find it?"

"I saw it on the ground, as I was walking to work about half an hour ago. When I showed my friend your photograph, he pointed over here and said 'Is that her?'" We look across to the young man's friend, serving at an adjacent bar. He waves to us.

"That's amazing. Thank you so much," says Ivonne.

The young man returns to the other bar, and Ivonne looks through her wallet. Nothing is missing.

"I just don't understand how I dropped it. I always keep it in this pocket, zipped up."

She still can't believe what just happened. We both agree

that it's astonishingly lucky that the man, who found her wallet, happens to work so near to where we are sitting, and that his friend saw and recognised her. Ivonne is keen to reward them in some way, so we move to their bar for our next drink and, as we leave, Ivonne gives them a generous tip.

By now, it's time for our reservation at Dall'Antiquario, a restaurant next door to our original bar. Ivonne recommended this place, because she had a good meal here on her first night in Lecce. We are meeting two other people for dinner, Giorgio and his girlfriend Simone, who live in the countryside outside Lecce. They have come into the city to meet us for dinner and, happily, they are already waiting at a table for four. The restaurant is packed and we sit in what must be the last two empty seats, opposite Giorgio and Simone.

Giorgio, whom I met through a language exchange website, makes his living from various activities, including helping with his family's vacation rentals and writing for a local magazine. Simone is a schoolteacher.

Despite our three different nationalities, the conversation flows freely all evening, and time flies. Inevitably, we start by relating the amazing story of Ivonne's lost wallet. Ivonne reflects on how the rest of her holiday would have been completely ruined if the two young Italian lads hadn't come to her rescue. Giorgio talks about his recent appearance on a local television news program. He was interviewed about a conservation project, where he is managing an ancient olive grove. Ivonne relates stories about the many famous pop stars she has been to see live. All I can contribute, rather sheepishly, is the comment that I went to the same school as two of the Beatles.

There is a lively atmosphere in the restaurant, perhaps helped by it feeling warm and cosy inside, contrasting with the cool evening outside. Our waiter is a cheerful young man, with short dark hair, tattoos and piercings. At several tables, he engages in lively banter with young diners, who clearly know him well. Sabino is his name, and wherever he goes there is laughter.

At the back of the restaurant, on the walls and the ceiling, there is lots of bric-a-brac. There are photographs, old advertising signs, American metal car number plates, all sorts of things. It's as if the owners can't bear to throw anything away. Also, every free space on the walls, below head height, is filled with graffiti written by diners. Most of this is in Italian, but some comments are in English: "Sabino I love your cooking!" and "No sad vibes."

Especially prominent are bicycles, decorated in various ways, hanging from the wall or the ceiling. I've noticed this motif in other Lecce shops and cafés, and occasionally elsewhere in Italy.

At the end of the evening, as we leave, I stop to speak to the man standing behind the bar, sporting a cap, a white beard and moustache. As I suspect, he is the owner, and we agree that I will return tomorrow afternoon so that I can interview him for the book.

The next morning, I visit another restaurateur, Andrea Favale, and at the end of our chat he asks me if I am speaking to anybody else in Lecce. I mention that I am going to Dall'Antiquario, to speak to the owner, and Andrea approves.

"They are very nice. It's a good restaurant, a small family business. If I had to recommend to you another place in Lecce, then I would choose them."

Late in the afternoon, I arrive at Dall'Antiquario, expecting the lunchtime service to be over. However, today is the May

Day holiday, and local families and groups of friends have chosen here for a leisurely lunch. The place is buzzing, as much as it was the previous evening, but now lots of young children are running around. The owner, Gianni, is still occupied, so I buy a drink, sit in the corner and just watch. People who probably have no leisure time, during the working week, are now laughing and joking together, enjoying the food and drink. Understandably, they don't want to leave.

Eventually, things quieten down. Gianni Gerardi and I go and sit outside, to talk. I begin by asking him about his parents.

"My father was a furniture maker, a craftsman with wood, in the village of Monteroni di Lecce, just outside Lecce. My mother was a housewife. They always lived in Monteroni, and that's where I was born. I have two brothers, one older, one younger."

After elementary school in Monteroni, Gianni attended middle-school, followed by a high school specialising in Art, both in Lecce. After finishing school, Gianni found work as the representative for a photograph-developing business, selling their services to shops in the area.

At around this time, he also met a girl called Antonella Manca. Although Antonella was only 15 years old, three years younger than Gianni, they started going out together. Their relationship was put on hold for a year, when Gianni went to Palmanova in Friuli, at the other end of Italy, for obligatory military service with the army. Having completed his national service, Gianni returned to Lecce, and Antonella.

"At first, I was a bit stuck. I didn't know what to do. However, aged 22, I decided to start an antique business. My father's profession had inspired my interest in the restoration of old furniture, and this felt like a natural next step."

In the beginning, Gianni operated out of a shop in Monteroni. Initially, the shop was almost empty but, bit by bit, he acquired pieces, firstly lamps, then chandeliers and furniture. He often travelled as far as Lombardy, to buy antique furniture which he could restore and sell at a profit in Puglia.

A few years later, ten years after they first met, Gianni and Antonella married. They subsequently had a daughter, Diletta, and six years later, a son, Sabino. Diletta, the name chosen by Antonella, means beloved in Italian.

After 15 years in business in Monteroni di Lecce, Gianni decided to relocate the shop to somewhere with more customers. He found premises in the centre of Lecce, previously used by a furniture restoration business. This is the place where we are sitting right now, which today is a restaurant. Here Gianni opened his relocated antique dealership in 1996, and happily traded for another 20 years. However, by 2015 it had become clear that the antiques market was collapsing. They couldn't continue in the same business.

Antonella had always had an interest in cooking. Mostly, she cooked at home, for the family. However, Gianni used to have a villa in the country and, every now and then, they organised large parties there in the summertime, inviting friends and family, and Antonella would cook for everybody. She had always been keen to learn and experiment, when it came to the preparation of food.

The couple talked, and Antonella convinced Gianni that they should completely change the business, from an antique dealership to a restaurant. They took the plunge and closed the antique dealership. It took them 12 months to convert the building, to make it suitable for cooking food, serving drinks, and seating diners. At last, in 2016, the new restaurant opened for business. On their first day, Antonella was in the kitchen with three helpers, while Gianni, Diletta and Sabino all served front of house. They still have a team of four in the kitchen. Antonella is head chef, working with one sous chef, one person peeling and preparing the vegetables, and one person washing dishes.

Whereas the antique shop required just one person, there to serve customers, now they needed lots of people, to cook and serve the food, clear tables etc. When they first opened it was a shock, coming to terms with a completely different lifestyle. After years of cooking for four or six people, suddenly Antonella was cooking for 50 people every day.

Having seen Sabino working in the restaurant, I ask whether his sister Diletta also still helps out.

"No, Diletta is now married, and they have a little girl, aged two. Diletta works in a leather goods shop in Lecce. Sabino and his partner also have a little girl. She is five years old."

We are interrupted by a happy group leaving the restaurant, who stop to thank Gianni. They clearly know him well, and have enjoyed their long lunch. It's now raining, and one of them opens up his umbrella. The underside of the umbrella has a picture of beautiful Renaissance buildings, lit by the sun, with a blue sky in the background.

"I have sunshine wherever I go. For me, there is no rain," he states cheerfully, walking off into the drizzle.

Gianni and I, fortunately, are sheltered by the awning above our heads.

The new restaurant was a success from the very beginning. It helped that Gianni and Antonella were well known in Lecce, and that Antonella is an excellent cook. Those friends invited for the day-one inauguration spread the word, and

Dall'Antiquario has never lacked for customers. The cuisine is traditional, their menu consisting of typical local dishes.

Gianni tells me about a national TV program that they recently took part in. *Alessandro Borghese: four restaurants* is hosted by, unsurprisingly, Alessandro Borghese. He is a famous Italian restaurateur and author, and the son of the German-American actress Barbara Bouchet.

In each show, Alessandro and his production team visit a different city in Italy, and choose four local restaurants. These restaurants take turns, providing dinner to the owners of the other restaurants and being rated by them. Dall'Antiquario was one of the four chosen in Lecce, and they emerged as winners!

"Have you seen the photographs on the wall?" Gianni gestures towards the door of the restaurant.

"No, I'll take a look when we've finished."

I ask about the seasonality of the business, whether they do well in winter and how much they rely on tourism. Gianni says that they are busy in the winter, and in this period almost all customers are local inhabitants. During the summer, locals spend time at the seaside and visit Dall'Antiquario less often, but this is more than compensated for by foreign tourists who eat at the restaurant.

Aware that Gianni is 69 years old, I ask him what he sees happening in the future. He seems surprised by the question, and says that he imagines things will continue as they are now.

"Might Sabino want to take over the restaurant one day?"

"I don't know. Children are strange!" he laughs.

More people pass us, leaving the restaurant.

"See you next time!" says Gianni. They all smile, and wave goodbye.

For the first time, I look closely at Gianni's cap.

"It's from Santo Domingo," he says. "Every February, we close the restaurant and take a month's holiday, going to a different place each time. Two years ago, we were in India. I like to travel. I've been to America."

"Do you take your wife and family?"

"Yes, my wife comes also, and we used to take the children. When we went to Cuba, for example, we took the children."

At this point, the restaurant having almost emptied, Sabino comes outside to join us.

I ask Gianni for the name of his shop, when it was an antiques business.

"Dall'Antiquario," he says.

"Oh! The same name as the restaurant?"

Sabino interrupts, and explains to his father that I was asking about the antique shop.

"Ahh. 'Gerardi Antichità,'" says Gianni.

Having run out of questions, it feels like now is the time to finish our discussion. I thank Gianni for his time and he offers me a glass of wine before I leave, so we go back inside. While sipping the wine, I gaze at a photograph on the wall, showing a group of people standing together, all smiling broadly and holding up glasses of sparkling white wine. On the left, an imposing man, with a big head of curly hair, holds the bottle.

"That's Alessandro Borghese," says Gianni.

"This is your wife Antonella?" I ask, pointing at the lady on the far right, who has the biggest smile in the picture. He nods. At this point, Antonella emerges from the kitchen, clearly pleased that, at last, the lunchtime work is over and she can relax.

"Congratulations!" I say, pointing to the photograph.

"Thank you." She smiles shyly.

Meanwhile, Sabino is clearing tables around the restaurant, and generally tidying up. He reminds me of somebody, but I can't think who until a few minutes later. Then I realise that he looks like Freddie Mercury, from Queen! I go over to say goodbye to him.

"Do you know the English word 'cool'?" I say to Sabino.

"Yes," he replies, looking puzzled.

"Well, you're 'cool' Sabino."

He laughs and walks off, to clear more tables.

There is definitely something alternative about both Gianni and Sabino. They don't dress like typical Italians, especially those running a family restaurant, and Gianni's passion for travelling abroad for a month, every year, is not something that many older Italians share.

Leaving the restaurant, I deploy my umbrella to keep off the rain as I walk back to the apartment. My thoughts return to Gianni and Antonella, and I reflect on the life-changing decision that this couple made, as they entered their sixties, when most people are thinking of retirement. Few would have the energy and courage to immerse themselves in a demanding new business, at that age. For Antonella in particular, this must have been a massive change.

Watching Gianni in the restaurant however, both last night and today, he seemed relaxed. He prepares drinks behind the bar, or walks around the room chatting to customers, many of whom are his friends. Perhaps his working life today is no more demanding than it was when he ran his antique business.

Antonella, probably the driving force behind the restaurant, now has a very different lifestyle. However, she looked extremely happy, holding that glass of bubbly, and celebrating her victory with Alessandro Borghese.

13 Delivering paradise

After a leisurely breakfast in the garden, chatting in the sunshine with Chantal and Didier, we load bags into the car and say our goodbyes. Jackie hasn't seen her friend Chantal for 20 years, but we managed to include three nights at their house, near Montpellier, as part of a month-long road trip through France and Italy. After such a long period since their last meeting, there was plenty to talk about, although Didier told us that Chantal had been worried that she and Jackie wouldn't have much to say to each other. How naïve.

Now we commence a five-hour drive to Alassio, on the Italian Riviera. I am driving the first section, beginning with back roads that take us from Chantal's house to the autoroute. These busy, twisting lanes require concentration but, once on the autoroute, my mind starts to wander. Inevitably, I recall events from the last few months, events that cast a dark shadow over the future.

In February, Jackie completely lost her appetite and didn't eat for a week. Her GP arranged blood tests, which showed that everything was normal except for something called CA125, an antigen that may indicate the presence of ovarian cancer. Normally between 0 and 35 units per ml, Jackie's CA125 level was 230. Her GP arranged for a scan to look into this further.

Jackie was due to retire in March, and we were planning a celebratory road trip to France and Italy in May/June. I say "we", but it's normally me that works out where we go, and books the accommodation. Given this new uncertainty in our lives, we agreed that I should only book accommodation that could be cancelled at short notice.

Later that week, Jackie sent me the link to a very expensive spa retreat in the Tuscan countryside. "I think we should spend a few days here," she said.

There are people who react to the news that they might have cancer by sinking into a pit of worry. For these people, it would be unthinkable to plan a holiday in such circumstances. But for Jackie, the CA125 news had merely increased the importance of time, of spending it wisely, and decreased the importance of money. Her priority was to live, to enjoy the present, not to worry about the future.

Although the hotel in Tuscany looked nice, it was extremely expensive and didn't seem to offer anything extraordinary. I told her that I would research luxury hotels and present a list of options. A few days later, we sat down to review this list on a spreadsheet, with the pricing column hidden. We checked out the web site and reviews for each hotel, and Jackie chose Villa della Pergola in Alassio, as I'd hoped she would. Unusually, she did not choose the most expensive option. Perhaps, by hiding the prices, I had made that too difficult.

I booked Villa della Pergola for three nights. Jackie had her scan and, one week later, we met the oncology team to hear the news. We were their last appointment on a Friday afternoon, and they were running late. It was 5pm by the time we went in. The junior doctor, looking at pictures from the scan, hesitantly explained that there was a lot of fluid build-up, which was consistent with the presence of cancer, but his tone of voice implied that it might not be cancer at all. The Macmillan nurse next to him, older and more experienced, felt that we needed clarity rather than hedging. She knew enough to be confident that this was cancer, and she said as much.

"It looks like peritoneal cancer, which is treated in the same way as ovarian cancer. We would like to do a biopsy, as soon as possible," she said.

"When would that be?"

"Next week. If this confirms it is malignant, then we would be able to start treatment about six weeks later."

"We were planning to go away for a month at the end of next week."

"That's fine. You should go! We'll take the sample for the biopsy next week and, if you like, we can discuss the results on a video call, while you're away?"

On the drive home, there was little conversation. Stunned, we were trying to digest what had just happened. Then Jackie got a message on the phone, from her daughter.

"Danielle is asking if I am with my mum this evening and, if so, whether she can call us. That means she is pregnant!"

"How can you be so sure?" I said.

"That's the only possible reason why she would want to speak to us both this evening."

She was right of course, and anticipating that good news made the drive home much easier.

Today's drive commands my attention, as the traffic slows and I see a queue ahead. We are not held up for long and, several hours later, having stopped along the way for lunch and taken turns driving, we are at last entering the small town of Alassio. Following the satnav, on a narrow winding road, we climb a hill with our backs to the sea, until blocked by an imposing gate between high stone walls. An intercom on the wall allows us to speak to reception, and we are admitted.

Further up the driveway, we park the car and walk further uphill to a stunning villa, set within a beautiful garden. Tall, pencil-thin cypresses frame an ethereal vision of marble pillars and balustrades. Paths wind along citrus terraces, past ponds with fountains, then disappear into luxuriant undergrowth, or a wisteria pergola. Turning around, the view over town and sea is equally lovely. Surely this is as close to paradise as we'll ever be.

In silence, punctuated only by the crunch of gravel underfoot, we approach the building. Two ladies exit the villa to welcome us, the more senior introducing herself as General Manager Nadia Finelli. Nadia is slim, impeccably neat with straight silver hair, dark blue jacket and trousers. The staff take our car, and our bags, and we are shown to our suite.

As soon as we're alone in the room, Jackie comments that Nadia was wearing a belt from Hermes.

"They start at £500," she says approvingly.

Sitting on the balcony, when not distracted by the stunning view, I am reading a book that relates the history of the villa. In the 19th century, Alassio became a haven for the British aristocracy, escaping their homeland's winter. Sheltered by hills to the north, and warmed by the Mediterranean, Alassio is pleasant even in the colder months. Every winter, the local population was supplemented by more than 1,000 wealthy British visitors, who transformed the town's economy.

Amongst the earliest visitors, who started this trend, was a Scottish General, William McMurdo. He it was who bought the land, constructed these beautiful gardens, and had the house built. British imperialism, the wealth of empire, flowed into this corner of Liguria, where it combined with Italian flair and know-how, to create a tiny piece of heaven. Local contractor Domenico Gorlero was employed to construct the colonial-style mansion, which attracted admirers from the beginning. Alfred Hitchcock directed his first film here, in 1925.

The British community in Alassio thrived until the 1930s,

when Britain and Italy fell out. Although aristocratic expats in Alassio thought Mussolini a splendid chap, they failed to convince the British government. When relations between the two countries broke down, Italy became less welcoming for the British. They visited Alassio in smaller numbers, stopping altogether once the war started, a decline which was not reversed after the war.

However, Villa della Pergola continued to be occupied by a Brit until the last owner, Ruth Hanbury, died in 1982, when the house and gardens were sold. In 2006, speculators wanted to redevelop the site, demolishing the villa and gardens. To ensure its preservation, the Ricci family bought the property in an auction, planning to convert it to a hotel.

I start thinking about what it takes to manage a place like this. There must be a lot resting on Signora Finelli's shoulders.

The next day, Jackie and I walk around the town of Alassio and, when we return, I ask to speak to the General Manager. Nadia says she is happy to chat to me about her life and her work, so we arrange to meet the next morning after breakfast.

During the night, I wake and, unable to get back to sleep, go outside onto the balcony. The lights of the town are twinkling below, and the moon adds its own silvery glow reflected from the sea. Hilly headlands along the coast are visible only as dark shadows, places without light. A gentle breeze rustles the branches of nearby trees. Breathtaking peace and beauty.

After breakfast, I ask to see Nadia. The lady at reception apologises as she explains that Signora Finelli is dealing with something, but she will be here soon. Sure enough, after ten minutes Nadia appears, smiling and suggesting that we talk outside in the garden. We choose a quiet table on the terrace, and I take care to ensure that Nadia has her back to the hotel, so that she is not distracted by the sight of her team coming and going. Accompanied by birdsong, and the rustling of wind-tossed leaves, we start discussing her life.

Nadia was born in the small village of Guarene, near Alba in Piedmont. Her father was a shift leader at Ferrero, the world-famous chocolate manufacturer. He died when Nadia was only 12, leaving his 36-year-old wife to bring up four children on her own. Fortunately, Nadia's mother was a strong woman. Her three oldest children all wanted to leave school, and start work as soon as possible, but Nadia enjoyed studying, in particular foreign languages. She attended a professional tourism school, in Alba, for five years. Her ambition, in those days, was to become a beautician.

Even at school, Nadia was a natural organiser. She arranged dinners, planned day trips with her friends, and holidays for the family. Aged 14, during the summer holidays, she found work experience in Alba's tourist office. Those few weeks convinced Nadia that she was destined for a life in tourism. She really enjoyed meeting and helping people and, of course, she loved organising.

Aged 18, Nadia finished school with the best grades for her year. The big Italian tour operator, Alpitour, had connections with the school and, based upon Nadia's qualifications, they immediately offered her a position – starting the next week! So, after finishing school, Nadia gave up the chance for a summer holiday, and immediately started full time work, on a three-month contract. She was an assistant in Palma de Mallorca, helping Alpitour to look after 2,000 Italian tourists per week.

Nadia's plan was to study at the University Institute of Modern Languages (IULM) in Milan, starting in the autumn. However, as summer drew to a close, Nadia realised that she was enjoying work too much. More importantly, she felt that she was learning a great deal from the practical experience of her full-on role, things she would never be taught in a university. She couldn't bear the thought of leaving to become an academic student, and a drain on her family's finances. So, she turned down her place in Milan, and stayed with Alpitour for six years.

During this period, Nadia moved around the Mediterranean: Crete, Mykonos, Santorini, Ios, Tunisia and also further afield, to the Dominican Republic, and Cuba. Each assignment was for six months and then, after three weeks back home with her family, Nadia would be moved on to a new location. In the winter, the work was in ski resorts, like Livigno. She saw many places, but everywhere life was dominated by work. Nadia's social life came from Alpitour colleagues and guests.

She looks back fondly on those days.

"I think I lived life at twice the normal pace, it was so full. I was never tired, and I was always happy. I loved it. Tourism is such a wonderful area to work in, because you meet so many different people. It gives you such a rich life."

After a pause, she continues.

"Even when they have a problem, once they realise that you are listening to them then they begin to trust you, and perhaps tell you all sorts of personal things. It's a real privilege."

Spending most of the year fully immersed in her work, Nadia found that she had less in common with friends and family in Alba, whom she met in the brief periods between assignments. Her life was completely different to theirs.

Eventually, Nadia decided that she wanted stability, to stay in one place for more than six months. She asked Alpitour for a role at their main office in Cuneo, just 70km from Alba. They gave her a contract manager position, her job being to find hotels suitable for hosting Alpitour holidays, in Italy, Switzerland and France, and agree contracts with them.

This represented a big change for Nadia. She was no longer dealing directly with their clients, the tourists, and Cuneo was a quiet town.

"When work is over, when the shops close, everybody goes home. Nothing happens in the evening. I've seen this in mountain towns, the people work hard, and otherwise stay home. If they socialise, they do so with friends in their own homes. The restaurants are empty. It's a closed society."

After a few years in Cuneo, she was approached by a friend of a friend, asking if she might be interested in becoming General Manager of a new hotel. Although Nadia had no experience of hotel management, she was intrigued and keen to learn more. A well-funded group of businessmen had purchased the old monastery of San Maurizio, in the village of Santo Stefano Belbo, planning to convert it into the first five-star hotel in the Langhe. The leader of the group was born in Santo Stefano Belbo, and he'd played in the monastery gardens as a young boy. His dream was to give the old monastery new life, as a luxury spa resort.

"None of them had any experience in the hotel business," explains Nadia. "One was a banker, another in the wine business."

"And you also had never run a hotel before?"

"That's right. But they knew of my experience with Alpitour and, after two interviews, they offered me the role. I took it, of course, and as a result I didn't sleep for the next eight years!"

She left Alpitour to join the project in 2001, one year before the San Maurizio hotel was ready to open. They employed a consultant who, having managed big hotels and now nearing retirement, was able to teach Nadia the basics of how to prepare rooms, how to manage the staff etc. After six months, Nadia felt she'd learnt all she could from the consultant, and that his approach was a little old fashioned, so they let him go.

"We opened in 2002 with 21 rooms, later adding nine more rooms and a spa. It was a huge responsibility for me, managing a team of 30 people, with clients and owners all expecting the highest standards, in this new high-profile hotel. I was 27 years old."

"How did you cope?"

"I don't know. I just decided that living there, in that hotel, was my life. There was nothing else."

"Was it easy, attracting guests?"

"At first, no. In those days, tourists only came to the Langhe in the truffle season, from mid-September to mid-November. It was a struggle attracting clients at any other time. Today there is more tourism, and the season is much longer, partly thanks to promotion by wine producers, and also because the Langhe now has UNESCO world heritage status. There are several successful five-star hotels in the Langhe today. It has become more like Tuscany."

In 2004, the hotel successfully applied to join the Relais & Châteaux group.

"For me, this was a big challenge, to be admitted to Relais & Châteaux. The owners were very pleased, when we were accepted."

Relais & Châteaux is an association of 580 luxury hotels and restaurants, with each member subject to strict annual quality checks.

"Being in Relais & Châteaux isn't just for business, it's like being part of a family. They hold an annual meeting lasting three days, each time in a different location, attended by the owner or manager of each establishment. Relais & Châteaux is worldwide, so the annual meeting could be anywhere. We meet other hoteliers and establish new relationships. Every year, new members join and are introduced. We also have special guest speakers, for example Colin Powell when the event was in Washington, and a lady from the imperial family in Tokyo. It's a great opportunity to learn more about the luxury hotel business, and really motivating."

However, Nadia found the work relentless. Even when the hotel closed for a few months each winter, there was work to do. Maintenance projects, changes to the building or furnishings, all this happens in the winter.

"It also takes time to prepare a hotel like this for re-opening. You must do a deep clean, for example, and that takes a month."

Nadia took only a few days off, each winter. In June 2010, after eight years, Nadia recognised that she had no work-life balance, and needed a break. She left the hotel.

"What did you do?"

She laughs: "Just think about myself."

"For the first time, I guess."

She laughs again.

"Yes. I stayed in Alba, seeing my family and friends. Also, my boyfriend and I spent a month on holiday, and then decided to find a house and live together."

"How did you meet your boyfriend?"

"I'd known Luca since I was 17. He was part of my group of friends. We'd all hang out in the main square of Alba. We lost contact, when I moved away. He's in the jewellery business. I decided to open a small jewellery concession in Relais San Maurizio, and that's how we met again. We recognised each other, and after that he visited often. At first, I didn't want a relationship, but he was persistent and eventually got his way! We've been together since 2007."

Six months after leaving Relais San Maurizio, Nadia was approached by a good friend, the owner and chef of a restaurant with two Michelin stars, Antica Corona Reale in Cervere.

"Nadia, are you bored?" he said, "Do you want to help me?"

His restaurant was doing well, but he had new projects that he didn't have time to manage. He wanted to join Relais & Châteaux, and he wanted to open a bakery shop, an atelier, as another food outlet.

Nadia was ready for the next challenge.

"When you leave that kind of role, it's very hard to relax. In no time at all, I was bored and wanting to organise something. However, I told him that I didn't want to go back to my previous life, with no time for myself, and he promised that we would keep my workload light. So, at the end of 2010, I started as his Chief Operating Officer, managing the team, with objectives to join Relais & Châteaux and open the atelier. We achieved both objectives. Of course, in no time at all the work became very intense. My one concession was that I took Sundays off!"

In the autumn of 2017, the owners of Villa della Pergola were looking for a new General Manager to run their luxury hotel on the Italian Riviera. Two friends of theirs, both in the hospitality business, also knew Nadia and each separately recommended her for the position. Both of these friends called Nadia, to ask if she was interested. They urged her to visit Villa della Pergola and check out the opportunity.

When she saw the villa, the location, the gardens, then, just like us, she was captivated. It is hard to imagine anywhere more beautiful.

"Yes, let's do it!" said Nadia, when the owners offered her the position. She left Antica Corona Reale in February 2018, and started at Villa della Pergola shortly afterwards.

I ask Nadia what happened between 2006, when the Ricci family purchased the villa, and 2018 when she arrived.

"In the first four years, from 2006 to 2010, they worked on the renovation of the historical villas and gardens. In 2010, it opened as a bed and breakfast, with 12 rooms. In 2016, they opened the restaurant. The owners are not hoteliers, but they love beautiful places with a history. They saved this place from speculators to preserve it for the future, and enable the public to enjoy its beauty. They had ambitions to improve further, creating a luxury hotel, which is why they wanted somebody like me."

"Did you relocate to Alassio, when you took this position?"

"Yes, I found a place in the village. Luca, who travels all over Italy with his work, moved to Alassio with me."

Two weeks after Nadia arrived, in March 2018, Villa della Pergola opened for the season. At the end of that season, she recruited a completely new set of people, changing the whole team apart from chef Giorgio.

The owners had ambitious plans, and Nadia delivered. They added three more rooms in 2018, achieved membership of Relais & Châteaux in 2020 and, in November 2020, the restaurant was awarded its first Michelin star.

"Giorgio was keen to earn his star. But when guests know you have a Michelin star, they become much more demanding. Giorgio realised he was no longer enjoying the work. He left at the end of 2021, to pursue other opportunities. Through my network, I heard that another young Michelin star chef, Giorgio Pignagnoli, was unhappy with his current position. We recruited him, and he's helped us to keep our Michelin star."

"Is Giorgio OK with the pressure?"

"As the restaurant is seasonal, in the winter the chef takes time off – he needs it – and he also designs new dishes, and attends special events. The kitchen is tough in the season. In summer, we open the terrace, and the restaurant is fully booked every night."

"How about you? Is this as intense as your previous roles?"

"During the season, I work every day. Last year, I had three days off in seven months. Adrenalin keeps me going. Often, I don't know what day it is. My team always asks why I work every day. This is my choice. If I spend a day at home, I cannot stop thinking about this place. Luca says 'Put your phone in the safe!' Only he knows the combination, and I have to ask for my phone back at the end of the day."

"When the season ends and the hotel closes, I am tired. Luca and I see more of each other in winter, going away at weekends."

Nadia reflects on the future.

"In August, I will be 50. Years ago, I said I would stop at 50, but now I'm not so sure. However, I do want to dedicate more time to myself, Luca and my family. I phone my mother every day, she's 75. In winter, I visit Alba often to see the family. A good friend of mine, just 53, has been diagnosed with a brain tumour. Time is finite, and this job cannot be my whole life. I know how to do a good job, professionally, but not how to live my life. I have to learn. I must find the right balance."

"This place is designed for relaxation, but I guess you can never relax here?"

"I do see the beauty here, but it is my workplace. I always see things that need doing. This place is mine, but I can never relax here."

After we finish, I walk back to my room, wondering when Nadia will transition to the next phase in her life. I reflect on the irony that the very thing that brought me and Jackie here, our heightened awareness of the brevity of life, is probably what will take Nadia away from her place in paradise.

14 The restless DJ

I don't understand why, but there is great pleasure to be had just from sitting in the sunshine, next to open water. Our table is at the lake's edge, with a fine view across the Gulf of Salò. I have to remind myself that Lake Garda in its entirety is huge, and that our view, across what is effectively a small indentation in the western shoreline, is misleadingly parochial.

Recalling our first visit to Salò, 11 years previously, I remember my anxiety as we neared the end of the journey in the hire car. We followed the satnav, telling us to leave the main road and descend a lane to the town centre, but this lane became narrower and narrower, stone walls on either side. Eventually, there was just one or two centimetres between each wing mirror and the wall, and I was dreading having to reverse back up the hill. Fortunately, keen to save money we had hired a Fiat Cinquecento, one of the few cars able to negotiate such a narrow passage.

On that occasion we rented an apartment with a garden on the lakeshore, where we could dine right next to the water. Walking into town, the first restaurant we came to on the lakeside esplanade was the pizzeria Papillon, which also had tables on the shoreline. Papillon is still here, and that's where we are now, waiting for the food to arrive.

Some places, like the Dolomites, are beautiful because nature made them that way. Whether mountains, lakes, forests or dramatic shorelines, they benefit from an absence of human construction. Other places are beautiful because people built them that way: grand houses, attractive city centres, sometimes even bridges and skyscrapers. What makes the Italian Lakes so special is that nature and humanity combine harmoniously to create pure elegance. The lakes, sheltered by hills to the north, enjoy a mild microclimate and provide a serene, welcoming environment.   With impeccable taste, the Italians have decorated their shorelines with quaint towns, beautiful villas, luxuriant gardens, dramatic twisting roads, and the inevitable cypress trees.

Lake Como has to be my favourite. Garda suffers from over-development in its lower reaches, Maggiore lacks hills, and Iseo is too small. It's as if somebody said to God, "Go on, what's the best you can do?", and Lake Como was the result.

But today we are on the shore of Lake Garda, fully aware that tomorrow is our last full day in Italy before we head home, to an uncertain future.   All we know is that Jackie will commence chemotherapy soon after we return. If that goes well, there will be a major operation, more chemotherapy, and then, hopefully, she will at least be in remission.

Today we forgot about that completely, and had a joyous ride in the hills to the south of Salò, on hired e-bikes. The weather was perfect, the views glorious, and the ride back to Salò, on a traffic-free tarmac cycleway across fields, was serene. I'm now looking forward to a good pizza and a glass of Valpolicella Ripasso which, combined with our view over the lake, surely makes this a perfect day.

We hired the e-bikes from Cyclingarda, a shop on the main road through Salò, where we were served by a friendly young man who advised us on the best route to take. Michele also commented on how quiet business was, compared to last June when they were incredibly busy.   This reminded me of something Nadia Finelli said, that 2022 was exceptionally busy, because everybody was desperate to travel after two years of pandemic restrictions. This season, 2023, is actually just returning to pre-pandemic normality, although I didn't say that to Michele. That was not good news, from his perspective.

Chatting to Michele today, it was clear that he is relatively new to the bike shop. I wonder what he had been doing before, and whether he is the owner of the bicycle business. Since Michele might be a tad bored tomorrow, sitting in his shop with very few customers, I decide I will go and see him, and ask if I can hear his story.

After a good night's sleep, and a pleasant breakfast at our hotel, I wander along to the Cyclingarda shop. It has just opened and, as expected, I find Michele sitting alone behind the counter, with no sign of any other customers.

"Are most days this quiet?" I ask.

Michele smiles. "Yes, so far this year."

"Are you the owner of the shop, or maybe the manager?"

"I am one of five owners. Three of us work in the shop."

I ask him if he minds sharing his life story, given that the shop is so quiet. He's happy to oblige.

Michele Brida was born in Desenzano, at the southern end of Lake Garda, and was brought up in Salò. Now retired, both his parents worked in finance. His mother was an accountant at a metal factory in Valle Sabbia, 25 km over the hills to the north of Salò, and Michele's father was a financial adviser. Michele has one brother, four years younger, who also lives in Salò, working in architecture.

Michele attended a high school specialising in languages, in Salò. He speaks English and Spanish, as well as Italian. After school, he decided to go to university, to study sociology, and won a place at the University of Bologna, reckoned by many to be Italy's top university, and certainly the oldest.

However, Michele hated being a student. After four months,

aged 19, he left university and decided to move to Barcelona, where he could practise his Spanish. There he found casual work, selling tickets for nightclubs, and stayed six months.

Then Michele returned to Salò, and worked as a waiter in the restaurant Ca' dei Manni for a year. However, he still had itchy feet and wanted to venture further afield. A friend of his father had opened a restaurant in Baja California, Mexico, so Michele went over to help out. He worked as a waiter there, and also in the kitchen.

After six months in Mexico, Michele returned again to Salò, in 2006. This time he tried various jobs. He worked for a time in a factory, in Valle Sabbia. He also spent some time as a postman, and he worked in construction. During this period, Michele at last found his true passion, which was to be a DJ. He purchased the equipment and, whenever possible, spent time developing his skills as a disc jockey.

After three years, Michele was ready to move on again, to explore somewhere new. Some of his Salò friends had moved to Sidney, Australia, working in restaurants there, and he decided to follow them. In Sidney, he initially found work as a carpenter, and then resumed restaurant work to get by. He also helped to provide security at a music festival. Whilst in Australia, Michele purchased DJ equipment, and practised, but never did any paid gigs. He was still learning. After six months in Sidney, he sold the DJ equipment to fund his trip home, and returned to Salò.

Once again, Michele tried various jobs to pay the bills, including work in a water bottling factory. I am struck by how Michele appears not just to have wanderlust, but also a desire to try many different types of work. However, he still had his heart set on being a DJ.

He got together with a group of friends, one from Salò, the other three from Brescia, to form a singing group, with Michele as their DJ. They began recording music and videos, posting on YouTube and listing on Spotify. Soon they started receiving requests to perform at venues throughout Italy, as far afield as Sicily and Sardinia, and even Switzerland. This group, the Fratelli Quintale, was so successful that Michele was able to give up his other paid work. They signed a contract with a major label, affiliated to Universal Music Group, which provided them with management, video production and a stylist.

In 2014, Michele was relaxing on the lake shore at Salò when he recognised a girl, Emma, whom he'd known when they were children. They started chatting, then went out a few times, and soon became an item. Emma had an unusual background. Her mother was from New York and her father from London, but they lived in Salò, where Emma was brought up. Emma's parents are now separated, her mother still living in Salò, and her father living between Brescia and Milan.

Speaking fluent English, Emma had decided to go to university in London, where she studied International Business and Chinese. As part of her degree course, Emma spent a year living in China. After graduating, Emma remained in London until she was 30 years old, when she returned to Salò. There, on the lake shore, she met Michele.

Meanwhile, in 2015, the Fratelli Quintale, having not made the big breakthrough they'd hoped for, decided to split and go their separate ways. One of their members, Frah Quintale, a rap singer, continued to pursue a solo career in music. He achieved great success in 2018/19, becoming famous throughout Italy. Videos from both Fratelli Quintale and Frah Quintale can be seen on YouTube.

What was Michele to do now? With the group disbanded, he was looking for a new direction. As always, Michele was open to change, eager to relocate to a new place, with new work. Emma, having spent a decade in London, was very fond of that city. Together, they decided to relocate to London. Emma quickly found a position, working for the financial investment company CMC. With his previous restaurant experience Michele was also able to find work, as a chef for the Honest Burgers restaurant chain. They lived in Shoreditch near Liverpool Street station, in the heart of the city, a highly desirable location for young people with an active social life.

Then, Michele and Emma took time off and travelled to French Polynesia. There they got married, in a simple ceremony with no guests. After one month in this sunny paradise, they returned to the big city.

Emma enjoyed living in London. However, as the months and years passed, Michele found himself becoming less happy. This was not where he wanted to be, nor what he wanted to be doing, in the long term.

They discussed their options and together decided to relocate to Barcelona, where friends had asked Michele to be the manager of their bar. Emma gave up her role at CMC and, in June 2018, they moved to Barcelona, and Michele started his new position. Emma settled down to enjoy the Catalonian summer, before looking for work in earnest.

However, in August Emma received bad news. Her mother's boyfriend had died. She returned to Salò, to be with her mum. Michele stayed on in Barcelona, managing the bar. Emma then had a difficult year, supporting her mother and separated from her husband. Eventually, Michele quit his position in Barcelona and returned to Salò, on Christmas Eve 2019.

As always, whenever Michele relocates, an opportunity appears for him, as if by magic. Five friends had recently opened a bicycle hire and repair business in Salò, called Cyclingarda. The driving force behind the business was a 45-year-old man, who had been a keen competitive cyclist in his youth. However, after managing the Cyclingarda shop for a year, he wasn't enjoying the business anywhere near as much as he'd hoped. Almost all his customers were tourists, many unable to speak Italian. But this shop manager could only speak Italian. After a frustrating and unhappy first season, he wanted out.

Using his savings, Michele was able to purchase this man's share of the business and take over as shop manager. Although Michele had no particular interest in bicycles, he did have a proficiency in languages and he enjoyed dealing with customers, so he was much better suited to the work. On 7th January 2020, Michele started work as shop manager for Cyclingarda.

Michele is the face of the business, manning the shop and dealing directly with customers. In addition to the shop, where they sell, hire and repair bicycles, Cyclingarda provides guided tours. Two of Michele's colleagues are mechanics, servicing and repairing bikes, and they also operate as tour guides.

I had noticed a set of bicycles available for guests to hire, at our hotel. I mention this to Michele.

"Yes, they are ours," he says. "We have a deal with several local hotels, whereby they hire a set of bicycles from us for the season, which they can rent to their guests. We service these bikes, providing a monthly maintenance check."

Soon after Michele started at Cyclingarda, Covid arrived and Italy was in lockdown. Obviously, the next two seasons were difficult for the fledgling business. In 2021, Emma found a job with a local pharmaceutical company, working at their office in Salò. She is responsible for export sales although, fortunately, the role does not require too much travel.

I ask Michele whether he has returned to DJ work recently. He explains that he hasn't, partly because they live in a small house where there is no room for the equipment.

"The kit is stored at my parents' house, in a small studio, but I don't go there often. I do miss it, and I hope that I can return to being a DJ one day. But right now, I am too busy with the shop."

"Presumably, the shop is quieter in the winter. Will that be an opportunity?"

"Yes, the shop is open less in the winter, and we tend to hire bicycles for longer periods, a month or more. However, as it happens, Emma and I have a project for this winter. We are building a house, so that we will have more space."

"Congratulations! Do you have other plans for the future? Maybe children?"

"Yes, possibly. Also, my wife owns some land where we have planted olive trees. Once they mature, in ten years or so, this could provide another business for us. I would very much like to be an olive farmer."

"That might be the only profession you haven't already tried!" I joke. "You have always moved on Michele, never staying in the same place or the same job for very long. Is that going to change?"

"You're right, I don't like to stand still. But now we have plans for the future, and I would like to get back to my music. Provided our income is OK, hopefully we can stay here and have a family."

I reckon Michele is in his late thirties. Is he ready to make a long term commitment, to put down roots?

It looks that way, but only time will tell.

15 Comrades

"I've decided I'm coming with you to Italy!"

This from Jackie who, on many occasions, has said she sees no point going to Italy in the winter, because you can't sit outside to enjoy a coffee or a spritz. She explains that the last eight months have turned her into "a caged animal". As the person sharing the cage, I can confirm this to be true.

After six cycles of chemotherapy, plus a gruelling nine-hour operation, she is now in remission. She is free and fit enough to travel. A bit of cold weather is not going to stop her.

I also did not travel during these eight months of cancer treatment. Now able to resume the Italian project, I've planned a trip to three cities in the north of Italy, in February, with the sole objective of gathering more interviews for this book. However, now that Jackie is coming, it will also be a holiday.

We arrive in grey, cold Milan on a Thursday evening, and are shown into the AirBnB apartment by its owner, Rosa Maria. The flat is warm and spacious, for which we are grateful because the forecast for the next two days is grim: rain, rain and more rain. Rosa Maria provides the WiFi password, and explains where we can find supermarkets and how to get tickets for the metro and buses. After she leaves, we unpack and immediately go out for dinner. Fortunately, we take umbrellas because, as soon as we leave the apartment, it starts raining.

Milan is the commercial capital of Italy, a centre for finance, fashion and design in general. Almost everybody is impeccably dressed. It feels like a big city, with efficient, functioning services. Work and money are the priorities here, whereas in most of Italy you might put family and food at the top of the list. In many ways, Milan feels more northern European than Italian.

That's especially true when the weather is like this: non-stop rain.

The next day, we travel across the city to a restaurant recommended to me by Silvia, a language exchange partner who lives in Florence but spends a lot of time in Milan. Having been told that the restaurant does not take reservations, and is very busy in the evenings, we decide to have lunch there. Even arriving at 12.30 on a Friday, the place is busy and we are lucky to get a table. It's a large L-shaped room, plainly decorated with yellow and white walls, supporting pictures and photographs, with tables everywhere. Almost every table has diners engrossed in conversation, so there is a real buzz.

The service is quick. We order simple pasta-with-sauce dishes, each priced around seven euros, and they arrive quickly. I have Tiramisu for dessert, something that every restaurant in Italy seems to do differently, so it's not a boring, predictable choice. The food is good and, given the prices, excellent value. After paying the cashier at the counter, I ask him whether they might be willing to feature in my book. He consults his colleague, one of the waiters, and they seem happy to take part. I get the impression that this waiter, possibly more outgoing than the cashier, is being nominated as the front-man for the establishment. He introduces himself as Alberto Bertatini, and we agree that I shall return later this afternoon, at 4pm, after they have cleared up following lunchtime service.

Jackie and I go back to our apartment, in the rain, via a supermarket to collect food for this evening and tomorrow's breakfast. After about ten minutes in the apartment, I leave to cross town again, in the rain, returning to Il Brutto Anatroccolo. Inside the restaurant, three middle-aged men are chatting: the waiter Alberto, the cashier and another man. Alberto waves me inside, with a friendly face and a big smile. Over lunch earlier, I'd noticed Alberto serving lots of customers, always unhurried, efficient, relaxed and cheerful.

I'm introduced properly to the others. The cashier, Alvaraldo Tocchi, stays behind the bar, working on something. The third man, Francesco Chieraschi, sits at a table with me and Alberto. Alberto explains that Francesco's parents used to run the restaurant, a long time ago, and he was born nearby. Although Francesco himself is not involved directly in the business, he knows much of its history and is a close friend of the owners. Today the restaurant is owned and managed by three partners: Alberto, Alvaraldo and Daniele Salvia. Daniele is not here at the moment.

I start by asking Alberto about his background, his parents, where he was born etc. Originally from near Varese, a small town between lakes Maggiore and Como, Alberto's parents were living in Milan when he was born. His father was a mechanic, and his mother worked for Singer, the sewing machine manufacturer. Alberto's grandfather ran a bar for a few years in the Varese area, when Alberto's father was a child. Growing up, Alberto's father helped out as a waiter in this bar.

Alberto attended a liceo specialising in accounting. Many of his schoolmates then went to nearby Bocconi university, to study economics and commerce. Alberto didn't follow them. He was offered two different jobs at Banca di Roma, but he said "no". Alberto simply was not interested in a career in accounting.

To provide background, Francesco tells the story of the restaurant. "My parents started working here in 1962, managing the place. In those days it was more a bar than a restaurant."

Most evenings, the tables were cleared away and people

would dance and drink in the bar until late. They also organised cabaret evenings, with stand-up comedians. Generally, food was served only at lunchtimes, but sometimes a slow cooked pork sausage called cotechino, a Milanese speciality, was served at midnight.

Francesco continues: "In 1978, I started working here. Then my parents left, and I brought in friends to help keep the place going."

During the 1970s, the bar became busy with students, from nearby universities, and also local people, but towards the end of the decade the students dominated. Francesco explains that, in those days, this area was a hotbed of socialism. There were often demonstrations in the streets, especially against America's foreign interventions. Sometimes police closed the roads, bringing in armoured vehicles and cracking down hard on the protestors.

"There was one period, around 1980, when the area was ungovernable, and police were stationed here permanently. Many youngsters gathered around our bar, and they would make a mess in the streets. It got so bad, with all these people blocking the road, that they had to change the bus route."

"One day, the police called me. They explained that they knew I didn't deal drugs, or do anything illegal, but they had 2,000 signatures from local people protesting that they wanted the bar closed. During the early 1980s things improved, and the area slowly became less dominated by left-wing students."

There was a period of about a year when everything was in flux, because Francesco's friends left and the place was closed. Then two other friends of Francesco, plus their wives, took on the business and reopened the bar. They paid Francesco's parents a fee to run the restaurant because, although no longer working there, his parents owned the licence. Rent for the building was paid separately to its owner.

Alberto was introduced to the business by his brother, a friend of Francesco. "We were all friends together, we worked here and we played football together."

I ask Alberto why he started working in the bar.

"In those days everybody had to do national service. I had asked to do civil, rather than military, service. I wanted to work at ACLI (the Christian Association of Italian Workers), helping children. While waiting for them to call me up, I thought I might as well work here temporarily. However, they never contacted me and, 40 years later, I'm still here!"

Apparently, after 26 months of not being called up, a young Italian was deemed to have completed his national service.

Francesco, however, did not go back to work in the bar.

"I didn't want to work in the evenings, a time when most of my friends were out enjoying themselves. Also, I had a girlfriend and I wanted to see her, at least occasionally! I became a musician instead. I played the piano. However, even though I've not worked here these last 40 years, I have always been involved. We are close friends."

Alberto continues his story.

"Two men and their wives were running the business, but then one of the wives left. So, I joined as a member. Then her husband also left, and Alvaraldo became a member to replace him."

In 1982, they obtained their own licence from the local government, the Comune. Alberto brings me a copy of this licence, with the names of the three business partners: Alberto, Alvaraldo and Antonore Santagostini. At this time, the name of the bar was changed from La Clinica to Il Brutto Anatroccolo, which is what's written on the licence they show me.

"Why is it called The Ugly Duckling?" I ask.

"Look at it!" Alberto gestures towards the plain walls, the relatively primitive decor of the restaurant.

"That was much easier than redecorating," he smiles.

Francesco gives another reason.

"At that time, other new bars were opening up in the area. Our place had been here for a long time and its traditional look made it stand out, as an ugly duckling."

"But many older people, of our generation and earlier, still come here and refer to it as La Clinica," says Alberto. "They have long memories."

I ask about the history of the building. They believe it was constructed in the 19th century, with the ground floor used initially as stables, associated with the canals nearby. From the 12th century onwards, canals were constructed to serve the growing city of Milan. Prominent intellectuals, including Leonardo Da Vinci, worked on the canals and the associated dams. Two major canals, the Naviglio Grande and the Naviglio Pavese, met nearby at the Darsena, a river port. Materials for building Milan's Duomo were brought in along the canals, and then transported by horse and cart to the construction site. Hence the need for stables in this area.

In the late 19th and early 20th century, most canals were filled in or covered over, having been superseded by the railways. However, the stretches that still remain, here in the south of Milan, now provide a pleasant leisure district, the Navigli, populated with bars and restaurants that come to life in the evening.

On one of the walls, I notice a poster looking like an advertisement for Coca Cola. But it says "DO NOT DRINK

COCA COLA"! Another poster displays a Coke bottle, together with messages in Spanish giving reasons it should be avoided: "BEWARE"; "Your bones will become weak"; "You will have gastritis"; "Do you want to become like me?" (with a picture of a fat man); "It destroys your teeth".

"We don't serve Coca Cola here," explains Alberto. "We stopped serving it in the 1990s, as a protest against American foreign policy. At the beginning it was difficult, because people kept asking for it. It would have been easier to say we had run out of bread! We were young, enthusiastic leftists in those days."

At this point, Alvaraldo leaves the bar and comes over to say something. He is interrupted by Francesco, who looks at me, while pointing at Alvaraldo.

"You know, he is English. He's an imperialist. He cannot change, it's in his blood!"

They all laugh, while I look puzzled. Alvaraldo explains that his grandmother's grandmother was English. She moved to Rome, to work as an au pair for a rich family, but the master of the house got her pregnant. She left and moved to Milan.

This reminds me that I haven't asked Alberto if he is married.

"Yes," he says, "I married almost 40 years ago."

"How did you meet your wife?"

"In school!"

I laugh.

"I've noticed that many Italians first meet their spouses in school."

"From my class, there emerged five married couples!" says Alberto. "Only one of those couples has divorced, with another couple presently separated."

"Do you have any children, Alberto?"

"I have a son Marco, he's a waiter here and you met him earlier today, remember? I asked if he could stay this afternoon, for our interview, because he speaks good English, but he wasn't available."

"Yes, I remember. He's your only child?"

"Yes, I didn't have time for another," jokes Alberto. "He's very useful because, when foreign students or tourists come in, who don't speak Italian, they usually speak English."

"How many of your customers are tourists, would you say?"

"About 30%, of whom two thirds are Italian and one third are foreign tourists. There are lots of AirBnB apartments in this area, nowadays. The big trade shows, such as fashion and furniture, bring many visitors to the city and, since the year 2000, there has been an explosion in short term rentals."

"Are many of your customers students?" I ask.

"In the evening, I would say 50% are students."

I then ask how they find staff, to work in the kitchen and front of house.

Alberto explains that he and the third owner, Daniele Salvia, take turns working in the kitchen, with the other front of house. Daniele replaced the original third owner, Antonore Santagostini, in 2005. Alberto's wife Daniela works in the kitchen every day, where they also employ a lad from Sri Lanka, who has been here for 20 years. Apparently, the Sri Lankan "boy" speaks excellent English, but not Italian! In addition to Alberto's son Marco, a number of students are employed as part time waiters.

"Does the menu change a lot?"

"It changes every day. There are a few fixed items, but most of it changes every day. Daniele and I decide what's on the menu."

Francesco explains why it's important to keep changing the menu. "There are some people who have been coming here for lunch almost every day for 20 years, because they work nearby."

Alberto shows me a typical menu, written out by hand. Dishes provided every day include Cotoletta (veal cutlet coated in breadcrumbs), and Ossobuco (slow cooked veal shanks) with risotto, both typical Milanese recipes.

"There are some longstanding traditions. For example, every Tuesday we provide tripe. Nothing is frozen, everything is cooked fresh, and sometimes we run out. Yesterday, we cooked 50 Ossobuco in the morning and, by 2pm, they had all gone."

I mention that I'd been told they don't take reservations.

"We don't take lunchtime reservations, nor do we take reservations for dinner on Friday and Saturday, but we do take evening reservations from Monday to Thursday. If you come back this evening, Friday, you will see a line outside, people queueing for here, all the way down the street to the next restaurant."

Alberto is looking towards the entrance. Following his gaze, I look above the door and see a load of silverware, clearly won in competition. Alberto notices what I am looking at, and explains.

"We have always had our own football team, called Il Brutto Anatroccolo, formed from people who work here, plus friends and family. We don't always do well, but in recent years we have had a strong team and been winning a lot. Last year we just lost out at the end. This year we are doing well, and hoping to win the league. Every Wednesday, the squad has lunch here. I don't play any more however, because I'm too old."

"Are you planning changes to the restaurant in the future?"

Alberto laughs. "We haven't changed anything in 40 years,

so why would we change now! We do change the posters on the wall, however. They are only there because Alvaraldo deals in antique posters. He searches the local markets and, whenever he buys one, he keeps it on the wall here until the day he sells it."

Our conversation draws to a close and, as I am preparing to leave, Alvaraldo brings over a big sheet of paper. He shows me what seems to be a black and white photograph of Leonardo da Vinci's famous painting, The Last Supper. On closer inspection, I see that all the figures are dressed in modern clothes.

"That's me," says Alberto, pointing to the second man from the left. It's a much younger version of Alberto, but he's recognisable.

"A photographer friend took this picture of the team in the 1990s," says Alvaraldo.

I love it. In the original painting, the hand gestures show that there must be a vigorous discussion taking place, and all the disciples seem to be talking at once. Italians always talk with their hands. Christ's announcement that one of them will betray him is supposed to have triggered this conversation, but is that plausible? It's easy to imagine the friends of Il Brutto Anatroccolo arguing energetically about politics or football, so the spoof photograph makes more sense to me than the original painting.

Back outside, umbrella held high, I push through the rain to the bus stop. I really enjoyed my time with Alberto and his friends. After 40 years, they still like each other's company and the laughter never stops. Alberto works with his family and with colleagues he has known for decades. He even used to play football with them. A happy man.

16 Reconnecting with your roots

Our final day in Milan was drier, but still grey. Now, arriving in Genoa by train, the sun is shining and the sky is blue. We trundle suitcases the ten-minute walk to our hotel, on Via XX Settembre, Genoa's principal shopping street. Via XX Settembre is characterised by beautiful marble porticoes, on both sides of the street, protecting pedestrians from the elements and hosting shops that include the world's most famous brands. Constructed 100 years ago, this beautiful broad avenue replaced an area of narrow streets and medieval houses.

Another elegant street is Via Garibaldi, lined with spectacular Renaissance and Baroque palaces, built when Genoa was a great financial and seafaring power. This area, the Nuove Strade (new streets), is a UNESCO world heritage site. The streets are no longer "new", but they were new in the 16th century when first named – rather like New College Oxford, which was actually founded in 1379.

Genoa's ancient harbour, the Porto Antico, benefitted from major investments in the 1990s, nominally associated with the 500th anniversary of when Christopher Columbus, perhaps Genoa's most famous son, arrived in America. As a result, Genoa has modern family attractions, the marine aquarium and maritime museum, plus a marina for the yachts of the super-rich, with restaurants and bars.

Genoa is a fascinating place to visit, and surely the most under-rated city in Italy. We first came during the pandemic, spending a few days here in September 2020. At the last minute, British Airways cancelled our flights but, refusing to accept defeat, we drove down from the UK. On that occasion, we rented an apartment in the medieval quarter, an ancient maze of narrow, dark alleys, stretching inland from the Porto Antico. This area is populated with immigrants from Africa and the Middle East, many struggling to get by. Rather like the Spanish Quarter in Naples, it feels edgy on first acquaintance but, in reality, it's generally safe.

This part of the city dates from the days when Venice and Genoa were rival maritime republics, battling for control of trade in the mediterranean. Venice eventually came out on top, towards the end of the 14th century, with long term consequences for both cities. Over the next 600 years, the story of each city followed many twists and turns, and today they are very different. The historical centre of Venice has only 50,000 residents. Genoa, one of the busiest ports in the Mediterranean, is Italy's sixth largest city, with a population close to 600,000. Inevitably, their city centres feel quite different. Most shops in Venice sell tourist bric-a-brac, whereas the medieval quarter in Genoa still has many traditional businesses frequented by locals. There's an impressive number of antique dealers, fabric shops, and musical instrument specialists, even a violin maker.

Near the Porto Antico is a covered arcade called Sottoripa, with stone arches facing the sea. Although dark and slightly forbidding, this place is alive with the shouts of traders, and aromas from street food, fresh fish, fruit and vegetables.

We are wandering through Sottoripa, on our first afternoon in the city, when an old shop catches my eye. The glass frontage informs us that Fratelli Armanino has been supplying the Genoese with dried fruit since 1905. I enter, to see a dazzling diversity of products arranged on shelves. In addition to dried fruit, there are candied fruits, nuts, dried pasta, mustards, jams, herbs and spices.

A middle-aged lady, with dark thick curly hair, sits on a stool at the far end of the shop. We start chatting. Her name is Alessia Armanino, and she is one of the owners. I explain about the book I am writing and ask if she would like to be included.

"I normally don't talk to journalists etc. but you seem nice so, yes, why not?"

We agree that I will return for an interview at noon the next day, when Alessia's colleague Cinzia will be there to serve customers.

The next day arrives, and it's a lovely sunny morning. I stroll from our hotel to the dried fruit shop, having time to stop and visit a beautiful church on the way. When I enter Fratelli Armanino, Alessia introduces me to her cousin Cinzia Dagnino, explaining that the two of them own and run the shop together. Alessia and I settle down, each sat on a stool, and I begin by asking how the business was founded.

Alessia's great-grandfather Placido Armanino was a mariner and a businessman, bringing bananas from Somalia to Genoa. She tells me that he was the first importer of bananas to Italy, and he was also involved in the dried fruit trade. It was Placido who had the idea to open a shop selling dried fruit, in Genoa, in 1905. Because he was still travelling on ship, his wife Santa ran the new shop, which was in Via alla Porta degli Archi, about 1km inland from where we are today. Although Santa ran the shop, the business was called P. Armanino e Figli (P. Armanino and sons), so she didn't get a mention.

Placido and Santa had four sons: Bruno, Edilio, Angelo and Valerio. As the boys grew older, they too became involved in the business, eventually taking over from their parents. This was when the shop acquired the name Fratelli Armanino (Armanino Brothers). It seems that, even today, the ladies who actually own and run the business don't get mentioned in its name!

In 1940, the shop relocated to Corso Buenos Aires, about 2km inland from today's store. This shop was managed by brothers Edilio and Angelo. A second shop opened in the Sottoripa, very near today's premises, managed by the other two brothers, Bruno and Valerio. Unfortunately, the shop in Sottoripa was destroyed by a bomb during the Second World War. As a strategically important port, Genoa suffered greatly from bombardment in the war, mostly by the British. Undeterred, Bruno and Valerio reopened their store in 1945, at the current location, and it's been here ever since.

Eventually, the four brothers became too old to work in the business. The shop in Corso Buenos Aires was closed in 1980. In 1984 the shop we are in, which was run by Bruno and Valerio, passed to the next generation. It was Edilio's son Placido and Angelo's son Massimo who took over the remaining store, in Sottoripa. Massimo had been working in the shop since he was a boy, but Placido was starting this work in his forties.

Placido was married to Margherita, who worked in her parents' fresh pasta shop, nearby. They had two children, Alessia and her brother Stefano. Alessia attended a classical liceo, then she studied law at university in Genoa. Stefano trained in medicine, and today he is a doctor.

I ask Alessia if, in those days, she had plans to work in her father's business.

"No! I wanted to contribute in social services. My ambition was to speed up adoption procedures for children, to make the government more effective in helping disadvantaged youngsters."

Sadly, this never came to pass. After her third year of university, Alessia was in Trentino for a holiday. She had been there many times before, on family holidays. On this occasion, she was having a good time and realised that she dreaded returning for another year of university in Genoa. A future in law was no longer appealing. The sons of lawyers found it easy to be admitted to the legal profession but, for Alessia, the daughter of a shopkeeper, it would be more difficult. She decided to leave university and relocate to Trentino.

From previous holidays, Alessia already knew people who ran the ski chairlifts in Val di Fiemme. She had even helped out occasionally, as a teenager, to earn a little money. Now, keen to stay in the mountains, she found long term work with them. Although, or perhaps because, it was unusual for a woman to work on the chairlifts, Alessia very much enjoyed the role. She stayed there for ten years!

As well as operating the chairlifts, Alessia worked in the Ski pass office. The chairlifts ran in winter and summer, but would be closed in spring and autumn. I ask Alessia what she did during the closed periods.

"I would return to Genoa to see my family, or go travelling. I love to travel."

"Do you ever find time to travel now you are working here, in the shop?"

"Yes! We close for 45 days in the summer, from mid-July to the end of August. I enjoy staying in Liguria, although I don't generally like the beaches because they are too crowded, but I also travel. For example, I've been to Easter Island, Polynesia, Hawaii, California and Africa. When you have a month and a half, it's possible to travel a long way."

During her time in Trentino, Alessia also studied in the evenings for a diploma in accounting. Thanks to her previous education and qualifications, she obtained the diploma within a year, where normally it would take several years.

"When I was young, and only had to study, I didn't really apply myself. But when I was working, and could only study in my free time, I was able to do it effectively!"

Alessia then says that, after ten years in Trentino, she went through a difficult period. She doesn't want to discuss details, and I don't press her, but she does say that her family helped her a lot at this time. Not ready to return to Genoa, she took advantage of her accounting diploma and found work in Lodi, south-east of Milan. She and a friend, between them, managed a private health club. The facilities included swimming pools, tennis courts, gym, a wellness centre and restaurants. Alessia spent five years, living and working in Lodi.

Meanwhile, Alessia's parents Placido and Margherita were getting older. Her mother was unwell, and her father was talking about giving up work and closing the shop. Alessia decided to take a temporary leave of absence from the club in Lodi, and return to Genoa to help her parents: "to give something back." She also wanted to revisit the dried fruit business, to see whether, after all, it was something she might wish to get involved with.

Placido, however, did not want his daughter to work in the shop. Alessia explains that this was partly the attitude of the older generation, who saw it as a man's job. The work is tiring and can be physically demanding, as produce is often delivered in big, heavy boxes. Placido also didn't want Alessia to be tied down. Although running the business gives freedom, in the sense that you are your own boss, it also commits you to long hours serving in the shop.

"It's no path to riches," says Alessia, "and you often have to work even when you feel unwell."

Without Alessia and Cinzia taking over, the business would almost certainly have closed. The Fratelli Armanino brand was well known in Genoa. However, Placido and Massimo did not want to sell the brand and the business as a going concern to people outside the family. Their fear was that whoever took over would not maintain the quality and the reputation of the shop, thus tarnishing the family name.

"As well as providing better produce than you'll find in a supermarket, here we have time to chat with our customers. Many of them become friends."

"How many years have you been working here?"

"Eight years, I think. I know how to find out." She takes me to the storeroom, at the back of the shop, and points to a row of bottles high on a shelf.

"At the end of every year, we buy a bottle of champagne."

There are indeed eight bottles.

As we exit the storeroom, Cinzia chips in.

"Alessia began here in September 2015. I remember because I had been working here for a year before she started."

They explain that, in 2015, Placido and Massimo were ready to retire and close the business. Cinzia was helping in the shop, but there was no way she could run it on her own. Fortunately, Alessia was keen to become involved and, with Cinzia as her partner, they could make it work.

"I could never have done this without Cinzia, I'm so lucky to have her as my cousin," declares Alessia, smiling at her business partner.

I ask Cinzia where she worked before coming to Fratelli Armanino.

"I worked for ten years in a historic porcelain and crystal shop, founded in 1878, in Piazza Manin. Then I moved to another historic porcelain and crystal shop, Radif in Via San Lorenzo, where I worked for several more years."

Founded in 1820, Radif is an even older family business, suppliers to hotels and restaurants as well as the domestic market. Cinzia informs me that Radif provided tableware for the Titanic!

"What made you come here Cinzia, to Fratelli Armanino?"

"That was really a leap in the dark. I had met my husband Davide Armanino, and married into the family, and I was looking for a change of scene workwise. We had a little boy, Riccardo, and I was also thinking that, with me working in the family business, that might give him the opportunity to continue here one day. For all these reasons, I came to work here in 2014."

"Do you think that Riccardo will want to take over here, one day?"

"Who knows? He is 20 years old and, right now, he loves playing basketball. He has toured Italy, thanks to his basketball!"

"He must be very tall then?"

"All we Armanini are tall," says Alessia, and she stands up to demonstrate. I suddenly feel short.

"My brother and Cinzia's husband are both much taller than me, and Riccardo is even taller."

I turn to Cinzia.

"Does Riccardo play professionally?"

"He wants to, but it's very difficult. Right now, he has returned to Genoa and he is studying, while still playing basketball. He's doing a course in photography, which he likes very much. Until last year, he only ever thought about basketball. He has to find his way."

"Because of the pension age in Italy, we cannot afford to retire until 2040, so he has plenty of time to decide," says Alessia. "As I did when I was younger, he comes here at Christmas to help out. He knows what it is all about. He has dried fruit in his blood!"

A lady comes into the shop and Alessia excuses herself, to go and chat with her briefly. There have been several customers since we started the interview, all clearly well known to Cinzia and Alessia. I suspect the relationships they have with their customers are the most rewarding part of the work.

"Are all your customers from Genoa?"

"We have many people who come from Milan, Turin, even Valtellina. Especially at Christmas, people will travel to buy the ingredients for seasonal breads and cakes, even salamis."

"Do you get many tourists in here?"

"Fortunately, yes. Thanks to the port, the cruise ships, the aquarium etc. There are fewer than there were before Covid, but it is growing again. We are big fans of the mayor, who is doing great things for Genoa. After the collapse of the bridge, he helped to ensure a replacement was built within two years, something thought to be impossible in Italy, given our bureaucracy."

Alessia is referring to the collapse of the Morandi motorway bridge in Genoa, which fell onto city buildings below, during a storm in August 2018. The disaster claimed 43 lives, and had a significant impact on the Genoese economy. I remember seeing the interview, on Italian TV, of a truck driver who was driving over the bridge when it collapsed. He stopped his truck when he saw that there was no road in front of him. The driver of a car behind beeped his horn several times then, in frustration, overtook the truck and plunged to his death. The truck driver was saying that he still had nightmares, as a result of this incident.

At this point, Alessia points out something that I hadn't noticed. The shop has no door – just an open doorway, leading onto the street. There is a metal shutter, across the complete frontage, that is pulled down to lock up overnight. However, during the day, you could not pop out briefly and close the door behind you, because there is no door!

"It's never had a door," states Alessia.

"There's never been a door?" I say incredulously.

"Never!" Alessia smiles proudly. I get the impression that this permanently open doorway is a symbol, of how the shop is always open and welcoming anyone who passes.

"Don't you get cold in the winter?"

"You can see how many layers I have on," and she starts counting, "1,2,3,4. . . and this is cashmere."

"Is there air conditioning, for the summer?"

"No."

I look around at the marble counter, the traditional wooden cupboards and shelves, plain whitewashed walls and arched ceiling. I can understand how these thick stone walls would keep the place cool in summer and, being next to the mediterranean, Genoa has a much milder winter climate than inland cities, like Turin and Milan.

"How old is the building?"

"It was built in 1133."

I express surprise that she can be so accurate and confident about the construction date. Alessia brings out a leaflet, describing the shop and its history, that she wrote in 2005, to commemorate the 100th anniversary of the business. The construction date 1133 is recorded in this leaflet. She explains that, at one time, this is where a fisherman stored his boat between fishing trips. In those days, the sea would have been much closer. Land reclamation, for various developments of Porto Antico over the centuries, mean that the sea is now 80 meters away, beyond the busy overpass that runs all along the shore. I try to imagine this room in the distant past, with the strong odour of fish filling our nostrils, and the sounds of seabirds and lapping waves, rather than cars and trucks on the overpass.

Alessia talks about how the mix of products they sell has changed over the years. When she was younger, they sold carob, which comes from the pods of an evergreen mediterranean tree. I confess I'd never heard of it. Apparently, some people say it is similar to chocolate, but naturally sweet.

"We sold a lot of it in those days, because it was cheap. We still get older people coming in and talking about how their father brought them here to buy carob, when they were little."

"What does it taste like?"

"It's disgusting!"

"I guess there is a lot of specialist knowledge required here, you have many different products?"

"Yes. Nowadays we have a wider range of products than in the past, because the world has opened up much more. In the old days, we would not have stocked mango, papaya or pineapple, for example. However, although they had fewer products then, they made more sales in industrial quantities."

I observe that the shop is open at least nine hours per day, six days per week, which must be quite a commitment for them.

"We do have a part time assistant, who serves for a few days each week. It wasn't easy to find somebody who knew about the products, but she is very good. Even with her help, we do work long hours."

I have no more questions to ask, and our conversation gradually draws to a close. After saying thank you and goodbye to both ladies, I exit the shop and walk a few steps towards the sea so that I can get a better view of this part of Sottoripa. Almost directly above the shop is an old stone tower. A quick search on my phone identifies this as the Morchi tower, and also gives background information on the Sottoripa. The construction date of 1133 is evidenced by a dated decree, from Advisers to the Genoese Republic, specifying how it should be built.

These buildings have witnessed so many human dramas, over their 900 years. Now Alessia has chosen to live out her life here, adding one more story to the multitude.

I recall that, when talking about the long hours she worked, it was clear from Alessia's demeanour that she didn't mind that at all. On the contrary, this was a pleasant way to spend the day. In the shop, much of her time is spent conversing with customers she knows well, people who are happy to linger, to chat and to listen. Alessia also has the companionship of her cousin, business partner and close friend Cinzia.

After decades of finding her way, Alessia has returned to her roots and settled into a comfortable, pleasant life here, within the ancient porticoes of Sottoripa.

17 A remarkable friendship

The big three - Rome, Florence and Venice - have been popular with visitors, for such a long time, that they almost take tourists for granted.   Often, the impression is given that holidaymakers are tolerated rather than welcomed.   Genoa, however, has the opposite problem. When it comes to tourists, there is almost a lack of confidence, an expectation that the city will disappoint, perhaps because, for so long, Genoa has been overshadowed by Italy's more famous tourist cities.

Of course, Genoa has no reason to feel inadequate, it's a great place to visit.   In particular, the quality of mid-priced restaurants is astonishing.   Maybe we have been lucky, but every restaurant we visited, on both our trips here, has provided fantastic food, and excellent wine. Yesterday, we had lunch at Le Rune, currently Tripadvisor's number one restaurant in Genoa.

Liguria is sandwiched between mountains and sea, and it feels like the hills are pushing you into the Mediterranean. Walking away from the sea in Genoa, you soon come across steep alleys, *salite* (slopes), that climb the hillside. Le Rune is tucked away at the bottom of one of these, Salita Inferiore di Sant'Anna. Once through the restaurant's unassuming entrance, we were greeted by a friendly lady, who showed us to our table and proceeded to serve a wonderful lunch.   We especially enjoyed the dessert that Jackie ordered, Pandolce Genovese, which tasted amazing.   The friendly lady informed us that, although most of the menu changes every day, that dessert is always available.   Apparently, were it to disappear, regular customers would be appalled.

This morning, I am returning to speak to Le Rune's owners,

and discover how they made this place such a success.

Simona Pelizza, the lady who served us lunch, introduces herself, and head chef Alberto Lovisa. They own and run the place, together. We sit at the same table where Jackie and I had lunch, and I start asking questions.

Simona has a round face that frequently breaks into a broad smile, although there is nervous energy just below the surface. I remember, when here for lunch, that Simona never ceased moving around the restaurant, finding things to do, even when Jackie and I, plus one other table, were the only customers.

Alberto also has a warm smile and cheerful disposition, with a reassuring deep voice and dark bushy eyebrows.

Simona was born in Genoa, and has always lived in or near the city. Her mother was a tour guide. However, one day, Simona's grandfather, who worked in a bank, persuaded his daughter to give up her work as a tour guide and get a job in banking. In those days, having a parent in an Italian bank made it very easy to get a job there yourself. Simona's mother started work at UniCredit and that's where she met the man who became her husband. They married and had a daughter, Simona, plus a son. Later, they fostered a girl, subsequently adopted, thus ending up with three children.

Simona might have considered a career in banking but, by the time she was a teenager, having parents in that profession no longer provided automatic employment opportunities. At the age of 14, Simona started at a liceo specialising in tourism, including instruction in three foreign languages: English, French and German.

I ask Simona why she chose this type of school.

"I always wanted to travel."

After leaving school, Simona lived at home for a year, in the countryside near Genoa, working for an agricultural business. Then she found work at a hotel in the city, helping in the restaurant. Later, she moved to work in another hotel in Genoa, the four-star Starhotels President near Brignole station. One of her colleagues left to go and work at a new restaurant, opening up on the other side of town, and he suggested that maybe Simona would like to join him. Accordingly, in September 1997, she got a job as a waitress at Le Rune. But this was not the same Le Rune that we are sitting in today.

It was at Le Rune that she met Alberto, who was head chef in the kitchen.

Alberto was born in Treviso, one of four children. His brother, ten years older, became a doctor and has now retired. His two sisters both work in schools, one as an administrator and the other as a language teacher.

Both of Alberto's parents worked in tailoring. His father made clothes for men, his mother for women. Alberto, however, had no interest in making clothes. From the age of 14, he attended a Hotel School (Scuola Alberghiera) at Castelfranco Veneto, 26km from home, being willing to travel because this school had such a good reputation. "I would wake at 6am, and take a 40-minute train journey to get to school on time. I always wanted to be a chef, for as long as I can remember. My mother prepared the meals at home, and I helped her with odd jobs in the kitchen. I was born to cook."

After leaving school, Alberto worked in kitchens for a couple of summer seasons at the beach resort of Jesolo, on the Venetian lagoon. He found these positions with the help of his school which, as a Scuola Alberghiera, has strong links with local hospitality businesses. Inevitably, Alberto enjoyed his summers there by the sea. Next, he found another seaside position at a restaurant in the village of Baja Sardinia situated, as the name suggests, on the island of Sardinia. Alberto worked there from May to September, and then spent another two months on the island as a holiday.

"You like beaches?" I suggest.

"Yes, very much!"

Alberto talks about how his time on Sardinia was relaxing, more about enjoying sea and sun than cooking. In Jesolo, however, he worked very long hours in the kitchen.

Leaving Sardinia, Alberto returned to Treviso and found a job in a popular restaurant near the station, called L'Incontro. Here, he cooked for a total of ten years. He tells me that L'Incontro is still run by the same owner, who is now 80 years old!

Towards the end of this period, Alberto was offered a consultancy role at the restaurant in Genoa's airport.

"Let's say I was a little tired of Treviso. I wanted to see other places, so I said 'why not!' and took the position. I worked there for four months, and that's where I met the girl who was to become my wife. She also worked there, and I suggested we go out for a drink. One thing led to another, and eventually we got married."

Meanwhile, after his four-month stint in Genoa, Alberto returned to L'Incontro to work for another year. His girlfriend also moved to the Veneto, to work at Marco Polo airport, and they married in Treviso, in 1989.

At this point, Alberto was offered the opportunity to open a brand-new restaurant in Cesenatico, on the Adriatic coast near Rimini. He and his wife moved to Cesenatico, where Alberto was one of three partners running the business. However, the venture didn't go well.

"It's difficult to make something work when you have three people in charge. We lasted just seven months and then gave up."

The couple returned to Treviso, but now Alberto couldn't find a position. He explains that Tangentopoli was happening at the time, and for a period of six months it was impossible to find work.

Tangentopoli, also referred to as "clean hands", was a huge corruption scandal in the early 1990s. The name Tangentopoli derives from *tangente*, a slang word for kickback, and may be translated as Bribesville. It is estimated that, in the 1980s, the equivalent of four billion US dollars in bribes was paid every year, to thousands of politicians and officials, by businesses bidding for government contracts. The resulting nationwide investigation into corrupt practices had a significant economic impact, reducing international confidence in Italy as a place to invest, and lowering the value of the lire.

Alberto and his wife decided to return to Genoa, where he found work in a restaurant in the hills, about 12km from the city. He stayed there for five years. Then, in 1997, a friend told him about plans to open a new restaurant, in Genoa.

"I heard they were looking for somebody, so I introduced myself and they chose me to be their head chef."

Signore Castagnetti, owner of the Best Western Plus City hotel in Vico Domoculta, wanted to establish a new restaurant as an adjunct to his hotel business. He was probably lucky to find a chef with Alberto's experience.

Alberto left the restaurant in the hills, and started working with Signore Castagnetti in May 1997, preparing for the opening of Le Rune just two months later. In September 1997, Simona started work at Le Rune as a waitress. She and Alberto worked there together for 17 years!

At this point, I ask where the name Le Rune comes from. Simona explains that runes, Viking/Germanic letters, had been found inscribed in Liguria, presumably brought there by Scandinavian seafarers. Signore Castagnetti, who had attended a Germanic school, decided to call his new restaurant The Runes (Le Rune). I can see runes inscribed on the wall opposite, and one particular rune has been chosen as the logo for the restaurant.

Initially, Simona and Alberto were simply employees of Signore Castagnetti. However, in 2004 the business was reorganised. Simona and Alberto became managers of the restaurant, with Signore Castagnetti stepping back from day-to-day operations, whilst remaining as proprietor. The owner did not see himself as a restaurateur, and wanted to focus on his hotel.

Simona talks about that time, which represented a big change for her.

"The restaurant was large, a lot of people worked there. Taking over that team meant acquiring new skills, learning to be a manager. At the start we made lots of mistakes. However, Signore Castagnetti was still around, and he's a great entrepreneur and businessman, good at managing the finances. We learnt from him, and we learnt from our mistakes. Years later, it started to feel like a problem having him in the business, when he was so hands-off, but we needed to go through that learning period while he was still around."

Their contract, agreed with Signore Castagnetti, expired in 2015. Simona and Alberto approached him, and asked if it could be renewed for a further 12 years. However, he made it clear that he did not want to renew: "I want you to walk on your own two feet, to become entrepreneurs and not just managers. I want to close the restaurant here."

Alberto describes how they felt.

"We found ourselves in difficulty. It was a lot of work just running the restaurant. We couldn't imagine having the strength and energy to open a completely new business, in a new location, and starting all over again. But Signore Castagnetti forced the issue. He told us that the restaurant must close on 1st January 2015, effectively giving us a kick up the backside! Sure enough, we closed the old restaurant on 1st January, and opened up here one week later."

"How was that achieved?" I ask, trying not to show my incredulity.

"It actually took us six months," explains Simona.

A sales representative, who sold coffee to the restaurant, told them he knew of another restaurant that had closed down two years ago, and the building was still empty. They went to see the place. It was dark inside, with no electricity, so they explored the interior with a flashlight. There were bags of rubbish, and old furniture, everywhere. It was a mess, but they decided to take it on. They had to clean the whole place, fit it out and furnish it, ready to become a restaurant again.

"How did you find the time, when you were still working at the old restaurant?"

Simultaneously, they both take deep breaths.

"We found the time," says Alberto with a sigh, looking weary at the recollection of how hard those months were.

"We also had help from a friend, who is a builder," says Simona. "He restored the colour of the walls. Two other friends are brilliant carpenters, and they did a great job restoring the furniture, the shelves and the bar counter. We had very little money. We paid Signore Castagnetti for the name and the logo, and he let us bring over all the crockery stamped with this logo. We also brought three members of the old team with us, to work in the new restaurant."

By that time, Le Rune had a good reputation in Genoa, so it was important that they were able to keep the name for their new business.

Inevitably, they had to borrow money for the new venture, from the bank and also from their families. These debts are now paid off, with the last loan repaid two years ago.

I observe that they must have had a lot of faith in each other, to invest so much in this risky new venture together.

"Absolutely," says Alberto. "We have known each other a long time."

"Yes, we believe in each other completely," adds Simona.

Alberto talks about what happened during Covid.

"For several months, all restaurants were closed completely, but we got by with home deliveries. I cooked in the kitchen, and she delivered the food on her scooter. The owner of the building refused to reduce our rent, so it was a difficult time, but we got through it."

Reopening after Covid, Simona wanted to make changes, to run a different type of restaurant. They spaced the tables out more, accepting that they would host fewer diners, but aiming to improve the experience for each customer. They put more thought into their choices for the menu.

Prior to the pandemic, the menu changed seasonally, every three months. After Covid, the menu changed every day, depending partly upon what Alberto came across in the local markets that morning.

As Alberto explains, "Our philosophy is to make customers

feel good, without being a really high-end restaurant. The overall quality of the menu has improved."

"And the prices are higher?"

"Yes. Everything has gone up. The olive oil we buy, for example, has doubled in price in the last few years."

"How big is your team?"

"We have three staff in the kitchen, and three in the dining rooms, plus other people help out from time to time, students for example."

I ask Alberto if he has children, and whether he is still married.

"My daughter Giulia, 24 years old, is studying in Venice. My wife and I divorced in 2005."

Turning to Simona, she answers the same question.

"I married in 1998, and we were together until 2004. We had a daughter, Stefania, now 19 years old and living in Rome, where she is studying cinematography."

Alberto points out that 2004 and 2005 was a period of great change, for both of them.

"An unimaginable period," says Simona, "emotional, and a huge commitment."

"But I always wanted to have my own business, ever since I was a young boy," says Alberto, "and now it's going well, it's working. It's taken me 30 years, but I have managed to find where I belong. I am very fortunate to have her because, on my own, I could never have done it. It's really important to look after your customers well, in the dining room, and to produce great food in the kitchen. You absolutely need both."

I comment on how their restaurant is number one in Genoa, on Tripadvisor.

"At the moment, yes," says Simona, clearly not letting it go to her head.

Alberto explains that, when Tripadvisor first started, in the early 2000s, Signore Castagnetti realised that it would become important and ensured the restaurant was registered.

"He saw what was coming," says Alberto. "Initially, we were number 100 or 120 in the Tripadvisor rankings for Genoa. Over the years we improved, but we still got negative reviews because, well, nothing's perfect. But the great thing about a negative review is it tells you what to watch out for, how to improve the customer's experience. In that way, we were able to take more care, to better look after our diners. Soon after we moved here, within two or three years, we entered the top ten in the rankings. We first became number one about four years ago, I think, and we've been in the top three ever since."

Simona points out that their online profile is vital for them, because the restaurant is hidden away, in a quiet alley where they get virtually no passing trade. I ask how many of their customers are tourists. Alberto estimates 40% on average, during the season from spring to autumn.

"The number of tourists in Genoa has increased a lot in recent years."

I ask if they have local customers who come every week. Simona laughs, and says that some customers eat lunch here every day!

"Other customers come 15 or 20 times per year, for special occasions like birthdays, or as a weekend treat. It's lovely."

I recall Simona saying, at the beginning, that she wanted to travel, but I assume it's difficult to find the time, when running a restaurant. I ask her.

"She's going to Rome, the day after tomorrow!" Alberto declares, with a broad grin.

"We are closed Saturday lunchtime, Sunday and Monday," says Simona, "so we have a sort of weekend for ourselves." Alberto adds that they often close on Tuesdays in the summer. However, unlike many Italian businesses, they do not close for the whole of August because that is a busy month for them.

"Moreover, in June and July, we usually close for ten days or so, to take a holiday. In September we often take a few days off, as well. We're not young any more, we want to enjoy life. Alberto will be 60 years old in a few months."

"Oh! Will you have a big party here?"

"Here, no," says Alberto, "I'm looking for a place out in the country, maybe an agriturismo, where we will celebrate. It will be August, so we should be able to have a good party outside."

I turn to Simona. "Do you travel a lot?"

"When I can," she says. "Always!" says Alberto, "you won't find her at home."

"We go travelling together," he adds.

I look surprised, so he emphasises the point.

"We are business partners, but we are also friends. We go together."

"But you're not lovers?" I ask, just to be clear. He smiles.

"No, we're not lovers. But we are very happy to spend time together. We spend our free time together, we eat together, we travel together. Always."

Simona reinforces the point.

"We have spent time together for many years. There's respect, there's trust, we get on well."

"We go on holiday together with our daughters," says Alberto, "almost like a family, but we are not a family. It's true that we are both here all day, but I am in the kitchen and she is out front, so we don't see much of each other. When we have time to eat, we do so together, with the team, usually for just 15 minutes. When we are on holiday, we don't normally talk about work. I like to relax, to read, to sunbathe."

"It depends where we are," says Simona. "If in the mountains we go walking, in a city we go sightseeing."

I ask Alberto whether he might think about retiring in the next few years.

"I don't know. I've worked for 45 years, but I wouldn't want to stop suddenly. Maybe I can find a way to ease off, to have more time for cycling, for swimming, going to the cinema."

It's a tough life in a restaurant kitchen. Alberto acknowledges that it might be difficult for him to work the same hours when he's in his seventies.

It's approaching the time when they need to prepare to open for lunch, so we wrap up.

It's clear that Simona and Alberto make a great team, and remarkable that they also manage to be such good friends. This is an unusual relationship. Without the complications and expectations associated with romantic attachment, perhaps it's easier for two people to stay close for a long time. Unlike many siblings, who might take each other for granted, having grown up together, there's still strong mutual respect in Simona and Alberto's partnership.

I can't help but be impressed by what they've achieved, in building their business and also their friendship.

18 Preserving your heritage

I wake early, on our last day in Genoa, and go out for a walk before breakfast. It's another sunny morning. The Mercato Orientale, near our hotel, is a lively marketplace where you find all sorts of fresh produce, and a food court. I love the atmosphere in these markets, and decide to wander and breathe it in one last time.

I'm reminded of when we were on holiday with friends, in an apartment at Lago d'Iseo, and we visited an open-air market there. Talking to the traders, trying to decide which meats and which cheeses to buy, was one of our best memories from that trip. Vendors, of high value produce, have time to chat, and will happily pass the day explaining exactly how one cured meat is different from another, and how this or that cheese tastes. Move to the bread counter however, where each transaction might be less than one euro, and you'll find the server impatient for you to make your choice, so they can move on to the next customer.

This early, in Mercato Orientale, there are few customers and the traders are still setting out their products. I tear myself away, to join Jackie for our last hotel breakfast.

Although we love Genoa, we are ready to move on now. A train journey, through the gorges of the Ligurian hills, takes us to our next destination, Turin. This is a very different city, influenced by French culture, and generally more elegant. Long, straight, broad avenues remind us of Paris. Our hotel is very close to the station, and it's another fine day, so, within 30 minutes of arriving, we have checked in, unpacked and gone out to explore the city.

My pre-trip research identified three potential candidates for the book, and our first stop is a grocery shop called Biraghi, situated in the portico of Piazza San Carlo, Turin's equivalent of Piazza San Marco in Venice. It is clear, from pictures on the internet, that this is a grand, traditional shop, with a lovingly preserved marble and wood-panelled interior. Selling a wide variety of high-quality produce, it is Fortnum and Mason in miniature.

I go inside and, although the shop is busy, I manage to find an assistant who has just finished talking to another customer. I compliment him on being lucky enough to work in such a beautiful place, and ask whether the owner or manager might be available. He tells me that neither is around, and that they are usually not to be found in the shop. Disappointed, I leave.

That evening, Jackie and I visit Porto Savona, a restaurant in operation for over 160 years and the second candidate on my list. We had a nice evening but, again, it wasn't suitable for the book. My third option is the hotel we are staying in! Traditional and welcoming, run by the same family since 1854, I was hoping they might provide an interesting story. Unfortunately, the manager is away for the whole period of our stay, and there isn't really anybody else who can help. In less than 24 hours, I have run out of options to investigate. Turin is proving difficult.

The next morning, we meet Alfonso, a Turin resident I know from a language exchange website. We've had a few video calls, to improve my Italian and his English, and now we are meeting face-to-face for the first time, over coffee, back in Piazza San Carlo. We have an outside table at Caffè Torino, one of Turin's many grand old cafés, which happens to be just a few doors along from Biraghi, under the same portico.

Alfonso is young, tall, handsome, energetic, and a huge Juventus fan. We talk about how they are doing this season, which is a distant second behind Inter Milan in Serie A, and unlikely to catch them. For Alfonso this might be considered disappointing, since Juventus have won the Italian championship more times than any other club. He knows I'm not really a football fan, so he changes the subject and asks how the book is going. I go through my tale of woe, explaining that my online research, carried out in the UK, has proved fruitless, and I list the candidates I had in mind.

"You're interested in Biraghi?" he says.

"Yes, why?"

"I know the manager at Biraghi, he's a friend of mine! I'll go and talk to him." Alfonso stands up immediately, and walks over to the shop. Returning a few minutes later, he tells me that his friend is really busy, because several staff are off sick today. However, he would be happy to talk to me. Alfonso provides his contact details. I cannot believe my luck.

Alfonso has a busy life and, 15 minutes later, we say our goodbyes. Jackie and I start our day as tourists in Turin. Later that afternoon, when the shoppers have thinned out and Biraghi is much quieter, I pop in for a second time. It's easy to find Alfonso's friend, Daniele Melchiorre, a young man, looking smart and professional in a suit, serving behind the till on the ground floor. He immediately guesses who I am, from my English accent, and he's happy to tell me his story, and how he came to be working in this beautiful old store. Daniele can find an hour for me at noon, in two days' time, which happens to be the day that Jackie and I take our evening flight home.

Two days have passed pleasantly, under clear blue skies. Now I'm sitting in the bar of our hotel, fortunately empty and quiet, and I see Daniele come into the lobby for our appointment. He settles down opposite, and I begin by asking about his family.

Daniele's parents, now about 60 years old, originally came from the south. His father was born near Bari, in Puglia, and his mother between Potenza and Matera, in Basilicata. All of Daniele's grandparents moved to Turin, to find work, when their children were still young. Daniele's parents subsequently met and married in Turin.

Daniele's father was a photographer by profession, his mother an administrator in a doctor's practice. Daniele was born in 1984, and his younger brother Stefano arrived five years later. In 2004, Daniele's parents divorced but, managing to remain friends, the whole family, including the dog, continued living in the same house they had occupied since Daniele was born.

Daniele attended a science & technology liceo, where French and English were also taught. He then started a course in political science and European studies, learning about EU institutions, at university in Turin. It was recommended that he spend time abroad, as part of his course, but he was unable to do this, because he had to work in a call centre to support himself through university. He spent seven years, obtaining a degree plus a master's in international relations.

"It was supposed to take five years, but I was slow," he smiles sheepishly.

Perhaps unfairly, since he's already told me he had to work to pay his way, I ask if he enjoyed the social life at university. He nods and smiles again.

"I attended the party at the end of every term. I met lots of people, not just Italians, but from all over Europe. Many Italians go to work in Brussels. However, at the end of my degree, I decided to quit this field."

I ask what he saw himself doing, when he started his degree.

"I wanted to become an ambassador, or to work for the European Commission or the European Parliament. I like interacting with people, especially people from other cultures, with different experiences. I really want to understand the differences between people, where they come from, so that I can learn and grow."

"So why did you change your mind, and decide this was not for you after all?"

"I met a lot of politicians, and I didn't like them. I saw a lot of corruption. They are able to do so much good for people, but they think first about themselves. I don't know if this is just in Italy, or everywhere. I decided that I could not continue with a career like that, working with such people."

After completing his master's, and having stayed in Turin throughout his studies, Daniele decided to go abroad. He moved to London, despite knowing nobody there, and speaking quite poor English. He stayed in a hostel, and went to an employment agency where he found a job in a French restaurant in Chiswick. This was Daniele's first time working in a restaurant. He waited on tables, served at the bar and helped in the kitchen. Now that he had some income, he was able to rent a room in an apartment, shared with another Italian and an American.   Daniele established a friendship with the American, a soldier who had recently finished service in Iraq, where his hearing had been damaged by a bomb. They went out drinking together.

"I also met a lot of Italians, working in the restaurant with me, and I'm still in touch with a couple of them. Although this was a French restaurant, most of the staff were Italian, Polish or Spanish. It was a good restaurant, it had one Michelin star!"

Curious, I ask Daniele for the name of the restaurant.

"La Trompette, in Devonshire Road. I worked there for

seven or eight months. The head sommelier liked the way I worked, and he took the time to teach me a lot about wine. They had three sommeliers, all French. Anyway, I developed a real interest in wine."

"Why do you think this sommelier noticed you in particular?"

"I think because I was passionate about the work, and I was really interested in what he had to tell me. Also, I was quick and efficient. It's important to be fast, especially in a restaurant in London."

After one year in London, three weeks before Christmas, Daniele realised that it was time to return to Italy. He wanted to go home, to see family and friends in Turin, and he also now had a clearer idea of the direction he wanted to take. Living in London, he had developed a passion for wine, and his English had improved. A career in wine exports, for example, looked very attractive.

He returned to Italy, and sent his CV to lots of wineries around Piedmont. Almost immediately, he received a call from a winery in Ghemme, near Lake Maggiore. The owner said he was looking for a young guy, interested in wines, that could speak English and French.

"As it happens, I also speak French, probably better than my English. He had customers in France, England, Sweden, Norway and Germany. In France they needed French, but everywhere else English was fine. I worked there for almost three years, selling wine for export, and also to local restaurants, bars etc. There was only me selling their wines. Generally, we sold via email or through trade shows. I travelled in Italy and also Germany, to promote sales. In Sweden and Norway there are state-owned retail monopolies, so wine is sold by bidding to a government agency and, if selected, delivering to a contract agreed with them."

"What type of wine did you sell?"

"Only wines made from Nebbiolo grapes. We produced Nebbiolo, Ghemme and Gattinara wines, all red. Ghemme and Gattinara are barrel-aged, and named after the village where they are produced. If the wine is not aged in the barrel, you just call it Nebbiolo."

"Did you live in Ghemme?"

"No, I lived in Turin and travelled every day, Monday to Friday. It took almost two hours there, and two hours back, by train and bus. I would wake at 5am, and get back home at 7.30 in the evening. It was tiring. Moreover, almost all my income came from the 15% commission I earned on sales. He paid only for my train fare, plus a few other expenses, about 500 euros per month."

After three years, in 2015, Daniele decided it was time to find another job, with better pay. In Turin, he met a girl working for an employment agency which had Biraghi as one of its key account customers. Biraghi is a dairy produce business, based in Cuneo, to the south of Turin. She introduced Daniele. They interviewed him and offered him a role, as a salesman, which he accepted immediately.

Daniele was given a company car and he began his new life, on the road. He travelled throughout Italy, selling Biraghi's cheeses: Gran Biraghi, Gorgonzola and Ricotta.

"We had weekly planning sessions, at which I decided where to travel that week. For example, I might be in Bari on Tuesday, Cagliari on Wednesday, Naples on Thursday, home on Friday. Sometimes, I would be travelling six or seven days consecutively. I could choose how to travel, by car, by train or by aeroplane. I spent about 80% of my time away from home. Typically, I would spend one day per week in the office, in Cuneo, which is 45 minutes from my home in Turin. I lived with my parents."

One day, in April 2015, he was at the home of a friend in Turin, when he saw a picture of a girl, one of her friends. "Wow!" he said, "who is this girl?"

"This is my friend Monica from Rome," she replied. "You haven't met her?"

Daniele immediately wrote to the girl in the picture, explaining that he would be in Rome in July, to attend the 30th birthday party of his friend who had moved from Turin to Rome, and suggesting that they meet up. "Yes, why not?" said the girl. Sure enough, they met at the party, and they got on well.

Then Monica moved to South Africa for four months!

"Why?"

"She was like me, with my trip to London after university. She was trying to work out what to do with her life, so she went to stay with a friend in South Africa. We kept in touch on WhatsApp and Facebook for those four months. Then she returned to Rome, and we started going out together. One year later, in September 2016, she decided to move to Turin to be closer to me. We found an apartment and moved in together."

"Did she have a job in Turin?"

"Initially, no, but she soon found a position in a DHL call centre."

Daniele now explains that they only lived together in Turin for six months because, early in 2017, they decided to quit their jobs and move to Australia! It had always been Monica's dream to visit Australia and, since they were only 32 years old, Daniele agreed they should give it a try. They obtained a one-year working holiday visa.

Soon after arriving in Sidney, Monica easily found work as a shop sales assistant. It was harder for Daniele to find a position, because he didn't want to work in a shop. He tried to find a travelling sales role, but that proved difficult. Eventually, he got work in the mornings as a cleaner in a psychiatric hospital, and an afternoon job in a warehouse.

"Having these two jobs proved too complicated, so I gave up and accepted that I should take work as a sales assistant. I found a position in Myer, which is a big department store, like Rinascente. I worked there for six months. After working for eight months altogether, to save some money, we then spent three months travelling, in Australia, New Zealand, Thailand, Malaysia and Singapore."

"At the end of that year, did your wife still want to live in Australia?"

"No. After one year, she felt that was enough, and she was ready to return to Italy. She had fulfilled her dream, and experienced Australia, but it was too far from everything else we knew. It's another world, and you don't fully appreciate just how far it is until you spend time there."

As soon as they returned to Turin, Biraghi wanted Daniele to go back and work for them: "Please come back!"

"I said 'OK.' But, rather than asking me to be a travelling salesman again, they wanted me to help manage the shop here. Because this shop only opened four years ago."

I am stunned! I don't understand, and this clearly shows on my face. The shop is obviously very old, so how can it have opened just four years ago?

Daniele takes pity on me, and explains. He goes through the history, of his employer Biraghi and also the old shop in Piazza

San Carlo.

Biraghi is a successful dairy business, founded in Cuneo by Ferruccio Biraghi in 1934. Ferruccio's children, Bruno and Anna, inherited the business, and they jointly own and manage it today. It has grown over the years, now employing 250 people, and selling milk, cream and cheese to clients all over the world. Bruno Biraghi is based in Turin, not least because it's a beautiful place to live. His sister Anna lives in Alessandria, a town to the east of Turin.

Where the Biraghi shop is now, there was previously a historical grocery store called Paissa. Founded in 1873, Paissa sold produce from all over the world. You could find anything there, from Calabrian anchovies to Tennessee whiskey, and they were official suppliers to the House of Savoy, the Italian royal family. However, in 2014, unsustainable debt triggered the failure of the business, and Paissa closed.

Bruno Biraghi thought the closure of Paissa was a disaster for Turin, but it also provided an opportunity. He was appalled that such a beautiful old shop, in the city's most prestigious piazza, was now closed and empty. However, he had an idea for how he could remedy the situation, and simultaneously help raise the profile of the Biraghi business. He saw how to help preserve the grand old tradition, of Paissa's past, in a sustainable way, as part of a modern, growing business.

Daniele returned to Turin at exactly the right time. A month sooner, or later, and he might have missed the opportunity to be part of this venture. When Bruno heard he was back, they arranged to meet and Bruno explained to Daniele what he had in mind. They would reopen the store, but renamed Biraghi. Rather than sell grocery products from around the world, they would find the very best that Piedmont had to offer, and display it all within this beautiful old shop. Biraghi's dairy produce would, of course, be part of the mix. At that time, Biraghi's only retail outlet was a shop within their factory in Cuneo, selling just milk, cream and cheeses.

Daniele's job, initially, would be to tour Piedmont finding suppliers, and agreeing terms with them for selling their produce through Biraghi's new shop in Piazza San Carlo. He happily took the role, and spent the next year on the road, finding producers of the highest quality and signing them up.

The new shop opened in October 2019, and Daniele's role changed accordingly. He now became joint manager of the shop, responsible for the suppliers and their products. There was another manager, and she was responsible for the team working at the shop. However, she left in the spring of 2022, leaving Daniele with overall responsibility for the whole operation.

The Piazza San Carlo store offers 1,500 different products, and only 25 of these are provided by Biraghi. It's the company's flagship store, showcasing Piedmont's best produce to international clientele. Bruno was primarily motivated by the desire to preserve a special piece of Turin's heritage, but he also understood how, in two ways, this endeavour would benefit the Biraghi business. Firstly, by placing Biraghi products together with the other high-quality offerings, it would automatically elevate the reputation of the Biraghi brand. Secondly, aware that more and more tourists were visiting Turin, he saw how well this would promote their brand internationally.

I ask Daniele how he copes, now that he has to manage everything in the shop.

"It's not easy, although I do have others in the team helping with day-to-day management. The shop employs 22 people. I work from 8am to 7pm, four days per week here, and one day per week at our Cuneo headquarters. But I enjoy it. Revenue for the shop is still growing, it gets stronger every year. We opened a gelateria in 2021, and this has been a huge success. It has a long queue, every day. The gelato is made in the Cuneo factory, using only our milk and cream."

"Can you estimate how much of your business comes from tourists?"

"I can tell you exactly, because we see from credit card receipts, and by analysing data from our loyalty program. Tourists provide 30% of the business, locals the other 70%."

I ask Daniele whether he and Monica are now married.

"Yes, we got married in May 2022."

"Are you thinking of having children?"

"As it happens, we talked about this yesterday evening. We recently went to see Monica's sister, who lives in Milan, and she has six-year-old twins. She asked whether we wanted children. My wife and I are 40 years old now. On the one hand, I would like to be a father, but I'm not sure I want to bring children up in today's world. Monica feels similarly."

"Does Monica work?"

"Yes, she works for a government agency that helps immigrants, especially from Africa and South America, to settle into Italian society. They arrange for them to learn Italian, and help them to find internships with local businesses. It takes time but, this way, they can become contributing members of society. She enjoys the work, and it's very rewarding."

Daniele and Monica encapsulate the demographic forces shaping Italy today. The native population is in decline, because young adults are having fewer children. Meanwhile, immigration helps to maintain the working age population required to support older generations.

I ask Daniele what his brother does nowadays.

"Stefano works in the import and export of domestic appliances, washing machines, fridges etc. Also, we own a bar in Turin, called Vaniglia. He and his wife, Serena, wanted to open this bar. She works there, and the three of us own it together. I help in managing suppliers, because I already have the network of contacts. My brother manages the finances."

I am surprised to hear about this additional responsibility Daniele has taken on, but I shouldn't be really. He has always had demanding work, with long hours, and I guess he takes this for granted.

As we are about to finish, I ask about his thoughts for the future.

"I could never have foreseen that I would be doing this role, but I am happy. I guess I have been fortunate. As for the future, who knows what opportunities will appear, and where life will take me. We will see. My wife and I very much like to travel, when we can. We try to take a long holiday every year. Last year, we spent three weeks in Tanzania, and, the year before, a month touring the USA. This year, it will be Chile."

Now we run out of time, and Daniele must go back to work. He returns to his intense, busy life, while I sit back and check my notes.

Where does he get the energy from?

I am just happy that Jackie and I still have a few relaxing hours, here in sunny Turin, before we have to head to the airport for our flight home.

19 Handmade

My first ever trip to Italy, in May 1987, was for a business meeting in Bologna. A colleague and I spent a full day with Italian scientists working in our field, then our hosts took us to a restaurant in the evening. I remember nothing from the technical meeting, but I distinctly recall ordering tortellini in the restaurant and lingering ecstatically over every mouthful. I'd never realised food could taste so good.

Astonishingly, given how many times I subsequently visited Italy, it was 35 years before my second trip to Bologna. It's a lovely city, famous for its food, Europe's oldest university, and also the portici. Many of Bologna's streets are lined with these loggias, covered arcades, providing shelter from the rain, and from the sun on a hot day. The main shopping street, Via dell'Independenza, has portici of course, and it is remarkably similar to Via XX Settembre in Genoa.

It's a cold Friday morning in March. I arrived last night, on a flight from Heathrow, and now I'm enjoying coffee and pastry in a café on Via dell'Independenza. Searching online, in the UK, I found a fresh pasta shop in Bologna that looked interesting. Influenced by the memory of that lovely meal in 1987, I see this as an appropriate establishment to represent Bologna in the book. Once breakfast is over, I wander along to the shop, Sfoglia Rina, just in time for it's opening at 9am.

The place is empty, with just one lady setting out products in the display area and on shelves. Hesitantly, I open the door and ask if I may enter. "Of course!" she says, with a smile. Inside, I admire the many different types of fresh pasta, set out on wooden trays beneath the glass counter. There are also cured meats, quiches and desserts.

I start chatting to the lady, whose name is Federica. She informs me that I won't find the business owner here.

"Lorenzo is usually at our *laboratorio*. I suggest you phone him there."

Laboratorio doesn't translate directly into English. It refers to a facility, where commercial products are made by hand. Sfoglia Rina has a laboratorio, outside the city, where they make their fresh pasta. They also have another shop in Casalecchio di Reno, near Bologna.

I go outside into the cool morning air, and telephone the factory. The lady who answers explains that Lorenzo Scandellari is not there, and I should email him.

At this point, I realise that I will likely never meet Lorenzo. In my experience, emails, or messages passed on by intermediaries, almost never lead to a meeting with the person I wish to interview. Only a face-to-face conversation, or talking directly to the person on the telephone, produces positive results. However, I compose an email and send it to the company's "info" email address, confident that this is as far as I will get. I move on to visit another shop in Bologna, that might be suitable.

After spending some time chatting in this other shop, I come out into the street to find a missed call on my phone. I have a voice message, which is from Lorenzo! He explains that he is busy all weekend but, if I am free this evening, he would be very happy to do the interview then. As it happens, I have arranged to have dinner with my friend Francesco, from Ferrara, this evening. However, after exchanging messages with both Francesco and Lorenzo, it becomes possible for me to meet with Lorenzo at my apartment, between 5pm and 7pm. I send Lorenzo the address, and say that I will wait outside for him at

5pm.

It's now 4.50pm and I am checking Google maps to see how traffic is flowing in Bologna. Almost everywhere, there is gridlock. I cannot imagine how Lorenzo will get here at 5pm, if he has commitments elsewhere this afternoon. I wrap up warm and take a book to read, so that I'm prepared for a long wait, then go downstairs and outside into the street. After a few minutes, I notice a tall, slim man in leathers, carrying a helmet, walking towards me and extending his hand.

"You must be Richard."

Travelling by motorbike, Lorenzo has managed to arrive bang on time.

We climb the stairs to the apartment, and immediately get down to business. Although Lorenzo's hair is greying, the impression he gives is one of youthful energy. He sports a beard and moustache, talks quickly, confidently, and often breaks into a smile.

We begin by talking about the founding of the pasta business, by Lorenzo's grandmother Rina de Franceschi together with her mother Giuseppina, in 1963.

"You must understand that, when my grandmother was a child, every peasant family made their own fresh pasta at home," explains Lorenzo. "Nobody had the money to buy pasta in a shop, but they had flour and eggs at home, because everybody kept chickens. Most of the people on the land were sharecroppers, receiving a proportion of the value of what they grew in exchange for their labour. My grandfather Anselmo worked the land, and he told me how the owner would lend them flour, so they had something to eat. Later, when the harvest was sold, the owner would cleverly deduct more than the value of this flour from their share. Anyway, everybody had flour and eggs, and everybody made pasta at home. In those days, it was taken for granted that the women would make the pasta, just as they did the cooking and ironing."

Lorenzo says that he is unsure exactly what happened in his family, before he was born. However, he does know that his grandmother Rina met and married Anselmo Scandellari, a lad working on the land, when they were both teenagers. Later, seeing the potential for more secure work in a town, the family moved to Casalecchio di Reno, near Bologna. Here, Rina found work in a brewery and Anselmo became a plasterer.

In 1963 Rina, together with her mother Giuseppina, decided to open a fresh pasta shop in Casalecchio.

"For me, this is an early example of the feminist revolution, these two women setting up their own business in the early 1960s," says Lorenzo.

The shop was open only in the morning, and in the afternoon the women went home to do their housework.

The name chosen for the business is actually a pun. The Italian word *sfoglina* refers to a female pasta-making matriarch using traditional techniques. Sfoglia Rina sounds similar, and incorporates Rina's name.

After a couple of years, they moved the shop to better premises, and there it remained for 30 years. At some stage, Anselmo gave up his work as a plasterer and worked in the pasta shop, with his wife Rina. I ask if Anselmo made the pasta, or just sold it.

"I've seen him do everything except roll out the pasta. He made the filling, made the dough, made the biscuits. He cut and folded to make tortellini. He also interacted with the public, selling in the shop in the mornings. By then, the shop was also open in the afternoons. Standard grocery shop hours were 7am to 1pm, with a long lunch break, then open again from 3.30pm to 7pm."

Meanwhile, Rina and Anselmo had two sons, Marco and Moreno.

The pasta shop was very small, and Marco and Moreno didn't like that type of work, so they did not become involved in the business. Marco did various jobs: he was a chef and also a gardener. Moreno initially worked in a factory and, later, opened a bar.

Moreno met and married a lady called Vanda, and they had an only child, Lorenzo. Vanda went to work in the pasta shop, with her in-laws Rina and Anselmo. From the age of six or seven, Lorenzo also helped in the shop. His first role was to break the eggs, needed to make fresh pasta.

Lorenzo attended a technical liceo and initially thought he might become an electrical engineer. However, when he was 17 or 18, his mother Vanda decided to leave the pasta shop. She wanted to do something different, and tried various other jobs, including cleaning, and helping to manage a stationery shop.

I ask Lorenzo why his mother wanted to leave.

"I'm not really sure. Perhaps she just wanted to do something different, perhaps there was a family dispute. I don't know. When you are making pasta together, there is a lot of conversation. You hear stories from the past, about family and friends. Sometimes the conversation strays onto contentious topics, and there is an argument. This is life in an Italian family!"

When Vanda departed, Lorenzo realised that his grandmother would be unable to manage the pasta shop on her own, especially the administration and bureaucracy. He offered to work there with Rina, for several reasons. Firstly, because of the requirement for him to perform national service after he left school, he knew that he couldn't pursue his own career immediately. He also saw the shop as an attractive, successful business, which it would be a shame to close. Finally, he felt sorry for his grandmother, who would have been upset to see her life's work come to nothing. He really wanted to help her.

Thus, Lorenzo went to school in the mornings, and helped deal with the shop's paperwork in the afternoons. When he finished school, because he was a conscientious objector, he avoided serving with the military. Instead, he was given civilian service duties, such as accompanying children to school, near Casalecchio, and he was able to continue at the shop.

"However, I always told myself that I wouldn't spend my whole life doing this."

"But did you enjoy the work?"

"Sure, I liked making pasta, but I can't say it was the dream of my life, to be at a board cutting out tortellini. However, I didn't know what the passion of my life would be."

When Lorenzo was 22, he met a Bologna university student from Brussels. Catherine was studying for a master's degree in history of architecture, and living with an Italian girl who was also in Lorenzo's friendship group. Inevitably, Lorenzo and Catherine met and, about six months later, they started going out. Soon after that, they rented an apartment together in Casalecchio.

After completing her degree, Catherine stayed on in Italy, working as a secretary for a couple of businesses. She and Lorenzo visited Catherine's family in Belgium, once or twice every year.

Lorenzo worked with his grandmother for a total of six or seven years, until she decided that it was time to retire, and then his mother Vanda returned to join him in the shop.

"I knew that I didn't want to let my grandmother down so, when she decided to retire, I asked my mother to come back. I guess I was thinking that my mother would take over the business, and later I could leave to pursue another career. Of course, I still had no idea what that career would be."

Around this time, while his mother was taking over from his grandmother, Lorenzo and Catherine took a three-month holiday in New Zealand. Vanda and Rina ran the business while they were away.

"It was a beautiful trip, in a wonderful land. We travelled around in a car with a tent, camping most nights. Physically it was tiring, but we met lots of people and experienced a completely different culture, which was invigorating. Returning to Italy, I found I had a great deal of energy. I wanted to create something."

When they came back, Catherine attended a course in cultural events, seeking the next step in her career. She worked for an association organising classical music concerts in Emilia-Romagna.

Returning to Sfoglia Rina, Lorenzo realised that the shop started by his grandmother was now too small to be a viable business. For one thing, changes in the law meant that some of the products they made in that shop could no longer be created on the premises. Lasagne with a meat sauce, for example, could only be cooked in a kitchen meeting the latest regulatory requirements.

"One day, walking around in Casalecchio, I saw an advertisement for premises having a commercial kitchen with a flue. So, we took this on as a second shop, and employed more people. In the original shop we still made pasta, and in the new shop we cooked the sauces, the meat etc. This all happened soon after I returned from New Zealand."

A few years later, a small premises adjacent to the new shop became available. Lorenzo took this on and put tables into the space, enough to seat just 20 people, but it meant they could serve food directly from the kitchen.

In 2013, they realised that the older shop was too small. They closed it, and instead opened a larger facility in Zola Predosa, west of Casalecchio, a laboratorio where all the pasta would be manufactured.

"Did you have to borrow money for these expansions?"

"Yes, absolutely. We had a load of debt! My grandmother told me that, during their 40 years running the business, she and my grandfather often had ideas and opportunities to expand. However, they were always afraid to get into debt, so it never happened."

In 2008, Lorenzo and Catherine married. They now have two daughters, Mila and Chloe, aged 14 and 12. I comment that his daughters have nice, simple names.

"When your surname is Scandellari, it's important to have a short first name," jokes Lorenzo.

With a Walloon father and Flemish mother, Catherine speaks French and Dutch, and she has also learnt Italian, English and a little German. Following their mother's lead, Mila and Chloe are learning multiple languages.

Catherine joined the pasta business in 2015, when they decided to open a store in Bologna.

"I am a boy from the suburbs. The big city, Bologna, has always fascinated me. We had customers from Bologna, we often made deliveries to Bologna. It was inevitable that we would want to expand into the city."

For several years, Lorenzo saw commercial premises advertised for rent in Bologna but, when he enquired, they were far too expensive. Then, finally, a place became available in Via Castiglione, a slightly quieter part of the centre. For Lorenzo, the location was perfect, because it was near, but just outside, the quadrilateral, the really busy part of Bologna which attracts tourists.

They went to see it. It was in a poor state, but both Catherine and Vanda liked it. In addition to the shop area, there was room to seat about 80 diners, just the right size for Lorenzo.

"Any bigger, and we would not be able to provide the level of service we want to give."

The owners were helpful, and they managed to come to an agreement. Lorenzo and his family spent a lot of money fitting the place out, with Catherine doing the interior design work. The Bologna shop, including a restaurant area for serving food, opened in December 2015.

"When you invested in the Bologna shop, that must have been a big risk for you. Did you have this great urge to grow the business?"

Lorenzo hesitates before answering.

"My wife and I are very similar in this respect. We make decisions based on gut feeling. I would say I am not an entrepreneur. I am, first and foremost, an artisan, a craftsman. When we opened the Bologna shop, and when we expanded in Casalecchio, I didn't produce a business plan, calculating the minimum and maximum potential returns. It just felt right . . . here."

He points to his stomach.

The sheer volume of pasta they were now selling forced them to double the capacity of the Zola Predosa facility the following

year, in 2016. Then, in 2018 they transferred the Casalecchio
shop and restaurant to bigger premises, growing the business
still further. The new Casalecchio facility is slightly larger than
the operation in Bologna. However, in Bologna they sell twice
as much pasta as they do in Casalecchio.

I ask Lorenzo whether everything manufactured in the
laboratorio is sold through his two shops, and learn that 20% of
the fresh pasta they make is actually sold wholesale, to other
vendors who ask him to supply them. One of these is the
Bologna branch of Eataly, an internationally famous Italian
brand. Lorenzo does not want to grow his wholesale business,
however.

"Do many tourists visit the Bologna shop?"

"Most of our business in Bologna comes from tourists! In
Casalecchio, it's almost all local people, but here we are
swamped by tourists. There is often a line outside the shop and,
while tourists are happy to stand and wait, the Bolognese just go
elsewhere when they see a queue."

"Do you have plans for more changes to the business, in the
near future?"

"Well, we are in a bit of a standstill period at the moment.
We would like to make more changes but, my wife and I, we are
both a little tired. We did a lot in a short period of time, and we
need to consolidate now. There's always a conflict, with ideas
pulling you to do more, but you have to have the energy!
Having said that, during the Covid period we created another
brand, Carina, in Casalecchio. Next door to the shop, we opened
a new bar where customers can enjoy an evening aperitif, with
food. However, we don't have the ambition to grow like crazy,
opening another ten shops for example. We are not doing this
just to make more and more money. We want to deliver

something of real value, and have a good quality of life ourselves."

"How many people do you employ, in total, across the laboratorio, the two shops and the bar?"

"90 people."

I am astonished. For 40 years, the business operated with just two people - one small shop in Casalecchio. Then, in less than two decades, Lorenzo and Catherine expanded it so much that they now employ 90 people.

Lorenzo sees that I am dumbstruck, and feels the need to explain.

"Half of these people work in the shops, which are also restaurants of course. The rest work in the laboratorio. We have consciously decided to continue my grandmother's tradition, and make all our pasta by hand. If we used automation, we could reduce the number of people working in production by two thirds."

"It can't be easy, managing a team of 90 people."

"No, it isn't. Previously, Catherine and I tried to manage everything directly ourselves, and this was very demanding. We didn't want a sort of military hierarchy. Our organisation was very flat. But that was too difficult. In recent years, we have put more structure in place, with a set of managers, covering each shop and the various streams of production. The danger is that we are not close enough to all aspects of the business, but we are aware of this risk. There are always problems, but I think the operation is a little easier now. The key thing is that we want the team to create things together, we want ideas from everyone and collaborative working."

Lorenzo also talks about how difficult it is, to separate work life from family life, with he and Catherine running the business together.

"I'm sure it's like this in any family business. It's really intense, but I love it. It was a series of coincidences that led to my wife joining me in the business, because she enjoyed her previous work, but I could never have achieved all this without her."

We've covered everything. Lorenzo picks up his helmet, and I accompany him down to the street where we say goodbye.

The next day, at lunchtime, I wander over to the Sfoglia Rina shop in Bologna, to see if I can speak to Federica and thank her for her help. As I approach the shop, I see a long line of people stretching down the street, and around the corner. Slowly, it dawns on me that they are queueing for a table in Sfoglia Rina. I enter the shop, to come across another small crowd, waiting to be served at the shop counter. I walk into the dining area, where every table is occupied. A hubbub of conversation fills the room. Servers whisk back and forth. This is what Lorenzo and Catherine have created, the thriving descendant of that little shop in Casalecchio, where just two people made and sold fresh pasta to local residents.

Even if Federica is here, she won't have time to talk to me, so I exit the shop and walk back down the street toward Bologna's famous two ancient towers.

So, what's happened here? Why has this business changed so much, after 40 years of staying the same?

At the beginning, Lorenzo was motivated by two things: affection for his grandmother, and respect for the traditional craft of the sfoglina. He didn't want Rina to see her life's work disappear, and he wanted to preserve the tradition of handmade pasta. However, he also had an irresistible urge to create something himself, to make something with his own hands. The trip to New Zealand, that three-month pause, gave him the perspective and the mental energy to take the leap.

As Lorenzo said himself, he's not interested in just making the business bigger. If that were the case, he would have opened a chain of 10 or 20 shops, like the original Sfoglia Rina, across Emilia-Romagna. Every change to the business has introduced a new twist, a new way of offering something to the public. The Casalecchio shop was extended to include an area where customers could sit down and eat, the Bologna shop allowed them to reach a different type of customer, the bar in Casalecchio provides another new service. All of this is possible because they have a dedicated production facility, able to provide the range and volume of fresh pasta consumed by all those customers.

Rina is no longer here, and Vanda has retired from the business, but the soul of their enterprise lives on. Today's Sfoglia Rina is handmade, by Lorenzo and Catherine, just like the pasta from the team in Zola Predosa.

20 The phoenix

Ravenna, not especially famous today, was Italy's most important city in the dying days of the Roman empire and the centuries that followed. It was capital of the Western Roman Empire in the 5th century, and also of the Ostrogoths kingdom after that. When the Byzantines reconquered territory in Italy, they also ruled from Ravenna.

Spectacularly beautiful Byzantine mosaics, surviving in several ancient churches and mausolea, attract tourists to Ravenna today. On my first visit, in May 2022, I arrived by train from Rome. The contrast between Rome's shoddy, dirty streets, and Ravenna's clean, well-preserved historic centre, couldn't have been starker. I spent three relaxing days in this wealthy little city, and knew that I had to return.

Now I am here again, strolling under a clear blue sky from the railway station to Ravenna's historic centre. Because of the city's reputation, as the mosaics capital of Italy, I contacted the owner of a large mosaics studio, asking if I could interview her for the book. A little early for our 11am appointment, I enjoy wandering around the centre before going to the shop in Via Giuliano Argentario.

As soon as I enter Annafietta Mosaicisti, I see the owner Anna Finelli and introduce myself. She is tall, with long flowing silver hair, and spectacles. The store is quite large, but Anna leads me upstairs to a workshop area, which happens to be unoccupied today. "We can talk here", she says, and offers me a coffee. I ask for water.

She is curious as regards why I contacted her, in particular. I don't have a good explanation. Browsing the internet, this seemed the most impressive mosaics shop in Ravenna, and that was the sum total of my research. We settle down, next to a table normally used for making mosaics, and I begin by asking Anna about her parents.

"My mother, Donata, was born in Ravenna. She went to England as a teenager, to be an au pair and learn English. She always thought English was important and, from the age of 12, I was sent to England every summer, to learn the language. I never studied English at school. There, I learnt French and German. Later, I married an Argentinian, so I also speak Spanish! These languages help me a lot today, because we have so many tourists here."

"My mother's parents, my grandparents, came from near Milan. They moved to Ravenna in 1930, and were antique dealers. In fact, their shop was on this very street. My father died when I was young, and my mother worked with her parents in the antique shop. I spent a lot of time with my grandparents, in their shop, when I was little. In the last ten years, tourism has become very important for Ravenna, but even in those days there were some tourists. Not many, but those who appreciated art and history. My awareness of the importance of tourism to Ravenna, gained in that antique shop, was an important factor influencing my decision, much later, to start this business."

After her father's death, Anna's mother remarried and had a son, Luigi, ten years younger than Anna.

Anna explains that she loved art as a child, because her mother and grandparents had a passion for the arts. However, she attended a scientific liceo because she was very good at mathematics, and she expected a technical education to give her more career choices. Upon finishing school, she didn't know what to do next. Because Anna loved mathematics, her mother suggested that she study economics and commerce at Bocconi

University in Milan.

However, Anna knew that a life preoccupied with money was not for her. After some thought, she decided to pursue archaeology, because she imagined that involved art and travel, both of which appealed. She obtained a place at Bologna University. At that time there was no archaeology faculty, so Anna studied ancient history, with an archaeological focus.

"I loved my time as a student in Bologna. It's a big city, much larger than Ravenna, and I had freedom. I really enjoyed studying history, I believe that has given me an open mind. I studied for four years and, in my final year, whilst preparing my thesis, I managed to get onto an archaeological dig. In 1988, as I completed my degree, a new archaeological course was created only for women. I got a place on this course, and spent a fifth year as a student in Bologna. At the end of that year, I got married."

"Oh!" I exclaim. "Tell me about your husband."

There is a canal connecting the city of Ravenna to the sea, and the docks along this canal form the port of Ravenna. Anna explains that Martin was an Argentinian sailor on a large grain carrier, that docked in Ravenna one day, and was then stuck there for months. The owners were going out of business and could not afford to pay the crew anymore, so the crew sequestered the ship and sued them through the Italian courts. Martin, like his ship, was stranded in Ravenna for 18 months, while the case went through the courts. During this period, he met other Argentinians living in the area, and some of these were friends with Anna. Martin and Anna met through these mutual friends.

"We met in February 1989, at a Carnival party in Ravenna. He was tall, handsome and charming. Irresistible."

They fell in love, and married in December of that same year, because Martin needed the papers to be allowed to remain in Italy. The trial also finished that year, with victory for Martin and the crew. Now settled in Italy, Martin developed a successful career as an interior painter and decorator.

Also in 1989, when her one-year course finished, ten of the students, including Anna, established a restoration business. They had help from the university, to get them started.

"We were ten young women together, founding this company. Nobody was in charge – we made all decisions together, which could be very slow! But it was a lovely experience, we learnt a lot. We were based in Bologna, but we had to travel across Italy for work. The first thing I restored went on display at Palazzo Grassi, in Venice."

Anna speaks slowly and clearly, giving me the impression that she is thoughtful and patient, important qualities if your job is to restore precious ancient objects. Alternatively, she might be speaking like that because she knows I would struggle with Italian spoken more quickly!

In the 1990s, there was a shortage of archaeological restorers, and they were in great demand. Anna did this work for eight years, during which time five of the ten team members left. There was a real mix of work, some enjoyable, some not so much. Eventually, Anna tired of the business, in particular the time it took for them to make decisions was frustrating.

"I like to decide quickly. Sometimes I'm right, sometimes I'm wrong, but I have to make a decision quickly. I sensed the need for a change. Then, it so happened that a change was forced upon me. I became pregnant. So, in 1997 I left the group and we moved to Ravenna, to be near my mother. My thinking was that I would continue to do restoration work, with my mother looking after the child whenever I had to travel. My daughter, Sofia, was born in January 1998."

Anna stops, and takes a deep breath.

"Then, in 1999 everything changed. My husband Martin died. Ours was a romantic story and it's really sad that it ended like that. Then, my mother died. It was awful."

I am stunned, and don't know what to say. After a few seconds, Anna continues.

"I felt desperate. In a short space of time, I'd lost the two most important people in my life. 1999 was difficult."

"Did you feel very lonely?"

"I was fortunate to have really good friends here, people I'd known since I was young. Ravenna is my home city. My friends were incredibly close, and helped me a lot. They supported me during Martin's illness, and for a long time afterwards. For many years we were like a family, together every Christmas. My brother, although much younger, was also fundamental."

"Do you mind taking me through the detail, of what happened when, in that period?"

I feel a brute uttering these words, like one of those journalists pressurising the victim of a recent tragedy to talk about how they feel, on camera.

Even though this was 25 years ago, there must be some pain revisiting these events, but she doesn't let it show. In the same calm steady voice, Anna recounts what happened when.

"In May 1998, Martin became ill, with cancer. In May 1999 my mother became ill, also cancer. In July, Martin died. 40 days later, in August, my mother died. Sofia was just 18 months old."

We are both content to let silence fill the room, for 10 or 20 seconds.

Having your first child is a major, life-changing experience, bringing its own stresses and strains. I cannot begin to imagine how somebody copes with a double bereavement, losing your two closest relatives, at the same time. In addition to Sofia, I suspect that Anna also needed work to bring purpose and direction to her life, to guide her through the storm.

"Can you explain how you decided to start the mosaics business?"

"When Martin became ill, I realised that I would be unable to travel, and so could no longer be a restorer. That was a moment of panic. I truly loved that work. What was I to do now?"

They still had the antique shop, which Anna's mother had taken over from her parents. Anna knew very little about antiques, but she had an idea for what to do next. She thought: "Ravenna is a tourist city, famous for mosaics, but nobody here is making mosaics that I like. The only things available are copies of the ancient Byzantine mosaics. I can open the first shop to make and sell original mosaics."

This decision was made in June 1998. Anna sold everything in the antique shop. She renovated the place, repainting the interior, and started a new business selling original mosaics. For years this shop had been known, to everybody in Ravenna, as Fietta's antique shop. Moreover, Anna's grandmother, also called Anna, was her ultimate role model, someone she revered. It felt right to name the new business Annafietta, in honour of her grandmother.

The first items she offered for sale were three little boxes, and three picture frames. Unable to make them herself, she found young artists at the Ravenna Academy who could make them for her. However, she didn't use students from the Academy for long. Business quickly took off, and Anna learnt how to make mosaics. Her experience as a restorer helped.

"When I was a child, the Basilica of San Vitale was open to the public, and I played there a lot. I loved the old mosaics, and perhaps that helped me to learn quickly. I was inspired also by prehistoric vases, where the decoration can tell you where it is from and when it was made, so I studied decorations a lot. I saw how a mosaic could become the decoration for a box, a frame, even a cat. We were the first to use mosaics this way, certainly in Ravenna and probably in Italy."

The shop had two rooms, one used for producing the mosaics, and the other for selling them. Over time, the business grew and Anna took on other people to help. Ten years later, when Anna had a team of three working for her, the business had outgrown its premises. Although Anna loved the old antique shop, imbued as it was with memories of her childhood, her grandparents and her mother, she knew it was time to move.

The owners, from whom Anna rented the shop, had another building in the same street, close to Basilica di San Vitale. This place had been vacant for years, and it had a second floor with an outside terrace, providing more space. Anna concluded an agreement with the owners and relocated in 2011. The original shop has since been divided, and is now rented out to two businesses: a fast-food restaurant (A Ció) and another mosaics shop!

Anna explains that much of the business comes from commissions, and now they have the space to construct large objects.

"I love being involved in the creation of something new. A mother will come to me and say 'I need something for my son's

40th birthday.' I ask her to tell me about her son and, together, we will design the perfect gift for him."

She also shows me the prizes for a children's football tournament, involving teams from all over Italy. Annafietta makes the prizes, including a trophy to be taken home by every one of the 60 football teams.

Another commission they have had, for many years, is to produce street signs for the city. Anna tells me to look out for these mosaic street names, as I walk around Ravenna – they were all made at Annafietta. In 2009, the municipality held a competition, to provide 20 street signs, and Annafietta won. They liked them so much that, since then, she has been asked every year to produce another 10 or 20.

"We also produce medals for the Ravenna marathon, which has been running for 25 years. They first asked me to do this in 2009, when we provided a medal for every one of the 400 runners. It has grown since then, and last time we provided 8,200 medals."

I express astonishment, and ask her if they use a machine to make them.

"No! They are all made by hand."

Another frequent commission is to produce a mosaic of a star, from the mausoleum of Galla Placidia, for the godmother at a baptism. There is also growing demand for mosaic portraits of people.

"In the 25 years since I opened the shop, Ravenna's attitude to mosaics has completely changed. In the 1990s, people didn't take them seriously – 'mosaics suck' - and they didn't consider Ravenna to be a city for tourists. Today, the people of Ravenna will say that mosaics symbolise their city, 'they represent us'. For example, if one of them visits a friend in London, they will take a mosaic as a gift. Mosaics may be used to frame a mirror in their home, or as an important gift. Last month, I received a call from a family in Rome, who remembered my shop from a visit three years ago. They are remodelling their home, and want to order a mosaic as part of the renovation."

After the move in 2011, Anna took advantage of the extra space to start providing short courses in how to make mosaics. The hands-on training lasts just two and a half hours, and is ideal for day trippers coming to Ravenna. Cruise ships that visit the port often take advantage of these courses, as part of their itinerary for a day trip to the city.

Sofia helped in the shop when she was young, but her mother never thought that she would end up working there. She started at university, but then the pandemic arrived which made it too difficult to continue. Sofia tried a couple of jobs, yet never found a career that interested her. In the end, she asked if she could come and work at Annafietta.

"After two years, she is very happy here. A good relationship has developed between my daughter and the rest of the team, because Sofia never behaves like she is the owner's daughter. It's nice to see. I am so proud of my daughter. She is a lovely person. She grew up without a father, without grandparents, she only had me, and I was always busy with work. I couldn't help her with schoolwork as much as I wanted. But she has grown up to be a strong, courageous and kind person."

I ask how big the team is today, and how they are organised.

"Because we have a small team, there are only five of us, it's important that everybody knows how to do everything: designing and making the products, and selling them. This gives us flexibility. If I am unwell, or decide to take time off, it's not a problem. The place can run without me. Of course, each of us has things that we are especially good at. For example, I don't know how to make a portrait, but Luca is very good at that. I very much enjoy selling, and I am the main contact for customers seeking commissions."

I ask Anna whether she has ever thought about opening a second shop, in another city.

"Yes, but it would not work so well. Here is a beautiful position for us, because people come out of San Vitale with the sight of those mosaics still in their eyes, saying 'wow!'"

"Can you imagine retiring one day?"

"My daughter says that I will never retire, because I am incapable of not working. However, I would like to try! I would very much like to travel more. Separating yourself from your home city gives you freedom, enabling you to more easily embrace new experiences. I have tried to take a holiday, staying in Ravenna, but I just end up coming here, to the shop! I especially like walking, and it's not important where. It could be the Camino de Santiago, or a walking holiday in Puglia. To have a backpack, to take your time, to move slowly through the country, taking everything in. That's my ideal trip. I also have lovely memories from my times in England, when I was young."

"Where did you go in England?"

"I attended a summer school in Exeter. Another year, I stayed at the house of my mother's friends, near London. I also spent time on the Wirral. An engineer, working at the Cabot factory there, sometimes visited the Cabot factory near here, and my mother had met his wife. She arranged that I should stay with them one summer, and their daughter also came over to stay with us. Whilst in the Wirral, I met Paul McCartney's brother, Mike, who was their neighbour!"

I tell Anna that, although I am from Liverpool, I cannot claim to have met any of the Beatles' family or friends.

"When I was 16, my mother gave me the address of an au pair agency, in London, together with the money to pay for my train fare and one week in a hostel. She instructed me to get a job there, to pay my way through the summer. Fortunately, my English was good enough and they found me work as assistant cook in a retirement home, near Sloane Street. After two months, I'd earned enough to spend the third month touring Scotland with a friend. This was in August/September – it was beautiful."

"It seems you like the UK?"

"Yes, but I have never been back. I must return one day. I know France, Germany, Spain quite well. I also travelled to New York once, to stay with American friends. They used to come to Italy every year, to visit their aunty who lived here, and that's how I met them and we became friends. I've also been to Argentina several times, visiting my husband's family, and travelling around, to see the Iguazu Falls, and Uruguay. I now have a passion for sailing, and I have been to Greece a few times sailing and swimming. Also, last year I had a lovely trip to Jordan, and visited Petra. Archaeology still fascinates me."

"You have had a wonderful life. Thinking of what happened to you in 1999, and how you've managed to recover from that, you've done very well."

"What happened in 1999 was dramatic, and I still miss the two of them very much, especially when I am happy. Happiness is something that must be shared. Yet, the course I have taken was only possible because I was left alone, I had the freedom to choose."

Anna pauses and is about to continue when a man enters the

shop, accompanied by a large dog, tail wagging, with a loud friendly bark. "Good morning! How are you?" says Anna, smiling at the man. "Good morning! I'm fine thanks. How are you?" he replies. Anna heads over to transact some business with him, and she returns a few minutes later.

We've both been immersed in the past, talking and thinking about the journey Anna's taken, but I sense the demands of the present are now encroaching. I don't want to keep her too long from her work, and my stomach is telling me it's time to eat. I ask if the Piadineria opposite is a good place to have lunch, and Anna assures me that it is.

I thank her for her time, and for sharing what must be a difficult story to tell, before saying goodbye and heading across the street to enjoy some food. Over lunch, I watch the tourists entering and leaving San Vitale. Many also enter Anna's shop. Outside it's a beautiful sunny day. Inside, the glittering colourful mosaics are just as beautiful, showing no trace of the tragedy that triggered their creation.

21 The artist

The air is cool and humid, as I stroll across Piazza del Duomo. Florence's cathedral towers above, in all its glory, upper walls lit by the rising sun. There is no other church like this. Clean lines of white, pink and green shoot into the sky. Tall and straight, the campanile stands guard and, suspended in the sky, is Brunelleschi's astonishing dome. The Duomo dominates because the Piazza is empty. I am the only tourist. A few Florentines scurry by, on their way to work, heads down and showing no interest in the masterpiece before them.

In a few hours, this piazza will be a milling throng. I'm fortunate that my hotel is right by the Duomo, and I woke early. I can enjoy the silence, and stride unhindered to circumnavigate the cathedral. There is so much beauty in details, on the doors of the baptistery, on the façade of the Duomo. It's a privilege, having the time and space to wander slowly around the outside of this stunning building, stopping to gaze at an interesting statue, or the carvings on one of the great wooden doors.

I think about the anonymous artist, long departed and forgotten, whose hands shaped the target of my gaze, creating a connection between us across the centuries. The life of that artist, for all its drama, passion, love, hate, envy, grief and joy, is now represented solely by this legacy before me, decorative work on a beautiful building. Most of us leave nothing of ourselves visible to future generations, yet I feel at peace with that thought. Even the knowledge that I will soon be forgotten, lost in the enormity of time and space, doesn't bother me right now. The tranquillity of this moment, in the still and quiet beneath the Duomo, brings harmony.

I come to an area where the building is covered in

scaffolding, and realise that it is subject to a major renovation project. The stonework looks clean and fresh for a reason. Beyond the scaffolding, at the rear of the Duomo, the walls are still grubby. Towards the end of my circuit, back in the renovated section, I stop to admire a huge set of wooden doors on the side of the building. They are covered in intricate carvings, of animals, plants and people, all different and entertaining. I'm thinking of how all cathedrals have enormous doors like these, but I never see them open. I always enter and leave through much smaller, everyday doors. The large doors are for show, demonstrating the grandeur of the project, and they rarely serve a practical purpose.

Then the enormous door opens! A man steps outside, perhaps seeking relief from the dark interior. He takes a deep breath, squints in the bright morning light, and then notices me.

"I wasn't expecting the door to open," I say. He smiles.

I talk about how much I like the carvings, and ask if he knows when the doors were made.

"You've got me there, I'm afraid."

"Of all the thousands of tourists who visit the Duomo, I guess hardly any of them take the time to look at these doors. But they are beautiful."

"You're right, of course. It's a shame."

It occurs to me that this man, presumably a worker inside the cathedral, has come outside for a cigarette break. Not wishing to intrude further, I wish him a good day and move on. It's time to find a café for breakfast.

After enjoying coffee and pastry, I wander around Florence. Now there are many more tourists on the streets and, although they speak in multiple tongues, by far the most common is English with an American accent. You'd be forgiven for thinking that Florence is an American city, judging by the voices you hear. The citizens of the USA certainly have a great affection for the place.

I find myself in Via Ghibellina, and recall that the street has an independent ceramic business I noticed on the internet, which might provide an interesting back story. I find the shop, M G Design, and see the owner inside, adjusting the arrangement of products on her shelves, ready for that day's customers. The shop is small, but everywhere there are plates, bowls and vases, all decorated with beautiful pictures. These paintings, mostly landscapes, or still lifes of fruit and flowers, are of high quality, good enough to grace any gallery.

Entering the shop, I introduce myself, and learn that the owner is called Maria Giovanna Cimino. Maria Giovanna has a round face and a warm smile. We chat for a few minutes. I tell her about the book I wish to write and ask if she might consider being included. Fortunately, she is interested, so we agree a time for me to return at the end of the day, when she expects the shop to be at its most quiet.

Late in the afternoon, I return to M G Design. Maria Giovanna points to a metal stool, where I can sit, while she continues touching up the paintwork on a plate. I ask her about her parents, and I'm surprised to hear that she is from the south of Italy.

"I was born and brought up in a village called Manduria, in Salento, between Lecce and Taranto. Manduria is famous for the wine, Primitivo di Manduria. My father Francesco owned and worked the land. Sadly, he is no longer with us. He and his brothers grew grapes and olives, to make wine and olive oil. My younger brother Antimo has taken over the land. He still produces Primitivo di Manduria DOC wine."

DOC labelling, *denominazione di origine controllata*, guarantees the origin of the wine.

Maria Giovanna explains that her mother, Cosima, is still alive. She ran a shop, starting in the 1960s, from a large room in their house, selling a variety of items, including fabrics and books.

"I remember hiding in the shop, when I was a little girl, and being attracted by all the colours in there. They evoked strong emotions. I loved to draw and paint, to copy these colours."

Maria Giovanna is animated. She speaks breathlessly, keen to convey as much information as possible, as quickly as possible, with the enthusiasm of that little girl in the shop.

She found most lessons at school boring, but came to life when required to be artistic or creative.

"I excelled at pretending to be a tree! I absolutely loved to draw and paint. My parents were very busy, working the land or in the shop, and they didn't have much time for me really. I lived in my own world, and I wasn't reaching the standards expected at school."

In middle school, an art teacher from the nearby village of Grottaglie, famous for ceramics, was amazed when she saw the oil paintings that Maria Giovanna produced at home. Signora Racioppi realised that this 13-year-old girl had a talent, that she was born to be an artist, and would always be obsessed with images and colours. She spent extra time with Maria Giovanna, even getting her to paint murals in the school corridor.

In the final year of middle school, the art teacher asked Maria Giovanna what she wanted to do next. Manduria had only a classical high school, there was no art school. The nearest art school was in Taranto, 35km away. Maria Giovanna really wanted to go to art school, but she knew that this would require her to get up at 5.30 every morning to travel to Taranto. She could not imagine her parents agreeing to this.

The teacher told her not to worry. One day, the teacher arrived at Maria Giovanna's house, asking to speak to her parents. She explained to them that their daughter had a talent, the likes of which the teacher had never seen before, and she surely had a great future ahead of her. Maria Giovanna's father was sceptical, and required convincing, but eventually he agreed that his daughter would go to art school and they would do what they could to help.

"I was so excited. This was my dream. When I started at the art school, I was expecting something like Giotto's workshop! Instead, I found students who were attending just to get a diploma, because they were no good at anything else. I already knew how to draw, how to paint, and it felt like I was learning nothing there. The teachers were not like my art teacher in middle school."

By the second year at art school, Maria Giovanna felt she was wasting her time. She wasn't learning anything interesting. They were asking her to do extra maths lessons, because she hated mathematics and could not pass the tests. She told her mother that she wanted to quit, she did not want to go to the school any more. Her mother said "That's fine, but what do you want to do?"

"I wanted to paint!"

"So, what happened?"

"One day, I heard about a large shop being opened, three or four kilometres out of town, and they were looking for somebody to paint ceramics. The shop was on a main road, near the edge of town, where people could stop and buy their products. The owners bought their ceramics in Grottaglie, and they wanted somebody to decorate them. I started working for them."

Meanwhile, Maria Giovanna's mother told her about her uncles, Cosima's brothers, who were living in Florence, and how they had a great interest in art. Whilst Rome is the political capital of Italy, and Milan the commercial capital, Florence is undoubtedly the artistic capital. Maria Giovanna wrote to her uncles, and they posted their art books to her, with images of paintings from the great masters. Maria Giovanna was thrilled, and copied as many of these pictures as she could. Her mother was delighted, and filled her home with these paintings.

Maria Giovanna entered an art competition, organised by the local government, winning second prize with her entry. She also sold a few paintings. However, she felt that Puglia was not the ideal environment for her, a place where producing good wine was highly appreciated, art less so.

Meanwhile, the ceramic shop, where Maria Giovanna worked, was struggling. Ceramics went out of fashion in the 1980s. The local people were no longer buying them, and there was no tourism in Puglia in those days. The owner told Maria Giovanna that he would have to change the products he was offering, and there would no longer be a requirement for her.

"My mother and I talked about what else I could do. I said that I had to spend my life painting. She said that she would contact my uncle Piero in Florence, that I should go to stay with him for a holiday, to think about what I wanted to do. So, I came here, in March 1990, but I never returned to Puglia!"

"You stayed with your uncle Piero?"

"Yes, he and his wife had a beautiful big house in Florence. He was a designer, already 80 years old when I arrived, and he had a heart problem. The plan was for me to stay with them for a few weeks. I explained that I wanted to find work, as a painter. He took me into his studio, a beautiful room with a leather armchair, an old wooden desk, shelves and shelves of books, and a telephone. We searched the telephone directory, for businesses that might want an artist. I found this entry 'Euro Lamp Art', and my uncle told me to call them."

Maria Giovanna telephoned, and they said they might be interested and she should visit them the next morning. The business was out of town, about 12km to the west of Florence.

Early the next morning, Maria Giovanna took the bus and arrived at the factory with samples of her work, and also a letter of recommendation from her previous employer. She met the owner, Mario Scelfo, showing him her work and the letter. When he read the letter, and saw the signature at the bottom, he was astonished. "What a small world," he said, "the brother of your previous employer is a good friend of mine!"

Maria Giovanna was offered a position, and began working at Euro Lamp Art. A successful business, they designed and manufactured lamps, chandeliers and other furnishings, exporting to customers all around the world.

Now that she was earning a salary, uncle Piero took her to the bank, to open an account, and explained how she must save money and not spend it all. The income enabled her to move out of her uncle's house, and move into a shared apartment with students. She still went to uncle Piero's place on Sundays, for a family dinner.

Maria Giovanna worked at Euro Lamp Art for two years. However, the decoration required for these objects did not make use of her talent, and the owner recognised this. "Listen!" he said to her one day, "You should be doing something that makes the most of your abilities. Leave it with me, I will find you something."

Mario introduced her to the owner of a nearby furniture business. They had a requirement for somebody to paint designs and pictures on their furniture. "Have you ever done this before?" they asked. Maria Giovanna had to admit that she hadn't, but she suggested that they show her a finished item and she would try to copy it. She managed to produce an exact copy, and was given the job.

Within a week or two, the owner came to Maria Giovanna and explained that, although they liked the quality of her work, she was too slow. "I'm sorry, but you must complete the work more quickly. We cannot afford for you to be so slow." She asked to be given more time to get used to the work, and improve her speed, so they agreed they would evaluate her progress after two months. Unfortunately, two months later she still wasn't fast enough, so they let her go.

Once again, Maria Giovanna was searching for work in Florence.

"In Via del Proconsolo, I found a shop selling nice plates, bowls etc. It was small, with a staircase leading up to a mezzanine, where the lady owner painted her ceramics. She came from a small village, near Naples. Her husband's father was a very famous sculptor, he made the statues you can see on the bridge near Ferragamo: Ponte Santa Trinita."

Ferragamo is a high-end Italian department store.

Maria Giovanna started talking to this lady, and showing what she could do. Seeing the potential for her business, she offered Maria Giovanna a position, painting ceramics.

From the beginning, Maria Giovanna painted her ceramics up above, on the mezzanine floor, invisible to customers. The owner painted her pieces in the sales area, where products were on display. Naturally, customers assumed that all the ceramics in the shop were painted by the owner.

Via del Proconsolo is a busy street, with many tourists. Americans, in particular, loved the ceramics painted by Maria Giovanna. It wasn't long before most items sold in the shop were painted by her, rather than the owner, who remained very busy in a sales role.

After a few months, Maria Giovanna started to feel this arrangement was unfair. She was working 12 hours per day, on relatively low pay, and with little recognition. She tried to negotiate a more equitable arrangement with the owner, but the lady refused to consider any change. Eventually, Maria Giovanna said that she would work only three hours per day, or not at all, and the owner had little choice but to accept this. With more free time available, Maria Giovanna went seeking work elsewhere in Florence.

"On Borgo San Jacopo, a street near the Ponte Vecchio, I found this shop with a large window and paintings inside. I introduced myself, and was able to obtain work there painting furniture, as I'd done before. There was an older gentleman, who would soon retire, and they suggested I could watch him and learn how it is done, with the idea of being his replacement. It was really interesting, because we started with all-white furniture, and had to finish it off with painted designs. I also learnt how to decorate mirrors with gold leaf. In Puglia, I had only painted simple designs on ceramics. In Florence, there are many artisans, and it's possible to learn a lot from them."

"So, now you had two jobs?"

"Yes, but I never told the lady at the ceramic shop that I had this other work! I painted ceramics in the morning, and furniture in the afternoon. Later, I quit my job at the ceramic shop and worked full time for the furniture business. In total, I was there for about two years."

"Did you enjoy this work? To what extent were you responsible for designing the decorations?"

"I loved it! The lady asked me to produce designs, on paper, that she would approve, and then I would implement them. They were very happy with me."

Around this time, Maria Giovanna was walking with some friends, near the Duomo, when they came across a group of three young men who started talking to them. These turned out to be two brothers, plus their cousin. They started socialising, meeting up often, and Maria Giovanna began dating one of the brothers, called Ciro. He worked for a construction business, renovating apartments in Florence. Eventually, Ciro suggested that they move in together, and they rented a room near Via Ghibellina. They married in 1994.

Maria Giovanna started thinking about her finances. Florence is an expensive place to live, and the couple could not afford their own apartment. Living away from her parents, to find fulfilment through her art, meant she was living almost in poverty. Perhaps if she were not an employee, but established with her own business, then she could realise the full value from her work and earn a decent living?

At this time, her cousin from Puglia, Antimo Cimino, was in Florence, and looking to pursue a career overseas. Antimo urged her to take the plunge and start out on her own.

"One day, we were walking down this street and we saw this empty shop. 'You should rent this place!' said Antimo. 'All these years, you've been working so that other people can make money from you. You are stupid! Open your shop here. It's time you saw the benefits!'"

"By the way," says Maria Giovanna, "you really should contact Antimo. He lives in America, and runs a travel business, organising trips to Italy that focus on meeting Italians. You and he would have a lot to discuss."

She continues with her story.

"I had my savings. I called the owner of the shop, and we agreed a rent I could afford, because this is a relatively quiet street, not in the busy part of the centre. Then I went to my employer, and told them I was leaving. 'No, please don't go!' they said. 'Surely we can come to some arrangement?' Eventually, I agreed that I would continue to work for them part time. So, I worked for them in the mornings, and I came here in the afternoon."

The new shop, M G Design, opened in September 1996. Once again, Maria Giovanna had two jobs. After a while, it became untenable to continue working for the furniture business.

"I told them that I was very sorry, but I just couldn't continue to do two jobs. It was too much. They really didn't want me to leave, but I had to. I cried."

The lady, who owned the ceramic shop in Via del Proconsolo, parked her car every day in the garage on Via Ghibellina. She noticed Maria Giovanna's new shop soon after it opened.

"She was shocked! She couldn't believe that I had my own shop."

"Was it difficult to make a living, in the beginning?"

"No. It was successful from the start. I had plenty of customers. The shop in Via del Proconsolo wasn't a problem for me, because she provided a different type of product. Her ceramics were simpler, she knew how to mix colours and create pretty designs, but she was not an artist. My pieces were of higher quality, and clients were willing to pay for that, especially Americans because the lira was so low against the dollar. Three years after the shop opened, we could afford to buy an apartment. It's a good size, near here, with a nice terrace. Two years after moving in, we had it renovated."

The ceramic shop in Via del Proconsolo closed a few years later, when the owner retired.

An unusual feature of Maria Giovanna's shop is the oven, taking up a significant amount of space, used for firing the ceramics after they are painted. I ask her about it.

"I had experience of using an oven from my first job, in Puglia. Soon after I opened here, I calculated the right size for the business, and ordered this, made to measure."

"Can you imagine retiring one day?"

"No! I sometimes feel very tired, last year was especially busy, but I cannot imagine my life without this. I package the deliveries at home and, coming up to Christmas last year, the house was full of products awaiting shipment. My husband said 'enough, enough!' Maybe he would like me to stop, although he doesn't want to stop working. He gave up the construction job a long time ago, because he didn't enjoy it, and now he has found something he likes. He is a security guard."

"Where do you get your ceramics from?"

"From Calenzano, north-west of Florence, an industrial area with several ceramic factories. My suppliers have changed over the years, as businesses come and go. At the moment, I buy a lot from a place run by a young couple, and also another business where the designer often creates new forms, new shapes. I am always looking for something interesting, something different."

"Where are your customers from?"

"Mostly the USA and Canada. Many of them return again and again. I often hear somebody say 'I was here 20 years ago!' Listen, I think that how a person relates to others is important. Florentines have a closed character. They keep their distance. I am from the south, where people are more open and welcoming. The Americans, they sense this, and they say to me 'Maria, we have come back to see you, because you are a friend!'"

"How did you learn English?"

"As a young girl, being a bit different, the crazy artist, I enjoyed listening to English pop music, and that's how I started. However, my English improved a lot through talking to customers, here in the shop."

"Do you find time for holidays?"

"The shop is closed for 20-25 days in August, because it is too hot, and my customers don't come to Florence then. September and October are very busy. Many people buy Christmas presents then, knowing that they won't find products like these elsewhere."

"Is any of your business online?"

"Yes, I get many orders through my Facebook page. This kept me going through the pandemic."

Outside, I can see that daylight is fading. I tell Maria Giovanna that I've asked all my questions, and maybe we should finish. She pauses, and takes a deep breath. There's clearly something she wants to ensure I understand.

"I always knew that the place I was born wasn't for me. That my true home was elsewhere. As a young girl, I often dreamt of being in Florence. Maybe everybody has a true path, waiting for them, and they have to find it if they are to be happy."

22 The curator

Leaving Maria Giovanna's shop in the dusk, I return to my hotel to shower and change. I have been invited to dinner at the home of a friend, Silvia, who lives out near Porta Romana. It's a 30-minute walk to her apartment. However, having done too much walking today on hard pavements, I decide to take the bus. Actually, it's two buses, because Google tells me I have to change part way.

I'm first in the queue at the stop, when the bus arrives. It's tiny, and packed like a can of sardines. One person gets off, leaving just enough room for me to squeeze on board. Nobody else even tries to get on. The doors close, pressing me into the pack of standing passengers. I'm reminded of a journey on the metro in Rome, in the 1990s, when I felt the wallet being lifted from my back pocket. I turned around and glared at the person behind, who let go of the wallet and looked away. He got off at the next stop.

That's the only time I've even come close to being a victim of crime in Italy, although tourists are always warned to watch out for pickpockets in the main cities. Maybe I've been lucky. A much more real fear, for me, is that of being "mugged" by officials on Italian public transport.

I recall another more recent occasion, again in Rome, when I had bought my bus ticket using an app. Just before boarding the bus, I validated the ticket, and the clock in the app started counting down the 100 minutes validity period. A few stops later, three uniformed ticket inspectors boarded the bus and demanded to see everybody's ticket. They often travel in gangs, perhaps for mutual protection. I showed the ticket on my app to the lady ticket inspector, and she told me that I had only just activated it, when I saw them get on the bus, and therefore it wasn't valid. She instructed her colleague to get my ID and fine me.

Indignant, I declared my innocence, but they weren't listening. I told them that my stop was coming up next, which was true, and the inspector taking my ID asked his boss what he should do. "You get off the bus with him!" she declared, as if this was obvious. He didn't look happy about that, but we both got off. He asked to see the app on my phone, and I noticed that the clock showed my ticket was only a few seconds into the 100-minute period. "Look," I said, "the app is not working. That clock is not moving. I activated the ticket about ten minutes ago."

He hesitated. Then he closed the app and re-opened it, to see that it now showed eight minutes into the 100-minute period. To be fair, he then accepted that I had a valid ticket, and told me that next time I should close and re-open the app after validating, to ensure it showed the correct time. I escaped a fine, but still felt aggrieved. I will go out of my way to ensure I pay the right fare on public transport, but in Italy the assumption seems to be that everybody is fare-dodging all the time. You are guilty until proven innocent.

Today, I have a paper ticket, but I have no idea where the machine is on the bus to validate it and, even if I knew, it's physically impossible for me to reach it. I am completely hemmed in, unable to move. I comfort myself with the thought that I am only travelling one stop and, even if an inspector is on board now, they can't reach me to check my ticket. I will validate it on the second bus.

We arrive at the next stop, the doors open and three ticket inspectors are waiting on the pavement. They corral those of us getting off, and demand to see our tickets. My protest that it was impossible for me to validate it, on the packed bus, is ignored.

"Do you think this is fair?" I say to the inspector, who is examining my ID and demanding I pay a 40 euro fine.

"I'm just doing my job," he says.

They knew that bus would be packed, providing them with easy victims. In Italy, it's gangs of public transport officials you need to fear, not gangs of criminals.

Early this morning, I enjoyed those moments of exceptional tranquillity, circumnavigating the Duomo. Now, I am angry at what I perceive to be an injustice. The highs and lows of a day in Italy.

My mood improves significantly, once I arrive at Silvia's and we sit down to enjoy dinner. We've spoken a lot on Skype, but never met face to face before. I tell her about the restaurant I ate in last night, and how I've arranged to meet the owner tomorrow to hear their story.

Another friend Francesco, a professor of the history of law at Ferrara University, recommended that I eat at Ristorante Cafaggi, and include it in the book. Francesco often visited Professor Paolo Grossi, a famous judge, at the University of Florence, and Professor Grossi always took him to dinner at this restaurant. Following Francesco's advice, I went to add Ristorante Cafaggi to the list of candidates for the book, only to discover that it was already there!

Presumably, somebody else had previously suggested I visit the place, although I don't remember who. I ask Silvia, "Did you recommend this place to me?"

"I don't know, perhaps I did. It is one of Florence's historical restaurants, so I might have mentioned it. I first went there about 40 years ago, and I don't think it's changed much since."

I ate at Ristorante Cafaggi yesterday evening and, after the meal, explained to the cashier that I'd like to understand their story, for a book I am writing. He seemed interested, and held out his hand.

"My name is Lorenzo Cafaggi, but you should talk to my brother," he said, indicating the other side of the room.

I wandered over and introduced myself to another gentleman, and explained what I was looking for. "I see. You should really talk to my brother Andrea. I'm Leonardo."

He pointed to Andrea, who was very busy, so I waited until he was available. The restaurant was clearly a family business, run jointly, by at least three brothers.

Eventually, I managed to get a few minutes with Andrea. We agreed to meet for a longer chat, and he gave me a copy of a book he himself had written: "A Conti Fatti", best translated as "All Things Considered". Then it became clear why Lorenzo and Leonardo were so keen that I talk to Andrea, as one author to another. I haven't had time to read the whole of Andrea's book but, dipping into it, I see that it is a collection of letters, pen portraits and general recollections from his life. The writing is gentle, self-deprecating and humorous. I'm delighted to find a short chapter on Francesco's mentor, Professor Paolo Grossi, who rose to a senior position in the national government, as President of the Constitutional Court of the Italian Republic. Sadly, Professor Grossi passed away in 2022.

The next afternoon, I arrive at Ristorante Cafaggi, in Via Guelfa, to speak with Andrea. He welcomes me, wearing an apron and a short-sleeved shirt, and gestures for me to sit down. Other members of the family are preparing the place for evening service. With his spectacles, grey moustache and beard, Andrea has a friendly, kind aura, although he rarely smiles.

I begin by asking how and when the business started.

Andrea explains that his great grandfather Angiolo owned a wine cellar and shop in Rufina, 27km from Florence, and a small farm in the country, all of which he managed with the help of his children. Angiolo had four girls and three boys. The youngest boy, Pietro Settimo, born in 1896, was Andrea's grandfather. He was lame, with a stiff leg, having broken it falling from a cherry tree when he was just eight years old.

"That stiff leg probably saved his life," says Andrea.

"How?"

Andrea recounts the story, taken from his next book, A Uscio e Bottega, which is soon to be published. As a boy, Pietro Settimo often went to the villa of Contessa Pantellini, to run errands, so the Contessa knew him well. After Italy entered the First World War, the Contessa went in her carriage to visit the wife of the commander of the barracks in Florence. As she arrived, she was startled to see Pietro Settimo amongst a crowd of other poor boys, in the courtyard.

"Settimo, what are you doing here?" she demanded.

"Lady Countess, we are all waiting to go to war . . ."

"But you can't fight with that leg! Wait here."

After a few minutes she returned with an officer who ordered Pietro Settimo into the carriage, paid his respects to the Contessa, clicked his heels and left.

Andrea continues: "The Contessa brought my future grandfather back to his father, and his life. The others would meet their destiny, and most would have had their name engraved on some monument to the fallen. But my grandfather was able to live, to have children, to take care of his home and his family. Many years later, narrating these facts to my father, he confided to him: 'Giancarlo, you know that in my life I have always tried to behave well, so that I need never be ashamed of my actions. But that day, getting into the carriage under the silent gazes of my unfortunate companions, I was ashamed, I felt like a thief.' My poor grandfather, completely without blame, spent his days feeling like a thief . . . a thief of life."

After the war, Pietro Settimo managed a food & wine shop, and then a dairy shop, both purchased by his father, to initiate the boy into a life independent of his brothers. Angiolo was keen to secure a future for all his children and, expecting the girls to be married off, that meant providing each of his boys with their own business. The oldest son inherited the wine cellar in Rufina, and the second son the small farm. For his youngest son, he bought a small business, a wine shop with a kitchen, near where Via Guelfa meets Via San Gallo. Andrea provides the exact date of this transaction: 19th June 1923.

Pietro Settimo married Andrea's grandmother Roma, in 1926. Together, they managed a successful restaurant at their premises in Via Guelfa. In 1927, Andrea's father Giancarlo Valmaro was born. Another boy, Renzo, arrived in 1931.

Recognising the need for bigger premises, Pietro Settimo and Roma purchased a place nearby, on the other side of Via Guelfa, and relocated their business there in May 1938. This is when Ristorante Cafaggi arrived at its current location. Two years later, Italy entered the Second World War and everything changed.

Although Mussolini came to power in 1922, there was still a strong anti-fascist movement in Italy. Pietro Settimo hated violence, especially political violence, and he disliked the fascist regime. Before and during the war, he sheltered dissidents and jews, protecting them from the authorities. This included friends, customers, and families from the neighbourhood, many of them persecuted by the racial laws of 1938.

One of Pietro Settimo's closest friends was Adone Zoli, a prominent politician, who chaired the Florentine section of National Liberation Committee of the resistance. Zoli was arrested by the Nazis in November 1943, and sentenced to death, but he was freed by partisans before the sentence was carried out. The National Liberation Committee, a political umbrella organisation uniting anti-fascist parties, led the Italian government from 4th June 1944, when Rome was liberated by the allies, until the general election in June 1946. Zoli had a long political career after the war, becoming prime minister of Italy in 1957.

In Florence itself, the war had a significant impact. Retreating Germans shelled the city, and Via Guelfa suffered badly. People died, and many buildings were hit, including the top floor of the Cafaggi restaurant. Despite this damage, Pietro Settimo and Roma kept the restaurant open, rebuilding the top floor and the roof after the war. Their sons also helped out, as soon as they were old enough.

Andrea looks back fondly on the period just after the war, which he experienced by listening to his father's stories.

"There was a beautiful spirit because everybody was working together, to rebuild the country. Political differences seemed almost forgotten. An important figure from our family was Bianca Bianchi, my father's cousin. She became one of only 26 female members elected to the first Italian Constituent Assembly, in 1946. She was a strong campaigner for education, and the protection of women and children. For example, she helped to introduce a law that stopped the nonsense of my being named as Andrea di Giancarlo, referring to my father's name, on my identity card."

Meanwhile, life continued to evolve for the Cafaggi family. In 1953, Giancarlo Valmaro married Maria Fiorenza and they had three sons: Andrea (1954), Leonardo (1958) and Lorenzo (1964). Pietro Settimo died in 1960, and Giancarlo Valmaro took over the restaurant, with his brother Renzo also helping out. In 1962, the family purchased the building next door, still badly damaged from the war, and rebuilt it to extend the restaurant. The new area was used for the kitchen, greatly expanding the space available to diners.

Andrea talks about the reconstruction work undertaken here, in the 1960s, explaining that, when they dug out the foundations, they found lots of wood. Rather as in Venice, wood was used to underpin the buildings because the ground was so wet.

"This might be why Florence has suffered relatively little damage from earthquakes. The ground here, north of the river Arno, is not rigid. There is lots of water and sand, dampening the impact of an earthquake upon the buildings. We have so many art treasures, in these ancient churches and palazzi, and it's vital we don't lose them."

1962 was also the year when Andrea began helping his parents at the restaurant, on Sundays.

"I started when I was eight years old. I started, but I never stopped."

"When did your grandfather stop working in the restaurant?"

"When he died! The same for my grandmother, and for my father. They never stopped."

I'm beginning to understand the family ethos. Obviously, Leonardo and Lorenzo also helped out in the restaurant, from an early age.

Andrea attended a classical liceo. Then he studied law, at university in Florence, for a total of ten years.

"It's not important. I never really finished my studies."

"But you enjoyed learning? You must have enjoyed it, to study for ten years."

"Yes, I spent ten years at the university. But I never had great faith in the law. As a way to make a living, it's fine, but the regulations are always out of date, they cannot keep up with the pace of change."

"Yes, it's difficult for the law to change quickly enough when you get new technologies, new ways of doing business."

"Moreover, the law cannot help people choose their leaders wisely. People find it difficult to judge whether a potential leader will put the good of society first, or put himself first to achieve power."

I assume that Andrea will go on to discuss how many political leaders become corrupt, and abuse their position, but he surprises me by giving an example of the opposite situation.

"Anyone who wants the good of others, and puts their life at the service of others without self-interest, is a hero who risks his life, or a saint. Look at what happened to Jesus."

I ask Andrea whether he ever thought of returning to a more academic lifestyle.

"Not really. If I did study again, it would be geopolitics and economics. I find these subjects very interesting, especially in today's world."

Andrea married Tiziana in 1980 and, at about this time, he decided to cease studying and focus on the restaurant.

"My parents were in their early fifties and I was 26, my wife 23. Leonardo was 22 years old, and Lorenzo 16 years old. My parents essentially ran the restaurant on their own, because my uncle, although still alive then, didn't work here often. I felt they were too old to be left doing all the work. I don't know where it would have led, if I'd carried on with my studies, but I chose to ensure the family tradition continued, to help my parents."

In 1984, Andrea's grandmother Roma died. He describes how this happened.

"One day my grandmother, who was 88 years old, said she felt unwell. My mother put her to bed, washed her, combed her hair and made sure she was comfortable. That night, she slept. The next morning, she was still alive but hadn't woken, so my mother called in the priest. My mother was very devout, a good catholic. The priest watched over my grandmother, and saw that she was continually moving her fingers, in her sleep. 'Ahh,' said the priest, 'perhaps she is counting rosary beads, and saying her prayers.' 'I'm afraid not,' said my father, 'I think she is dreaming of shelling beans.'"

As Andrea said, she never stopped.

Andrea's uncle Renzo died young, in 1985, from pancreatic cancer. His father Giancarlo Valmaro, however, lived to the ripe old age of 94, passing away in 2020. Andrea's mother Maria Fiorenza is still alive, although she is not well.

"She was the heart of this restaurant. The women have always played fundamental roles, in the family and in work."

Andrea has owned the restaurant since 1994, and his brothers work there with him. I ask how many grandchildren Maria Fiorenza has, across the three brothers.

"There are eight in the next generation, six boys and two girls."

"Will any of them continue with the business?"

"No, it seems they are choosing other ways," says Andrea with sadness in his voice. "Many of them have worked here from time to time, but not at the moment. My daughter, she graduated with top marks, and that's partly because of her experience working in the restaurant. Here, she learnt not to be shy, to explain herself clearly, to be precise, and also to be kind."

I comment that, in researching for this book, I often hear of children that pursue their own career, outside the family business, but later return to take over and continue the tradition.

"I can understand that. It's important that the family business continues," says Andrea.

We talk about the kitchen and the menu. Andrea's mother was head chef, when she worked here, and now brother Leonardo is in charge in the kitchen, supported by a team of cooks. The menu changes regularly, but it is always based on traditional Tuscan dishes.

I ask Andrea how many customers are tourists, and whether they have many regular customers.

"In the season, perhaps 60% are tourists. In the winter, very few. Lots of locals come here regularly. This includes university professors, many of whom were children with me at school."

We start discussing Andrea's second book, that he is in the process of finishing, which will cover much more of his family's history.

"How do you find the time to write, when you are also working in the restaurant?"

"Some things matter more than others. I just have to prioritise my time, and I know that this work, this book, is too important for me, and perhaps for others too. Things must be recorded for the future, or they will be lost forever. Like tears in the rain."

Soon, the restaurant must open for the evening, so we have to finish our discussion. As so often, time is our enemy. The uncertain future is always there, in the background, with hinted menace. I sense Andrea feels this more acutely than most of us. He pulls open his shirt to reveal a long scar, clearly from a major operation.

"My heart. Three years ago."

I walk very slowly back to my hotel, reflecting on our conversation. Back in my room, I come across a video on YouTube: Ricordo di Giancarlo Cafaggi. This three-minute sequence of family photographs is a nice tribute to Andrea's father. It must have triggered a cascade of memories, for anybody that knew Giancarlo in life.

Andrea has great affection for the people and traditions in his life. If you were fortunate enough to be his friend, then I suspect he would do anything for you. Through his books, Andrea is determined to capture the things that matter, to honour and preserve them, as a gift to the future.

23 Life is beautiful

It all started with a photograph.

This picture, on the front cover of an otherwise unremarkable coffee table book, captures for me the essence of Italy.

I confess that, over the years, I've acquired quite a few large glossy books on Italy, all packed with lovely images. They're an easy Christmas or birthday gift for somebody like me, who is otherwise hard to buy for. I never tire of browsing through them in the winter, transporting myself to a warm, sunlit piazza.

Anyway, the photograph on the cover of this book - Best Kept Secrets of Tuscany - is a view down the full length of a loggia. Plates rest on tables with white tablecloths, there are wicker chairs and occasional potted shrubs. Everything is ready for lunchtime service. Sunlight streams in, through the row of arches to the left. One or two tables are occupied by people chatting, sipping coffee, looking cool and relaxed as only Italians can. It's a glimpse into heaven.

A note in the book informed me that this picture was taken in Arezzo, a small city in Eastern Tuscany. Obviously, I had to go there and find this loggia.

In the summer of 2022, friends kindly invited us to help celebrate their 50th wedding anniversary, in Tuscany. Together with their family and other friends, we all stayed in a villa for a week, during which Jackie and I took a day trip to Arezzo. The weather was perfect. Wandering around the city, it was easy enough to find the loggia in the photograph, on the main square Piazza Grande. A little later, we were talking about where to have lunch, when Jackie said she had seen a lady making fresh pasta, in this loggia at Piazza Grande. What better advertisement could there be for an Italian restaurant? As a result, we had an enjoyable lunch at Ristorante Logge Vasari, sitting at one of the tables in the very photograph that brought us to this city.

When it came to doing research for the book, I remembered the loggia and this restaurant, and contacted the owners to ask if they might consider being included. We fixed a date for me to visit, as part of my trip to Florence in March 2024. That's why I am now on a train from Florence to Arezzo, to meet with Andrea and Michela Fazzuoli, owners of Ristorante Logge Vasari.

My second time in Arezzo and, once again, the weather is perfect. Walking from the station to the restaurant, I come across a statue I don't remember from our first visit, perhaps because we arrived by car on that occasion. Reading the explanatory plaque, I'm surprised to discover that the inventor of musical notation, a monk called Guido, came from Arezzo! He lived around 1,000 years ago. All of this is completely new to me.

A surprising number of famous Italians are from Arezzo, including the poet Petrarch, and the Renaissance painter and architect, Giorgio Vasari. Employed by Tuscany's rulers, the Medici family, Vasari designed the loggia of the Palazzo degli Uffizi in Florence. In 1573, commissioned by Cosimo Medici, he designed the Palazzo delle Logge for his home town, Arezzo. Unfortunately, he never saw his design brought to life. Vasari died in 1574, and the building wasn't completed until around 1600. It is the photograph of this beautiful loggia that originally brought me to Arezzo, and to Ristorante Logge Vasari.

Scheduled to meet the owners at 11am, I arrive at the restaurant about 15 minutes early. The building is already open, and a friendly waiter greets me. He explains that neither of the owners is here just yet, and offers me a coffee. I sit at a table under the loggia, enjoying the morning sunshine. A few minutes later, a young lady comes over and explains that she is the owners' daughter, Elisa, and she's very sorry but her parents have been unavoidably delayed, and they might not arrive until around 1pm. Since I have all day, that's not a problem and I decide to walk around the town until noon and then return to the restaurant for lunch.

Piazza Grande is an interesting space. On all four sides, the buildings are old, in various shades of ochre. A 1,000-year-old church stands over the western corner of the piazza, with a nice little fountain beneath it. The piazza slopes steeply from the northern corner, where Ristorante Logge Vasari is located, down to the southern corner, where there is a cluster of shops. This is unusual. Most Italian piazzas are constructed on level ground, although the main piazza in Siena, like Arezzo's, has a significant gradient.

I'm now back in the restaurant, at a table beneath the beautiful loggia, having ordered some fresh pasta for lunch. Before the pasta arrives, an energetic, attractive lady comes over to the table and introduces herself as Michela Fazzuoli, one of the owners. She apologises profusely for being late, and declares that she is ready to chat whenever that's convenient for me. We agree that I will finish lunch first, and then we'll talk.

The food is delicious, of course. As I'm finishing the final mouthfuls, I notice a middle-aged man walking through the loggia, stopping to speak to people at the other tables, most of whom he clearly knows. At one table, a lady is eating alone. The man stops to speak to her, and they both look serious, even sad. He moves on, continuing in my direction. When he sees me, he screws his eyes up slightly in puzzlement, then smiles broadly and declares that I must be Richard. Since I'm a lone stranger, and obviously not Italian, I guess it was easy for him to identify who I must be. Andrea Fazzuoli and I shake hands, and he urges me to take my time, to have dessert and coffee, and then pop into the restaurant when I'm ready to talk.

Although I've seen each of them for just a few seconds, it's clear that both Michela and Andrea are full of life. They have an infectious energy and warmth, that lifts everybody around them.

When lunch is over, I wander inside and find Andrea, who takes me upstairs to a large, stone vaulted room. We sit down, and I begin by asking about his family.

"My mother Bruna was a chef. She was born to cook. When 15 or 16 years old, she started working in a restaurant, washing dishes. She had learnt cooking at home, and the restaurant soon realised that she would be useful in the kitchen. Gradually, she worked her way up the hierarchy to become head chef. That restaurant kitchen was her school, where she became a great cook. She married my father, Guglielmo, who worked as a car mechanic, and they had three sons: Marco, Maurizio and me, Andrea, the youngest. Because mamma was always working in the restaurant, the rest of us did not eat at home. We ate in a small trattoria in the Colcitrone district, not far from here."

Andrea explains that his father was not content with this arrangement. He wanted the family to spend more time together, and he was willing to change his career to make that happen. When the opportunity arose, they decided to take over the small trattoria in Colcitrone, where Guglielmo and the boys always ate. Thus, in 1980, Bruna and Guglielmo opened their first restaurant together, called Trattoria da Memmo, because Guglielmo is often shortened to Memmo.

"From that day onwards, the whole family was in the restaurant and bar business. I was helping my parents, in that restaurant, when I was nine years old."

After four years of running Trattoria da Memmo, they had the chance to rent premises in Palazzo delle Logge, the perfect place for a much bigger restaurant. So, in 1984 the business relocated, becoming the Ristorante Logge Vasari that we see today. In 2013, they were able to buy these premises outright.

Andrea tells me that the palazzo, where we are sitting now, was originally used for government offices. Later, it became the customs house, where salt traders paid the tax due on their product. In the days before refrigeration, salt was valuable because it was just about the only way to preserve food.

More recently, the building housed a number of antique shops. Since the 1960s, Arezzo has hosted the most important antiques fair in Italy, attracting up to 800 exhibitors. This world-famous fair still takes place every month, using multiple venues across the city.

Nowadays, Palazzo delle Logge is split amongst 19 individuals, each owning a separate section, plus the local government which has offices on the upper floors. Most of the private owners, like Andrea and Michela, use the premises for their business, although there is still one family that lives there.

Andrea is telling me all of this with great fluency, as if it's a story he has recounted many times before, rather like a tour guide.

I ask Andrea about their education. "Marco attended an Accountancy School (scuola ragioneria). Maurizio and I went to a Hotel School (scuola alberghiera). Maurizio's wife, Marzia, and my wife, Michela, both studied at Accountancy School."

"How did you and Michela meet?"

"We had friends in common and met, for the first time, in Corso Italia, when we were 18 years old, in 1989." Corso Italia is the main shopping street in Arezzo, where people congregate most evenings for the passeggiata. "From then onwards, we were boyfriend and girlfriend."

I ask about Michela's parents.

"They both worked in a shoe factory, something quite different. Michela's mother is still alive, in fact she is outside now having lunch, but her father passed away recently, I'm afraid."

Now I recall the lady at a nearby table, eating her lunch alone, who Andrea stopped to speak to just before he said hello to me.

"Did you only ever think about the restaurant business, or did you consider other options for your future?"

"When I was young, I tried football!" exclaims Andrea. He pats his tummy. "When there was 60kg less. But I wasn't that great. Then, in 1990, my parents were involved in a huge car accident, while on holiday in Naples. My father died, and my mother was in hospital for a year. She needed me to work in the business, so I gave up football. I was 19 years old."

I didn't see that coming. Andrea moved smoothly from joking about how it's hard to imagine him playing football now, to the tragedy that shaped his whole life. He has had over 30 years to assimilate that event, so he takes it in his stride now, but in 1990 it must have been traumatic. That was true especially for Bruna, lying in a hospital bed for months, thinking about how they would rebuild their lives.

Bruna recovered, came home and resumed work in the restaurant. The business continued to go from strength to strength and, in 1992, the Fazzuoli family opened a bar next door, in an adjacent part of the palazzo, for Andrea's brother Marco to manage. In 1993, they opened a new restaurant next door to the bar, at the end of the loggia, called La Lancia d'Oro and run by Andrea's other brother Maurizio. The family now owned a restaurant, a bar and another restaurant, all next to each other along the loggia, each managed by a different brother!

However, for young lovers Andrea and Michele, life was not perfect. Andrea worked in the restaurant six days per week, with time off only on Tuesdays, when it closed. Michela worked in accounting, and she was free only on Sundays. In 1993, when La Lancia d'Oro opened, Michela joined the family business.

"It's very hard for one person, in a couple, to work in the restaurant business when the other doesn't. They never see each other. It became much better once Michela was able to join us. At the beginning, Michela helped with the accounts and administration, but then she wanted to go into the kitchen, to become a cook."

"Who does the cooking at home, you or Michela?"

Andrea starts laughing. "Let me tell you a story. In 1989, just after we first met, Michela invited me to her home for lunch. She cooked pasta – ravioli - and then took cold cream out of the fridge, to pour onto the pasta, together with some prosciutto. I laughed, saying 'no! no! no!' I told her to sit down, and I got up to cook lunch."

"Today, she's a better cook?"

"Today, she cooks beautifully. Fantastic. Every three months, there is a new menu in the restaurant. Michela and the chef design it and select the ingredients, and taste the recipes, together. It takes two or three weeks to design a new menu."

"Does everything change, or are some dishes retained?"

"Around 50% of the menu is changed. There are some traditional dishes, like Ribollita and Chianina, that will always be on the menu."

"How is your restaurant organised? Who does what?"

Andrea explains that Michela is responsible for the kitchen, and he is responsible for the dining area. The kitchen employs a total of nine staff, including head chef Federico. There are eight waiters in the dining area so, including Elisa, Andrea and Michela, the restaurant employs a total of 20 people.

"We have two people who just prepare fresh pasta. We make a lot of pasta, every day. See this menu: out of ten dishes, eight have fresh pasta. What did you have for lunch today?"

"Pasta filled with pumpkin. Tortelli di zucca. I love it. Delicious! I don't suppose you'd let me have the recipe?"

"In addition to pumpkin, the filling includes a cheese called Blumarena, made using sour cherry syrup. We tried other cheeses, even meat, before finally discovering that Blumarena was the perfect combination for pumpkin. With any new dish, we also have to consider what the ingredients cost, how long it takes to prepare, and if the cooking can be scaled up to the volumes we need. Cooking for 150 people is not like cooking for 20. This is what it takes to develop a new menu."

"How long has your head chef been here?"

"Federico has been with us for ten years. We were looking for a cook to head up the primi piatti team, he applied and we gave him the job. Later, when Lorenzo departed, Federico took his place as head chef. He is a Sicilian, from Palermo."

"How long was the previous head chef, Lorenzo, here?"

"Also, ten years."

"So, the team doesn't change a lot?"

"Thank goodness! It's important to have a steady hand, so we don't want too much change. But you also need individuals to grow, to be able to rise through the team, so there needs to be some change."

"Michela learnt by working with my mother Bruna, when she ran the kitchen here. But the team is always learning, always improving. For example, yesterday we had a training day on meat fermentation. Nowadays, there is a lot of science in cooking. Top Italian chef, Massimo Bottura, he has a scientist, a chemist, in his team! You must keep learning to stay at the forefront. Everything changes."

"Did your mother embrace these new methods?"

"In her later years, mamma would keep watch over the kitchen rather than stay hands on. She saw people doing things differently and she would accept it, saying 'OK, so they do it differently.' In the old days, mamma would cook a meat sauce for seven hours. Today, the team does it in one hour, using new techniques. Once, she cooked this sauce the traditional way, just to show the team. 'Yeh, that tastes better,' they admitted." We both laugh.

"In the early days, was the menu a lot simpler?"

"Yes, I'd say it was more rustic in the 1980s. Fewer dishes, and they would be traditional. You must remember that, in those days, there were very few restaurants in Arezzo, just five or so. Now there are 200!"

"It feels like this is an important, perhaps a famous, restaurant?"

"In a sense, yes. We've received numerous awards. Large organisations, like the local government, banks, insurance groups, they reserve a dining room here for major events. On the walls downstairs, you will find photographs of numerous famous people who have dined here. Ronald Reagan, for example. In 1987, we even had a team from NASA, seven astronauts, brought here as guests by a local business."

"How many of your customers are tourists?"

"In the winter, virtually all our customers are local. In the summer, I'd say that 60%, maybe 70%, are local, with the rest tourists. Some tourists return here year after year, stretching back 40 years, and they bring their children, who continue to visit as they become adults. It's beautiful."

I tell Andrea about the photograph that brought me to Arezzo, and to this restaurant, explaining that the image of the loggia encapsulates, for me, the essence of Italy.

"Yes, absolutely. La bella vita. This loggia, people call it little Uffizi, because the design is so similar to the Uffizi in Florence."

We talk about what changes have happened over the years. As the brothers grew older, they took on more and more of the business, with Bruna able to step back. In her final years at the restaurant, 2013 and 2014, she worked at the counter, making coffee and taking payments. Bruna passed away in 2016. In 2010, Andrea's brother Marco and his wife Katia sold their bar. They moved to Brazil, where they had friends, to run a business there. However, they returned to Arezzo in 2020, and now live here in retirement.

Today, the two restaurants are still operated as a single business, with four partners: Maurizio, Marzia, Andrea and Michela.

I ask a cheeky question: "Which restaurant is better?"

"The truth is they are very similar. We both make our own fresh pasta and fresh bread, every morning. We use similar ingredients, and we both have a quality wine cellar. La Lancia d'Oro is smaller, that's all."

The next generation is continuing the tradition, with Maurizio's daughters Valentina and Martina, and Andrea's daughter Elisa, all working in the family's restaurants. Maurizio's son Filippo and Andrea's son Riccardo are in their final year at school, and it's not clear what they will do next.

"Elisa went to university in Siena, to study economics, but Covid arrived in her first year and basically stopped all lessons. She left, and now wants to work in the restaurant. The clients really like her. We were hoping, still are hoping, that she can go back to studying, to gain new experiences. But she is very happy here."

I ask about plans for the future, and Andrea explains that over the next year they will refurbish and open additional space, that they have procured, to use as a cocktail bar. Apparently, this used to be a warehouse within the palazzo, and it has old frescoes from the Vasari period. "It will be a beautiful room," says Andrea.

He notices that I am looking around, at the room we are in now, which has a grand vaulted ceiling, and truly feels 400 years old.

"In the 1870s, this room was an apartment. I found the plans. Over there was the kitchen, here the bathroom, there, as you can see, was the chimney for the fire."

Looking around, now I can imagine how somebody once lived here.

"Also, Roberto Benigni used this room as his headquarters, for two months, when he was making the film Life is Beautiful. He chose to shoot in Arezzo, because he was fascinated by Piazza Grande. At least 30 minutes of the movie is set in the piazza. When it was released, we were invited to the premier, here in Arezzo."

"It's a lovely movie. I have it on DVD, at home in the UK."

This 1997 Italian film uses humour to tackle a difficult subject. Co-written by Benigni, who also directed and played the lead role, it tells the story of a Jewish book shop owner and his family in Arezzo, during the Second World War. They are taken to a Nazi concentration camp, where he invents stories to shield his young son from their nightmare. Benigni's father spent two years in Bergen-Belsen, which partly inspired the story. It achieved international success, grossing over $200M worldwide.

At this point Michela joins us, and Andrea confesses that he has told me the story about her wanting to put cold cream on ravioli. After chatting for several minutes, we go downstairs where they show me around the dining room, and I look at the photos on the walls. The sun is still shining, calling me outside. Reluctantly, I say goodbye to the Fazzuolis, who have been very pleasant company.

Strolling back to the station, I am struck by the coincidences connecting the people I interviewed yesterday and today. Both called Andrea, they are each one of three brothers, all in the restaurant business. They both love life and throw themselves, with complete commitment, into something they passionately believe in. But they couldn't be more different. One is thoughtful and introspective, the other ebullient and charismatic.

Yet each, in his own way, brings joy to the people in his life.

24 Undefeated

Padua is home to Italy's second oldest university, founded in 1222. It's a beautiful city, with amazing frescoes in the Cappella degli Scrovegni, and Palazzo dei Signori. From 1405 onwards, Padua became part of the Venetian republic, and it was a Venetian nobleman who created the city's most elegant space. In 1775, Andrea Memmo had an area of boggy land drained, by digging an elliptical canal and creating a green island in the centre, where he rented space for market stalls. This helped to pay for the project. Over the years, the canal became lined with marble statues. Today, whether you call it a park or a piazza, Prato delle Valle is a lovely place to pass the time.

Because I like the city so much, I was keen to feature an establishment from Padua in the book. On the internet, I came across an interesting high-end restaurant called Belle Parti. YouTube provided an interview of the owner, an effervescent, attractive young woman. How did somebody so young come to be running this successful, quality restaurant? Perhaps she is from a wealthy family, and her parents purchased it for her? I had to discover the story.

I telephoned Belle Parti and explained my project and the book. Fortunately, the owner, Stefania Martinato, was willing to talk to me. Belle Parti is closed on Sundays, so we agreed to meet on a Sunday morning, at the restaurant.

Today is Saturday, and I am travelling by train from Florence to Venice, where I plan to spend a few days. I have booked a table for lunch at Belle Parti, so I leave the train at Padua station. With plenty of time in hand, I wander around the city centre, eventually arriving in the narrow, cobbled street called Via Belle Parti, which gave the restaurant its name.

Leaving the street, and entering the restaurant, is like being transported to another world. The dining room is spacious and elegant. The high ceiling is supported by enormous old wooden beams, tables are laid immaculately with pristine white tablecloths and sparkling glasses. The atmosphere is calm, professional, and friendly. I'm shown to my table, where I am placed near another English-speaking gentleman, also on his own. Inevitably, we start chatting. Jim Rice is an American, here on holiday, and we have plenty to talk about, since we both love Italy.

Then Stefania comes over and introduces herself. I had thought she might not notice my name on the reservations list, but that was naïve. I explain that I wanted to experience the restaurant as a customer, and this was my best opportunity. She smiles, and expresses the hope that I enjoy my meal, before leaving to greet more customers.

The environment at Belle Parti sets you up to expect a great meal, and I am not disappointed. The waiting staff, the food, the wine, and my dining companion at the next table, all combine to create a memorable lunch. As I'm leaving, Stefania and I exchange a few words, just to confirm our appointment tomorrow. Soon, I'm back on board a train to Venice.

The next morning, I take another train back to Padua, and arrive at Belle Parti at 11am. Stefania is there to let me in, dressed more informally today. The grand dining room feels so different when it is empty, with just two of us sat at one of the tables. We talk softly, almost in whispers, as if in a sacred space, a church, where we don't want to be noticed.

"Tell me about your parents."

"My parents, Raffaela and Gianfranco, were just 20 years old when they had me. My mother's family were poor farmers, living in a small village in the Veneto. She was one of seven children, three boys and four girls. My mother, together with my uncles and aunts, ran a bar in this village, Trebaseleghe. When I was very young, my parents, together with my mother's brothers and sisters, and her parents, they opened a bigger place called Stecca. This was in the village of Pianiga, near Padua. You could play bowls there, they served spare ribs, sausages, french fries and other food. My grandparents worked in the kitchen. It became quite famous. Then, my parents decided to leave that business and manage a hotel together, in San Nazario, in the mountains near Bassano del Grappa."

"What was the hotel called?"

"Mirabrenta. I grew up there. I was very free, because my parents were working all the time. However, they were not getting many customers. My father decided to open a pizzeria, because they had an oven inside the hotel, that was used to make bread. This was the 1980s, and there weren't many pizzerias here in northern Italy. So, they opened this pizzeria, they put a sign on the street advertising pizza, and loads of people started coming, hundreds of them. There were only three staff, mamma, papa and a waiter. They didn't know what to do. My father called his mother, to ask for help, they needed more people. At last, they were earning some money."

Having seen how popular pizzas were, even when sold from inside a hotel, they decided to open a proper pizzeria in a small village called Galta, back near to Padua. Stefania explains how they decorated their new restaurant.

"At the time, there was a famous interior designer, who fitted out restaurants as if they were children's playgrounds. Inspired by him, they gave their pizzeria a sundial, a Botticelli, a reproduction of the Mona Lisa, it was like entering an ancient palace. Today we would consider this tacky but then, when everybody was used to red and white checked placemats and wicker chairs, this was fantastic, like entering a magic kingdom. Only 2,000 people lived in this village, but the customers flocked in. They came because they looked forward to the experience. At that time, you could only pay in cash, and I remember my father taking the money away in wheelbarrows."

Stefania hesitates, then says "There's something else I should tell you . . . "

She describes how a local criminal gang noticed how well their business was doing, and decided to rob them. They raided the restaurant early one Sunday morning, and held the family hostage. Stefania ran away and called the police, and then returned to the pizzeria! She was just 10 or 11 years old. When the police arrived, with helicopters and guns, the criminals were angry. They wanted to take Stefania with them, as a hostage, and held a gun to her head. Her father refused and insisted that they take him instead. It all ended in a shoot-out with the police, and one of the criminals was killed. Fortunately, Gianfranco survived without injury. That evening, after this ten-hour ordeal, they opened the pizzeria as usual, as if nothing had happened.

I am stunned, and I don't know what to say. Presumably, if this happened today, there would be concerns about post-traumatic stress disorder. The authorities would want to ensure that the family received some kind of support, to help them recover mentally. In the 1980s, they were just left to get on with their lives.

Meanwhile, Stefania is searching on her phone for something, which she eventually finds and sends to my phone. It's a photograph of a full-page newspaper article from that time, reporting the crime.

Stefania moves on, and is now talking about how, as a young child, she helped to make Tiramisu for the restaurant, lifted up onto the table to whisk eggs. She also assembled pizza boxes, for take-away pizzas.

Working extremely long hours, her parents were always tired. Stefania would get herself ready for school in the morning, and travel to and from school on her own.

"As an only child, with my parents working all the time, I felt alone. I hated their business, because it took them away from me. I would never have thought that I would do this work myself."

Stefania's father wanted to grow, to find an alternative location where they would get more customers. He found a place near the river in Bassanello, a district of Padua. It required refurbishment but, because it lay on a busy road, there would be a lot of passing trade. They renovated this new place, while still running their old pizzeria in Galta.

Stefania was enrolled in a school in Padua, although this required a 90-minute journey each way while they were still living in Galta.

At that time, Stefania only spoke the Venetian dialect. She learnt Italian at school.

"My mother tongue is dialect. When speaking Italian, even today, I feel like a different person."

"Arriving at this school, I was confused. They called me by my surname, instead of my first name. It was a school for rich people, because by now my parents had earned a lot of money, but we were from a simple background. I was so innocent."

She talks of how she found a dirty, sick pigeon on the street, and took it to the vet, begging them to save it. The vet had

Stefania vaccinated, and the bird put down! Meanwhile, the school didn't know where she was.

After a few months, when Stefania was 12 years old, they were able to move to Padua and open the new pizzeria, Ristorante Pizzeria Il Bassanello. Now they had seating for 300 in the restaurant, plus two floors of accommodation above for the family. However, her parents had to purchase the building, they weren't able to just rent it. They couldn't afford this, so they went through a period when money was very tight. Determined not to take Stefania out of her school, at home they had no beds, no sofa, and not really enough to eat. All their money went to pay off the loan from the bank, or to school fees.

By working incredibly hard, they made a success of the new pizzeria, and gradually improved their financial position. Then somebody, they don't know who, started a fire that consumed the building. Living above the premises, their lives were endangered by the smoke, but they managed to escape.

In Italy, it is mandatory to have insurance when you open a restaurant, although the insurance never covers everything. Stefania's uncles, plus lots of other people, rallied around to help them clean up and rebuild. Taking a deep breath, her parents reopened the pizzeria and went back into business.

Aged 14, Stefania left middle school in Padua and attended a languages high school. She had no idea what she wanted to do with her life, but she was interested in languages. There, she enjoyed sport, especially volleyball.

"The coach was marvellous. He inspired me, giving me the confidence to express myself."

"Did you have many friends at school?"

"Yes, I was very sociable, always seeking friends. However, I felt different. They were the children of doctors and lawyers, but I was still working in the kitchen, helping to make pizza. On Sundays, my schoolfriends went dancing, and I was a pizza chef. I would go to watch them dance until 4pm, and then I had to return to the pizzeria to work. Now I know that you should never be ashamed of your roots, always be proud of what you do, and this I tell my children."

Leaving school, Stefania decided that she wanted to study law at the University of Padua. However, as she was beginning her studies, her father found the perfect place where he wanted to open a second pizzeria, in the centre of Padua. He came to Stefania, and asked if she would take it on.

"I said OK."

"You said yes straight away, without even thinking?"

"Yes."

"Do you understand why you didn't even think about it?"

"I don't know. It was a choice of the heart."

"Was it perhaps because you always did what your parents asked of you?"

"No, it wasn't that. I was always rebellious. It was completely my choice. I was happy, because it gave me an important role for the first time. I was 19 years old."

"To be honest, I can't imagine you as a lawyer."

"No! I would have been a poor lawyer."

So, after just a few months, Stefania left university and started working with a team, renovating the building for the new pizzeria.

"I learnt how to get things done, even if you don't know how to do them. When the bricklayers arrived, I stayed and worked with them. I watched the electricians and the plumbers. I helped to lay the floors. I've seen how to build a pizza oven, with stones. My father took me to the bank, to arrange the finances.

He wanted me to do it all, to understand everything that is required to create a restaurant."

Although afraid of making mistakes, her courage grew and she took responsibility for everything. However, as an attractive young girl, she found it difficult getting the workmen to take her seriously.

The new restaurant, called La Cova, was not far from today's Belle Parti. Stefania managed this pizzeria, her mother managed the pizzeria in Bassanello, and her father would shuttle back and forth between the two sites.

"We worked incredibly hard. The place was so popular, everybody in Padua ate there. It was small inside, just 60 seats, but outside we used the whole street. Every now and then the police came to fine me, because I had added too many tables outside. But we needed the money from these extra tables, to pay off the loan."

For three years, this continued, but the strain on the family was too great. Stefania's mother could no longer manage the pizzeria in Bassanello on her own, and her father was exhausted from shuttling back and forth.

La Cova, established as a successful restaurant in the centre of Padua, was sold as a going concern. Stefania's father was delighted because, at last, he was financially secure. Deciding to step back from their other operation, they rented the Bassanello building to a family from the south of Italy, who wanted to run a pizzeria. Stefania's parents used the money to construct a small house in their home village, Trebaseleghe, planning to enjoy a well-earned retirement.

Stefania decided to find a job, and she went to work with her cousins who ran a small pizzeria in Piombino Dese, a village near Trebaseleghe. There, she worked as a waitress.

"I remember when I was given my first tip, just half a euro. I was disappointed, but it also made me think about the contrast with previously, when I was the owner of the restaurant, receiving no tips. Back then, I was working incredibly hard, trying to learn how to do everything, from bricklaying to dealing with the banks. It was so difficult, feeling like a little girl in a world of men, who didn't take me seriously. Anyway, I was determined to make a success of my new role. I learned how to be a good waitress. I also came to understand the challenges employees face, to see the world from their point of view. That was really important."

Stefania came to enjoy her time at the pizzeria, working for her cousins. The regular customers were nice, and life was pleasantly busy. Meanwhile, the family running the pizzeria in Bassanello had stopped paying rent to Stefania's parents, so they had to evict them. They decided to come out of retirement, and return to the restaurant business.

But Gianfranco had bigger plans than just managing the Bassanello pizzeria. One day, Stefania's parents came to tell her they had found the perfect restaurant for sale, in a 15th century palazzo in Padua. They persuaded Stefania to take it over, to become the manager, while they returned to running their pizzeria in Bassanello. Stefania's father told her that they would help her when they could, but they had no experience of running a restaurant like this. Running a pizzeria was much simpler.

In 2003, the family bought Belle Parti, a restaurant named after the street where it's located. Stefania and her father made few changes to the restaurant, retaining the name, the furniture, the overall design. There was a handover period of 15 days, while the previous owner continued running the restaurant and

Stefania worked with him, as a waitress. Stefania watched everything he did, to learn as much as possible.

"I was shaking like a leaf. Anyway, I started managing this restaurant. I fell in love with every corner of the place, because it feels magical, but I wanted to leave. I wanted to leave, but I couldn't."

"You wanted to leave, because you were afraid?"

"Yes, I was afraid. It was hard. Everybody in the team was older than me. I was the boss, but I was the youngest. They made fun of me, I could hear them, but I ignored that and kept my mouth shut. I told myself I just had to keep going, keep learning, and one day they will respect me."

In the early days, they had few customers and Stefania was struggling. They had to find a way to fill the restaurant. She and her father contacted local travel agencies, offering a discount for any customers they referred to the restaurant. A lady at one agency gave her a book, listing all the tour operators in Italy. Stefania sent faxes to these tour operators, advertising Belle Parti for conferences etc. In addition, one of her regular customers, Carlo Alberto Portalupi, the owner of a big company in Padua, saw how hard she was working. He arranged for her to give a talk at the local chamber of commerce, and for her to receive the addresses of local businesses. Stefania had photographs taken of the restaurant, created a brochure and sent it to these local businesses. Thanks to these initiatives, more and more people came to Belle Parti.

The clients referred by tour operators, and the guests brought by local businesses, were nearly all foreigners. In those days, very few Italian waiters spoke a foreign language. In evenings, after work, Stefania watched foreign language films in their original language. She was determined to build on her education at the languages school, to learn to speak English, French, Spanish and German well enough to converse with her customers.

This was important for the local businesses that brought foreign guests to the restaurant. With those guests able to converse in their own language, ordering food etc., they felt more at ease, and therefore more likely to do business with their Italian hosts.

At that time, Stefania lived in an apartment near the restaurant. One night, in July 2007, she was woken by loud popping noises coming from outside. Her window was open, she could smell burning and heard people shouting "get out". The popping sound was wine bottles, exploding with the heat. Stefania went outside and tried to get into the restaurant, but it was too hot. All she managed to get was singed eyebrows. Firefighters arrived, and eventually managed to put out the blaze.

Referring back to the fire in her parents' pizzeria, she jokes "The fire walks with me."

"If you ever come to England, you are not allowed to visit our house."

Then the police arrived and, to begin with, they thought perhaps the fire had been started deliberately, for a fraudulent insurance claim. Still in shock from what had happened, Stefania now faced a barrage of questions from the police. Feeling completely alone, she called her parents, but there was no answer. Fortunately, a friend of the family, Leonardo Carraro, was able to come over and stay with her.

The cause was traced to an electrical fault, in a lamp in the dining room. "It started here," says Stefania, pointing to the wall, just behind where I am sitting.

When Stefania did manage to contact her father, he said "You need to sort it out. It's up to you to get this fixed."

"My father has always been very strict with me, somewhat Germanic."

Stefania needed to rebuild the restaurant, to restore it, to how it had been.

"I liked what I did so much, I loved this place. It was part of me. I wanted to recreate what was here before, out of respect for all those who worked here. I feel very close to those who do my job, it's a dedication, a vocation. There is a thread that connects us. If I look into the eyes of someone who does my job, I know what they feel, and they know how I feel. There are some things that cannot be explained, but we share things that others will never know. We see so many people, we see the intimate moments when they eat, when they come alive."

"I like to see joy. I like that people share moments in my place, that I, however briefly, become a part of their lives. I believe this all comes from loneliness, you know, I've always been afraid of being alone, of being forgotten, of being left aside. Perhaps because, since I was born, loneliness was an inevitable part of my life. I need to see people, to have them together with me. I like to create situations in which people are together and know each other, and don't feel alone."

I remember how I was placed next to Jim Rice, another English-speaking lone diner, at lunch the previous day.

Stefania contacted the architect who did the original design, in the 1970s, and he provided the drawings. She called a lawyer, who helped her to find contractors to do the work. She even managed to find the carpenters who did the original woodwork. Once again, Stefania was managing a renovation project, but this time she had more experience. Within six months, the restaurant was almost ready to reopen.

I look up at the ceiling, at the great wooden beams.

"So, those beams are new?" They don't look new.

"No, do you see they are black? That was the fire. It took 12 months for the acrid smell to go away."

The insurance company required time to process the claim, so Stefania needed a loan to reopen the restaurant. Every day she remained closed cost her 2,000 euros. She went to the bank.

I can see tears welling up in Stefania's eyes.

"I will never forget that banker, and what he called me. 'Darling,' he said, 'we can't possibly lend you such a large amount in these circumstances.'"

For this banker, the fact that Belle Parti was a successful business, that the insurance payment would arrive one day, these seemed not to matter. All he saw was an attractive girl in her twenties, on her own, asking to borrow a lot of money.

A tear is running down Stefania's cheek. She has told me about the pistol once held to her head, about feeling lonely as a young girl, about trying to manage a team that didn't respect her, about the fire that destroyed her pride and joy, all with equanimity. But recalling that injustice, from the banker, was one straw too many.

"It's not that the banker hit on me. It's that he treated me like a little blonde girl, and not like a business person."

Stefania went to another bank, but this time she took her father, aware that they might not take her seriously if she were on her own. They lent her the money and, 12 months after the fire, the insurance payment arrived.

Meanwhile, having reopened the restaurant, Stefania was working harder than ever. Then she discovered that she was pregnant. She had become close to a young man called

Tancredi, a customer at the restaurant, before the fire. She liked him very much, although she didn't have much time available for him. They managed to spend a few evenings together, enough for Stefania to now be expecting his child. Her parents didn't even know she was dating.

"I took my father to a bar near here, where we found a quiet corner. I took him by the hand, saying 'there is something I must tell you.'"

Aware that Stefania's father was the strict parent, not the obvious person to show understanding and support, I ask why she didn't tell her mother first.

"I don't know. Perhaps it's because I saw my father as the more difficult parent to deal with. I like to face the biggest problem first, to take away that shadow, and then I can see the light. So, we are sitting in this bar, and I tell him everything, not knowing how he will react."

There is a long pause.

I am tense, uncertain what's coming next.

"He says 'I'm happy for you.'"

Now it's my turn. I feel a tear running down my cheek, perhaps because, as the father of two daughters, I can completely understand the emotions involved.

Stefania continues.

"I could never have given up this child. My father, knowing this, gave me this beautiful response. 'But,' I said to him, 'how can I continue with the restaurant?' 'You make it work,' he said!"

She laughs.

Stefania returned to the restaurant, her stomach growing bigger by the day, and worked there right up to the day the baby was born. She left the restaurant to go to hospital and give birth to her little boy, Tancredi, named after his father.

"The greatest joy of my life."

The very next day, Stefania went back to work, and continued in the restaurant while she raised her son. Most of her earnings went to pay somebody to look after the baby, while she was at work, but at night she and the baby were alone together.

"When you become a mother, something triggers inside you and you need to always have your child with you. So, I slept little and every morning, when I left the house, leaving my child behind, I cried. Then I had to come here to the restaurant and be happy, because my customers, they come here for a good time. A visit to this restaurant is, for them, a memorable day, a celebration. They need me to be cheerful so, every day, I had to transform myself. I had to take breaks from work to go into the office and express milk, using the breast pump. Some days, when the child minder wasn't available, I brought him to the restaurant, and put him in the office, in his pram."

Stefania still lived alone. Her boyfriend fully supported her decision to have the child, but he was away most of the time, travelling with his work.

"He was a boy with big dreams, like me."

As the manager of a formula two motor racing team, Tancredi travelled a lot. He used to work in formula one, and introduced Stefania to famous drivers, including Lewis Hamilton. Stefania and Tancredi had a second son, Cesare Franco, in 2012, and they are still close today.

Something that helped Stefania through this period, when Tancredi was a baby, was having a good team around her at the restaurant. By now, they had grown close, and felt like a family.

"People stay here a long time. I always say that those who

work at Belle Parti, will stay at Belle Parti. Here, you get the chance to see the world without travelling. People come from across the globe. Martin Scorsese for example, he dined here with his family."

After taking on Belle Parti in 2003, Stefania went through several different head chefs, but none lasted more than a few years. However, in 2014, she employed an ambitious young cook called Daniele Doria. Straight after leaving school, Daniele worked for two years in the kitchen of another restaurant in Padua. Then he moved to La Cova, Stefania's old pizzeria. From there, he was recruited to the Belle Parti team as an assistant cook, aged 21. Daniele fitted in perfectly, rising to become head chef, and he still leads the kitchen here today.

"He is honest, hard-working, and a very kind-hearted person, who creates harmony in the kitchen. Together, we realised that we love classical Italian cuisine. We fundamentally believe in simple food, using the best ingredients, cooked perfectly, without unnecessary complications."

Stefania's phone rings. She answers, explaining to the caller that she is still here at the restaurant, but she will be finished soon. I realise that we have been talking for a long time, and that I probably have everything I need, so we should draw to a close. I say this to Stefania, once she finishes her call, and thank her for her time.

Stepping outside, into Via Belle Parti, I feel drained. I always get involved in the stories of the people I interview, but this was especially emotional.

Now on the train back to Venice, I recall with embarrassment my initial speculation that perhaps Stefania came from a wealthy family, and that Belle Parti had been handed to her on a plate. I had no idea of the battles, the setbacks, the unrelenting hard work, everything that she and her parents went through, to get them where they are today.

In one respect, however, my speculation was correct. She did receive a huge gift, or rather several gifts, from her parents: courage, determination and resilience. By what they said, and how they lived, her parents taught Stefania that you must never give up. Whatever life throws at you, don't let it beat you. Work hard, keep faith, and in the end you will triumph.

25 Dynamo

Breakfast over, I am wandering through the sunlit streets of Ravello. It's spring, and the aromas of wisteria and lemon blossom are everywhere. Citrus trees are still covered by protective netting. It's easy to forget that we are 1,000 feet above sea level here.

The streets are clean and attractive, dotted with potted plants and shrubs. However, if you look over a wall, you may see a piece of wasteland, strewn with discarded furniture and rubble. That's Italy.

As I approach the main square, I see a ceramic shop, just opening up for the day. On our honeymoon here, in 2007, I was especially struck by the pots, plates and bowls displayed in these shops. Their strong primary colours – yellows, blues and greens – are rarely seen in northern Europe, as if we are ashamed to be so bold and simple. Jackie reckons that colours like this only work in a mediterranean climate, but I'm not so sure. Seeing them lifts my mood, like a dose of sunshine. Surely, we would benefit from having more of this in the UK?

Although I have already discussed Ravello, in Chapter 4, the memory of these beautiful ceramics has brought me back. I want to speak to the owner of one of these shops, to understand the back story, so I am heading towards what appears to be the most important establishment: Ceramiche d'Arte Pascal. As I approach, I spot a man sitting down, outside the store, gazing at his phone. He looks up to greet me, and I ask if he knows where I can find Pasquale Sorrentino, the owner of the shop.

"That's me," he smiles, "why would you want to talk to him?"

Pasquale stands up and we shake hands. I explain about the

book, and he seems happy to help. Behind the spectacles, Pasquale's eyes are bright and energetic. He talks quickly, with confidence, like a man who knows what he wants and how to get it.

"Why don't you join me for dinner this evening? We can talk then. We can eat at my restaurant, over in Scala."

That sounds perfect to me, so we agree that I will return to his shop at 6.30 this evening.

Now I have a free day ahead, and I decide to visit another town in the area. I return to the main piazza, turn left and walk through the tunnel. On the other side, I arrive at what must be the bus stop with the best view in the world, looking down over the Gulf of Salerno. From there, I catch a bus to the village of Atrani, on the coast near Amalfi.

Alighting from the bus, it's not at all obvious how I get from the road into the village. Then I see a set of steps leading down into the ground. Following these, I can cross underneath the road and reach the shoreline, and from there the village of Atrani. There are no cars here, only narrow streets and steep stairways. I come across the main square, Piazza Umberto I, which is tiny. Now I recall Ivana Mostaccioli telling me about her husband Antonio's first restaurant in this piazza: "little more than a cave".

My plan is to walk over to the neighbouring town of Amalfi, so I leave the piazza heading in that general direction. Nowhere is horizontal, every way is either up, or down, on steep steps. It's impossible to keep a sense of direction, or visualise myself inside a 2D map, because I am moving in a 3D world. I feel like I am in one of those Escher drawings which don't correspond to reality.

Then I notice that many of the houses have flood protection

door barriers. These are commonplace in Venice, but I am surprised to see them here. These houses are located on a steep alleyway, where water should immediately run away, down the steps. Clearly, rainfall here can be so heavy that the water forms pools as it gushes down the alley, and people need to prevent the water pouring in through their doors.

Eventually, I find a way up through the maze of stairways, and along the coast to Amalfi. It's early in the season, the beginning of April, but Amalfi is astonishingly busy, perhaps because it's the central transport hub for the whole Amalfi coast. After wandering through crowds for an hour or so, I pop into a restaurant for lunch, Il Tari. Soon after I sit down, another solitary gentleman arrives and sits at the next table. Inevitably, we start chatting.

He is a retired anaesthetist and he has travelled here, from his home town of Salerno, just to spend the day in Amalfi. The waiter comes over, and he orders a particular bottle of white wine. When offered water, he shakes his head in disgust, as if he never touches the stuff! Over the course of lunch, I watch him drink the whole bottle, with the exception of one sip, which he kindly pours into my glass to give me a taste. It *is* a nice wine. But, to drink all that alcohol with no water?!

Returning to Ravello late in the afternoon, I have time to visit the little cloister at the Church of San Francesco, next door to an art gallery. This is one of my favourite spots in all of Italy, so tranquil and unassuming. I recall my last visit to the cloister, in 2017, when I was captivated by background music, a piece I'd never heard before. The lady in the art gallery gave me the name of the composer, Ludovico Einaudi, who was new to me. Of course, Einaudi has been famous since the 1990s, but I only started listening to him in 2017.

It's 6.20pm, and I arrive at Pasquale's shop early so that I can look around inside. It's much bigger than the other ceramic shops in Ravello, more like a warehouse. The bright colours I love are everywhere, and there are many interesting, quirky designs.

Returning outside, I see Pasquale talking to a young man. As I approach, he introduces me to his son Guido. Then Pasquale explains that, since he has ridden his scooter to the shop today, I will have to get a lift to Scala with his wife, Madalina. Sure enough, about ten minutes later, Madalina arrives and asks me to follow her to the car. Sporting short, brown hair, she is intelligent, attractive and business-like. I learn a lot from Madalina, during the short drive to Scala.

She talks about local history, explaining that, in the Middle Ages, Scala and Ravello formed a single large settlement, a key part of the Amalfi republic. The population then was much greater than it is today. Now, fewer than 2,000 people live in Scala, which is slightly smaller than neighbouring Ravello. Enjoying more spectacular views over the sea, Ravello has proved a greater attraction to tourists, artists and writers, over the years.

As we pass through Scala, I think back to my chat with Ivana Mostaccioli, in Venice 18 months ago. I wonder just where in the village she lived as a little girl, and where her father's bread shop was located.

I ask Madalina where she is from, and am surprised to hear that she is Romanian! She explains that she is Pasquale's second wife, and they have been together for over 20 years. Madalina is taking me to their five-star hotel, located in Scala's oldest building, which used to be a bishop's palace. After completing major renovation works, she and Pasquale opened this hotel, Palazzo Pascal, six years ago.

Entering the hotel, I can see that it has been restored beautifully. I am taken to a corner of the hotel's restaurant, Gli Ulivi, where I sit at a rectangular table laid for eight people. Madalina heads off, to speak to somebody in the kitchen, then Pasquale arrives and sits opposite me. He explains that most of his family will be joining us for dinner. Now I'm wondering how I can get through the interview, asking questions of Pasquale, when there are six other people at the table. This is going to be interesting.

I suggest that we start talking about Pasquale's life now, before the others arrive, and he agrees.

Pasquale's parents lived in Ravello, where his mother's family ran the only delicatessen in town, during and after the Second World War. Pasquale has a sister Carmela, two years older than him. He also had a younger sister, Loredana, who sadly died a few years ago.

As a young boy, he spent a lot of time with his extended family, grandparents, uncles and aunts, who grew olives and tomatoes. Pasquale recalls working in the mountains, collecting chestnuts for 30,000 lire (about 15 euros) per day. They would start at 6am, and work through most of the day, in the strong autumn sunshine.

When Pasquale was seven years old, because there wasn't enough work in Ravello, his immediate family moved to Brescia, where his parents opened a restaurant. In the late 1960s there was an economic boom in the north of Italy, and growing demand for restaurants.

"My father would make 700 or 800 pizzas in one evening," he says.

Because Pasquale spoke the Neapolitan dialect, and not

Italian, he had to repeat his first year at elementary school in Brescia.

After five years in Brescia, Pasquale's mother was unwell so they returned to Ravello. However, his father saw how he could still benefit from the vibrant economy of the north. He bought a refrigerated truck, and started a food haulage business. Each month, he would do two trips, from Campania to the north of Italy, and back. He might take fish from Naples to the north, then return south with nets, from Lake Maggiore, to protect the lemon trees. The drive each way took 13 hours, and Pasquale sometimes went with him.

From the age of 14, Pasquale attended the accountancy school in Amalfi. He wasn't interested in the classics or science.

"Accountancy school was very helpful for me. It means you don't need a certificate, if you want to open a shop, for example. My sister and I both benefitted from that."

At school, Pasquale loved sport, especially tennis and football. He played football for a local club, Inter Costiera, even becoming captain of the team.

"There were other players better than me, but I succeeded because I worked hard. My right foot was sweeter than many in Italy's top league, but only my right foot!" he smiles. "We won the Campania regionals, against Naples, Avellino, Benevento, Salerno – beautiful."

He also went running in the hills.

"I know these mountains like the back of my hand."

At this point, we are interrupted by two new arrivals at the dinner table, introduced by Pasquale as his sons Luca and Marco.

Once they are seated, we continue with Pasquale's story. After finishing school, he wanted to go to ISEF, an institute for higher education in physical training. However, places were limited and he didn't score well enough in the necessary examinations. Pasquale spent three months backpacking around Europe, by train, with another lad. They visited Germany, Denmark, Belgium, England and finally Scotland, where they stayed with friends.

"That was a lovely time," he recalls.

After their trip, Pasquale worked in London for three months.

Meanwhile, his father had purchased a shop near the main piazza of Ravello. The previous owners had struggled to make a living, because the tourist season in those days, the early 1980s, was very short. Like Pasquale's parents in the 1960s, they had decided to move to the north of Italy, and open a restaurant.

When Pasquale came home from London, he worked in his father's shop for six months.

"What did you sell in this shop?"

"It was a bazaar, we sold lots of things. Because tourists were only around for three months in the year, we had to sell things that local people wanted, like shoes."

Then, his parents told him to go and work out what he wanted to do with his life!

"I was especially interested in ceramics, to me they were beautiful. So, I went to Deruta in Umbria, a ceramic centre, to see and to learn. In those days, there were 350 registered artisans there. That's where I placed my first order, with a company in Deruta. I also remember the very first plate I bought, which cost 350,000 lire. I could have bought a car for 350,000 lire! My father gave me the freedom to do this, and I didn't know whether I had made a huge mistake. When we sold that plate in our shop, one week later, for 800,000 lire, I was jumping for joy. I'd done something that nobody else would have done because, at that time, Ravello was seen only as a place for cheap souvenirs."

"I have always sought to go further, to find things that please people, modern designs for modern houses."

"Look at this panel," he says, pointing to the wall to my right. "I bought this over 30 years ago, in Umbria. It's by a very good artist, Claudia Ciotti, who does wonderful things, like Madonnas and Byzantine designs. I liked this so much, I had to buy it, although I had no idea where to put it. It has been in my house all those years, and now we have it here."

Pasquale met a girl, studying at the Salerno ceramic art institute, who had a talent for painting ceramics, and she became Pasquale's first wife in 1981. He continued to travel around the country, seeking pieces that he liked, to sell in the shop in Ravello.

Five or six years after buying the shop, the family purchased the building itself. They also broadened the business, opening a separate shoe shop and also a restaurant. Pasquale and his sister, however, continued to focus on ceramics. That was always their passion.

As their parents got older, he and Carmela took over the running of the shop. Both parents passed away in their sixties, their mother in 1995 and their father in 1998.

During the 1990s, the shop stopped selling a range of souvenirs and focused solely on ceramics. It became the first shop in Ravello to specialise in this way.

As the years passed, the tourist season became longer and longer. During the mid-1990s, European economies were doing well and business was good. However, in the years after 1999, Pasquale noticed that people had less money to spend. He changed his business model. For each expensive design, he purchased only one piece, for display. If somebody wanted to buy it, then they had to wait until Pasquale could have another piece made for them. This meant he was less exposed financially, when customer tastes changed, and he kept his prices low.

"I made my fortune this way, because my investment was low, and I provided more choice, increasing the chance of a sale. Now, everyone who comes to the store says 'Oh my goodness!' A Florentine gentleman today, he said 'This is not a shop, it's a museum.'"

Pasquale talks about the importance of understanding how the market evolves, how tastes change.

"You must follow the change in tastes, or you will be lost. Even an artist must understand the customer. Today, Americans want beautiful homes, to have beautiful things to decorate those homes. It's not easy, but we must provide pieces they want to buy."

In 2001, they decided that the restaurant was too much work, and closed it. The restaurant building was used to open a second, bigger ceramic shop, in addition to the one near the piazza. A few years later, Pasquale and Carmela decided to split the ceramic business. She continues to manage the shop near the piazza, and he manages the shop he has today. They normally use different suppliers, different artisans, and therefore sell different products.

"We are in competition!" says Pasquale, laughing.

Madalina and Guido arrive. It's clear that Pasquale has a complicated family, so I ask about his children. He explains that his sons Luigi, not here today, and Guido are from his first marriage. Three other sons, Stefano, also not here today, Marco and Luca are from his second marriage. Then there is Madalina's son, Anthony, from her first marriage. Finally, they have also adopted a boy from Vietnam, son number seven.

I ask about the future of the business, and whether his family will continue with it.

"I hope so. But whatever they choose to do, that is the right thing for them."

"How many people do you employ in the ceramic business?"

"The work is highly seasonal. I have four or five permanent staff, including my son Luigi. In addition, I'd say there are about 50 artisans that supply our products."

I ask if all these artisans are local, based in Campania. Pasquale explains that the local artisans tend to be somewhat cheaper, and quicker. They provide the simpler pieces, the souvenirs. However, he also sources products from Umbria and Tuscany, where artists expect more money, and the objects are much more expensive.

"In the winter, I travel a lot, seeking new pieces, and new producers. In October and November, that's a busy time for shipments, especially to the USA. Nowadays we do 4,000 shipments each year. In my first year we did only 100."

"Where do most of your customers come from?"

"Right now, I'd say 80% are Americans, 10% Canadians and Australians, only 5% Europeans."

He goes on to explain that houses in Europe are smaller, and it feels like they are already full. Two or three decades ago, it was different and many of Pasquale's customers were European.

"Also, I'd say about 70% of our orders are for customised pieces, in response to a specific request."

Pasquale then starts talking about the artisans who create the products he sells, and how important it is to keep the old skills alive.

"Making ceramics is hard. It looks easy, but it's hard. It requires years of experience. And if the money isn't there, to keep it going, then they will stop, and the knowledge will be lost."

He tells me what happened when he returned to the shop for the first time, after it had been closed for six months because of Covid.

"When I opened the door, and went in, I started crying. I hadn't seen them for six months, and when you see them every day you take them for granted. But seeing these creations for the first time, after six months, I was very emotional. They are so beautiful."

His son Guido concurs.

"When I go away, for a vacation, and then come back, I see them with fresh eyes."

I turn to Pasquale. "Do you ever take a holiday?"

"Sometimes, in the winter, we spend a week at Sharm El-Sheikh. I completely switch off, and relax. But if I spent two weeks there, I would die! I like to go where I can travel around, to find art, to see and to touch."

"So, you won't retire?"

"No! I could never retire. I would like to have less stress, and more time to travel, to seek beautiful and interesting works."

There is now a discussion about whether anybody else is likely to arrive, and the conclusion is that we should not wait any longer, and should start dinner. Then we all talk about what we are going to eat, and drink. Soon, the meal begins.

While tucking into a delicious pasta with lemon sauce, I ask Pasquale where he found his chef.

"Jesus sent him to me. He's a miracle. He's young, and he loves his work."

"And how is the hotel doing?"

"Most tourists want to be by the sea. Here, we serve a different type of client, people who enjoy walking in the mountains, who want to eat and drink well, to relax. We plan to add a lovely spa, soon. This is the perfect place for such people."

The conversation around the table broadens, and we pass a pleasant evening together. At the end of the meal, Guido offers me a lift back to Ravello. Pasquale accompanies us outside, to Guido's car, and as we are parting, he says "You must return to Ravello, and stay with us next time."

"Thank you, Pasquale! That's very kind of you."

"Friends are worth much more than money."

Back in Ravello, I look up Palazzo Pascal on the internet. It's rated highly in reviews from guests, which doesn't surprise me. Pasquale knows how to run a business, and he knows how to please his customers.

I reflect how, in each chapter of this book, I only scratch the surface of somebody's story. It's simply not possible, in a few pages of text, to convey the richness and complexity of a person's life. This must be especially true for Pasquale. He has an insatiable curiosity, a passion for exploring and learning, and bundles of energy. There will be many interesting stories, from his 40 years in business, that are missing from these pages.

26 I left my heart in Sorrento

This morning, I am on my way to Sorrento, for the first time. I'm drawn by Sorrento's reputation, as a romantic resort with gorgeous views across the Bay of Naples.

However, before I get there, I am meeting Fabio and his family for Sunday lunch. I take a bus from Ravello to Amalfi, then another towards Sorrento, but I get off this bus near a village, up in the hills of the Sorrento peninsula. There, I have a drink in a nice, modern café, then Fabio arrives in his car to collect me.

As I get in the back of the car, I am introduced to Fabio's wife, Teresa, two charming young daughters, and the family dog, a young black poodle. Teresa encourages the girls to ask me questions in English, which they are learning at school. Aged nine and eleven, they are both surprisingly good at my language, and at thinking up interesting questions. I ask them about the dog which I know, from online conversations with Fabio, is a recent arrival.

I have a theory that whenever a family acquires a dog, but one of the family members didn't want that dog, then the person who didn't want it is also the person who ends up taking it for walks. Sure enough, Fabio was outvoted when they were discussing whether to get a dog, and he is the one who takes it for walks.

As we get close to our restaurant, on the coast at Marina del Cantone, we hit a long queue of traffic going down the hill to the bay. Approaching the shoreline, we see each car ahead of us stop, then the driver speaks to a policeman, then the car turns around and drives back up the hill. When it's our turn, we are told that there are no parking spaces available by the bay, so we should park at the top of the hill. Fabio drops the rest of us off, before heading off to find somewhere to park.

Teresa leads us towards the restaurant and suddenly, as we get close, Fabio appears on foot. He explains that he ignored the policeman's advice, drove into one of the car parks and immediately found the only free space available.

"This normally happens to me Richard. I can always find somewhere to park. The only time I don't is when I am with somebody who has negative thoughts, and tells me that I will never find a space."

It's this approach to life that makes Fabio such good company. He always expects good things to happen and, even when they don't, it doesn't bother him. Always calm, always cheerful, how I envy him!

We walk into the restaurant and it is absolutely packed, with every seat occupied and lots of people standing waiting. Delayed by the queue of traffic, we are late for our booking and, understandably, they have given our table to somebody else. Looking around, I notice that the people standing and waiting are in small groups, randomly scattered around the restaurant. There is no queue, and no evidence that the staff have a list of names for those waiting. The waiters are too busy dashing back and forth, carrying plates and looking harassed.

At this point, Teresa starts lobbying the waiters, as they scurry past. Fabio leans over and explains to me that Teresa is much better than him, when it comes to getting service from shops and restaurants. After about 15 minutes, a table becomes free and, as if by magic, we are the ones called over to sit at it. I look at my watch. In theory, the restaurant closes in 45 minutes, but it is still packed, with plenty of people waiting to sit down. I cannot imagine how it will close in 45 minutes.

Anyway, we have an enjoyable meal. As we are leaving, we hear loud singing and look over to the restaurant next door. Everybody in that restaurant is singing the same song, in unison.

"This is what we do, in Naples," explains Fabio.

That sums up the whole experience, for me.

On their way home, they go out of their way to drop me in Sorrento, for which I am very grateful.

Straight after checking in to my guest house, I head out to explore the town. It's early evening, and the passeggiata is already underway on leafy Corso Italia. People are strolling with their ice creams, looking in shop windows, chatting to friends, and enjoying the aroma of orange blossom. I head towards the sea, wanting to see the view across the bay to Naples. As I get there, I realise that the sea is actually 50 metres below the town. Volcanic, tufa cliffs drop straight down to a narrow shelf of land on the shoreline.

Although a famous seaside resort, Sorrento has little in the way of beaches. To make up for this, the concrete piers and docks are covered with regimented rows of sunbeds. As usual in Italy, space by the sea is managed to extract maximum value.

I return to wandering around the town, and come across several shops specialising in the craft of inlaid wood mosaics, called *intarsia*. This is the chief artistic tradition of Sorrento, stretching back over 500 years. Skilled practitioners can produce astonishing works, that take your breath away. It's hard to believe they are constructed solely from pieces of stained wood.

Back on Corso Italia, I pop into an intarsia shop that I know has been there a long time. It's called La Botteguccia, which simply means the small bottega, i.e. the small shop. High up, on the wall inside, are two amazing intarsia pictures. One shows an elderly lady, sat at a table, with an elderly gentleman leaning over and touching her cheek. The detail, including the lines on their faces, and how his jacket hangs in folds, is spectacular. There's a poignancy that you rarely see, even in paintings. The second picture shows a portly monk, hiding behind a huge barrel in a cellar, taking a cheeky swig of wine from a bottle, while an amused young boy looks on from behind a wall. Again, small features are astonishing: the monk's toes poking out from his sandals, a sieve hanging from the wall, where every wire is visible.

I ask a lady in the shop about these works. She explains that they were made by an exceptionally experienced craftsman, in his final years, but he is no more.

"There might not be anybody left nowadays, who is that good. Those pieces are for sale, they have been for a long time. As you can see, nobody has bought them. We're happy to keep them here forever, because they are so beautiful."

I notice that the price tag is 600 euros, much less than people pay for a really good painting.

I tell this lady about my book, and ask if I could talk to one of the shop's owners, to understand their story. She introduces herself as Anna, the daughter of one of three sisters, all involved in the shop. She suggests that I return tomorrow, after lunch, when her mother Jasmine will be there. Jasmine has worked in the business for many years, and she will be able to tell me all about it.

It's now the following day and I am waiting, outside La Botteguccia, for the shop to reopen after lunch. In theory, this happens at 2.30pm, but it's now 2.40pm. A lady in a grey jacket, with light brown hair and freckles, arrives with a key to open the door. I introduce myself, and she tells me her name is

Jasmine Scala. She apologises for being late, and lets us both into the shop.

I am invited to sit down, although Jasmine is happy to stand. After my explaining why I'd like to talk to her, we settle into discussing the history of the business.

She explains that she is the oldest of three sisters: Jasmine, Maria and Giuseppina.

"This is my father," she says, showing me a photograph. "He started producing inlaid woodwork when he was 20 years old, working in a bottega. He and his three brothers, they all worked there."

I am told that Jasmine's mother cleaned houses for a living.

"Times were difficult, just after the war. There was no money. When I was 14 years old, I left art school and went to work in a shop selling bait, here in Corso Italia. I remember they paid me 7,000 lire per month, which I took home. We were grateful for that money. There was much hunger in those days."

"Is the shop still here?"

"Yes, but now they sell perfume."

I am amused by that transformation, from selling something that smells awful to selling something that smells nice.

"Can I ask, how old are you now?"

"I am 83 years old."

I'm astonished. Jasmine's brown hair is soft and shiny, without a trace of grey. I cannot see any wrinkles in her face.

"You look amazing!"

"I've had my problems," she says. "Three years ago, I had breast cancer. Now I have to go for regular checks."

I ask Jasmine how she came to be working in a shop selling inlaid wood. She explains that in 1961, when she was 20 years old, she and her two sisters opened their own intarsia shop, right above where we are now. Although the sisters had learnt the craft from their father, most of the pieces they sold were made by other local artisans. Initially, their main product was gaming tables, for roulette.

One day, an American lady came into the shop, with her husband and young son. Jasmine, who spoke English, greeted them with "Hello, my name is Jasmine, how are you?" Jasmine thought she recognised the lady, from somewhere else, but it turned out that they had never met. This American family just happened to be on holiday, in Sorrento.

They got chatting, and the visitors showed a real interest in intarsia. Jasmine took them to a workshop, and showed them how inlaid wood is made. As it happened, this lady worked for NATO. That meeting, in the early days of the business, established a connection that generated decades of income for La Botteguccia. The U.S. Navy's sixth fleet, based in Naples, has regularly bought items from the shop, over the last 60 years. Jasmine used to travel to Naples, to sell directly to personnel at the base. They are still important customers. Just yesterday, somebody came to collect a significant order for the sixth fleet.

"Have you worked here continuously since 1961?"

"I worked here until I got married, to Vincenzo, when I was 24 years old. We had two children, Anna, who you have met, and Liberato. My son Liberato, he is a dentist. This is why I have such good teeth," she jokes.

I laugh, but it's true. Her teeth are perfect.

I assume that, once the children were old enough, Jasmine returned to working at La Botteguccia. She starts talking about changes that happened in the 1980s.

"The building containing the shop was badly damaged in an earthquake. A new shop was built, to replace it, and this is the shop we have today. Obviously, we rent these premises."

"Do you live near here?"

"Yes, fairly close. I have an apartment. Maybe I should tell you about Giovanni."

"Who is Giovanni?"

"When we were both young, Giovanni and I were good friends. I guess you would say that he was my suitor, but we didn't become involved romantically. Then, when he was 20, he emigrated to America, where he made his living as a hairdresser. He moved to New Jersey."

I'm intrigued. What has this got to do with where Jasmine lives now?

"Did you keep in touch?"

"No. As you know, I married Vincenzo in 1961, and we had two children. Many years later, Vincenzo left me."

Jasmine then explains that Giovanni visited Sorrento every year and, on one of these trips, he heard that Jasmine's husband had left her. When he returned to New Jersey, he started telephoning her to ask how she was. He called her three times per day, every day! Then he moved back to Sorrento permanently, and bought an apartment.

"He asked me if I would like to marry him. I wasn't really sure, but he was such a nice man. So, I said 'yes.'"

Jasmine moved in with Giovanni, and they married in 2002.

"He was a lovely person," said Jasmine. "His family, from his first marriage, is still in New Jersey, and he has grandchildren in Chicago."

Sadly, in 2014, Giovanni died. Jasmine still lives in the apartment they had together.

Without thinking, I glance up at the lovely intarsia picture on the wall, of an elderly gentleman leaning over a table, touching the cheek of an elderly lady. Giovanni carried a candle for Jasmine, for 40 years. Then, when he heard she was on her own, he returned to Sorrento to look after her.

I tell Jasmine how much I admire the picture on the wall, with the elderly gentleman leaning over a table.

She agrees that it is beautiful, but she looks sad, explaining that she fears it is a dying art form.

"Young people aren't interested in learning the craft. They say it is too much work, for too little money."

Jasmine explains the various stages required to create intarsia, including drawing and colouring the design, staining wooden veneers to match, and then cutting each piece of veneer with a jig saw. She shows me the incredibly fine wire used to cut these pieces, which are then glued to the base, pressed and varnished. It's clearly very time consuming, and it takes many years to become an expert.

She picks up a small, glossy wooden box, decorated with an abstract pattern.

"Even such a little piece requires days of work. It was made by this boy, Antonio. I call him a boy, but he isn't."

"How old is he?"

"He's about 70. He's been working for us for 43 years."

"Does he sell all his work through you?"

"No. Through us, and another shop. He makes a lot of stuff. We can't take all of it. It's just him and his wife, they have no children. He starts at 4am, and works all day."

Jasmine explains that, in total, they have five or six artisans working to provide all the stock they sell.

In my mind, I visualise all the inlaid wood I have seen in the shops across Sorrento. The totality is huge. It doesn't look like a dying industry, but perhaps the remaining practitioners are all old, as Jasmine seems to think.

I ask, and Jasmine confirms that virtually all their business comes from tourists, or the sixth fleet. In the winter they sell very little.

"My daughter Anna and my sister Maria are now the owners. I have retired. I have an American pension, from my second husband. I still come here to the shop, because I cannot stay home alone every day."

Potential customers come into the shop, so Jasmine goes over to talk to them. I linger for a few minutes, examining the huge variety of inlaid wood pieces, all quite beautiful. When I get the opportunity, I thank Jasmine for her time and leave.

After two minutes strolling down Corso Italia, I come to the cathedral and pop in to have a look. Even here, there is intarsia: images of biblical scenes on the cathedral doors. This artistic tradition runs deep, in the veins of the city. Surely it will endure.

27 All you need is love

A few years ago – let's not be precise – Jackie wanted to celebrate her 60th birthday by having a family gathering, at a villa in Italy. I searched online, and came across no end of farmhouses in Tuscany, converted to holiday accommodation through the addition of a swimming pool, air conditioning and ensuite bathrooms. They were lovely but, somehow, they didn't feel special.

One day, an image jumped out of the screen and grabbed my attention. This holiday villa looked more like a palace, or a stately home, rising behind a manicured parterre garden. Reading the details, it had the right number of bedrooms and lay in the countryside just 20 minutes from Verona airport. Jackie agreed that this was the place, so I telephoned the owner, Marina Cicogna, and booked Villa La Zambonina for the week of her birthday.

We had a lovely time there, with our five daughters, Jackie's sister and their six partners, although we didn't meet the owner, who was in Rome. For my 60th birthday, a couple of years later, we went back and this time Marina was there, staying in her own rooms next door. I always wondered how she came to own such an amazing villa, but never felt able to ask.

When I started doing the research for this book, it didn't occur to me to include Villa La Zambonina. Why, I don't know. But when Jackie mentioned it, in the context of her 70th birthday, I realised that I should ask Marina whether I could include her story. Fortunately, she said yes. Now I am on my way to her apartment, in the suburbs of Rome, so that we can talk over lunch.

I am let into the apartment by Marina's manservant, a

reminder that she and I come from very different worlds. But there is nothing remote or stuffy about Marina, who is definitely a people person. She greets me with a huge smile, and I feel at home immediately. We sit down in the lounge, where the whole of one wall is covered by a beautiful old bookcase.

Marina's cute little dog Clemmy, whom I first met at Villa La Zambonina, is keen to renew my acquaintance. She jumps up repeatedly and, although Marina and I have been conversing in English, Marina switches to Italian to tell the dog to get down.

I am offered a coffee, but ask for water, which the manservant brings straight away. Then I begin with my usual first question.

"Tell me about your parents."

"My parents? I *love* my parents. They were a fantastic couple. My mother, Maria, was very beautiful. She was the youngest of four, in a wealthy family."

"How did the family become wealthy?"

"They were industrialists. My grandfather had a large, successful business. They were involved in the trade of agricultural machinery with the United States, amongst other things."

"Where were your mother and her siblings brought up?"

"In Verona, during the winter. They had a house in Verona, but they came to Zambonina in the summer, and they also went to Lake Garda where they had another house. My grandmother liked the countryside, and she was interested in agriculture, and the growing of rice. My grandfather bought Zambonina, the villa and the land, soon after my mother was born in the 1920s, to commemorate her birth."

Villa La Zambonina was the centrepiece of a substantial rice farm. I ask Marina about the history of the villa.

"The original, central part of the building was a farmhouse, acquired in 1528 by the Giusti family, wealthy nobles from Verona. The wings were added in the early 1700s, and it has been in its present form since 1709. After the Giusti family, ownership of the villa changed several times, before my grandfather bought it."

"Do you know where the name comes from?"

"No, that's a mystery. It has been referred to in documents since at least 1396, but we don't know its origin."

"Did your family only use the villa as a summer retreat?"

"Mostly. However, during the war, the men continued working, but the women in the family lived at Zambonina. They had to share the villa with the German army, who used it as a HQ for one of their generals. German officers were considerate and respectful, keeping the place clean. Later, when the Germans fled, the Americans arrived and they also based officers at the villa. The Americans were noisier, but much more friendly."

As the youngest of four children, Marina's mother was given more leeway by her parents, and grew up to be somewhat capricious. She went through a series of boyfriends, breaking off engagements if they weren't quite right, and she was still single when she entered her thirties. Then, one day, she met her soulmate.

Attending a dinner party, Maria was introduced to an aristocrat called Gianpaolo Cicogna, from one of the noble patrician families of the Venetian republic. He was handsome, elegant and fascinating, with lots of stories to tell. Maria fell in love immediately.

Marina tells me about the Cicogna family.

"The important thing, is that we have a Doge in our family," she laughs. "Just as in Rome, it's important to have a pope in your family, in Venice you must have a Doge. Pasquale Cicogna was the Doge who built the Rialto bridge."

Gianpaolo's father was a research chemist who died tragically, from a disease he picked up in Africa, when Gianpaolo was just one year old. His widowed mother had a degree in pharmacy. She took the open *concorso* examination for public appointments, and won a pharmacy position in Vicenza. She moved to Vicenza, with her young boy and his nanny, to begin her career as a pharmacist.

Gianpaolo grew up in Vicenza, with aspirations to become a doctor. When the war arrived, being opposed to Mussolini's regime, he joined the partisans fighting in the mountains. He survived those dangerous times and resumed his studies after the war. However, soon after the war finished, Gianpaolo's mother died. He decided not to complete his training to become a medical doctor, but instead to take advantage of the qualifications he already had, and take just one more examination to become a pharmacist. After passing that test, he was able to take over his mother's pharmacy in Vicenza.

Gianpaolo was close friends with a family connected to Maria's sister, which is how he came to be at the fateful dinner party where they first met. They became a couple, and married in 1953 after a brief courtship. Gianpaolo retained some involvement in the pharmacy, so they decided to live in Vicenza.

The couple had three children: Alessandra, the oldest, then Marina and finally Alvise, one year younger than Marina. The tradition in Maria's family was to bring children up with German-speaking nannies. As business people in the north of Italy, they felt it was important to speak German.

"It's not an easy language, and it's much easier to learn German when you are young," explains Marina.

At home, the family mostly spoke German. Maria and Gianpaolo followed this tradition, and employed German-speaking nannies for their children.

Summers were spent in the family's houses, at Zambonina and Lake Garda. Marina describes an amusing incident from one holiday, when her parents and their children were at the house by Lake Garda.

"My grandmother was very particular, and she wanted the house to be locked up and secure when she went to bed. However, one evening, my father wanted to go to the dance in the local village. My parents had to sneak out, and then climb over the gate and sneak back into the house when they returned. This was a couple in their thirties, with three children!"

The children went to state schools in Vicenza. Alessandra did very well academically, unlike Marina who was less interested in schoolwork. Aged 14, Marina went to a scientific liceo, but she was still not doing well in exams. Her parents decided that, as a somewhat rebellious teenager, Marina might benefit from being sent to boarding school. From the age of 16, she spent two years at a boarding school near Asolo, and was made to sit extra exams at the end of her second year.

With Marina still not getting the grades her parents hoped for, they decided to give her one last opportunity. Gianpaolo had a French business partner in the United States, where they were trying to promote electric wheelchairs. Her father told Marina that she should have one final year of schooling, in the USA, where she would stay with the family of this business partner, in Great Neck near New York city. If she didn't get the grades, then she should expect to go to work on the rice farm, at

Zambonina!

Marina arrived in Great Neck speaking hardly any English, but determined to make the most of the situation. However, the family she was staying with was not at all like her own family. Relationships were fraught, there was always tension, always conflict. In her own family, people got on, they quite liked each other! Life was also difficult at school because, being older than all the other students, she had no friends. Inevitably, given all these difficulties, Marina was homesick.

"This was probably the most difficult year of my life."

Despite everything, she excelled at school and achieved good grades.

"Everything they were teaching, I had already studied before in Italy, so it was easy for me."

Her father was delighted: "You've found your place! Please stay there, and apply to a university in America."

Marina studied business administration at the American University in Washington D.C., sharing a house with Italian friends. She enjoyed the USA very much. The process of applying to universities, of managing her own life in a completely different country, developed Marina's confidence and independence.

Because of Marina's success, Gianpaolo decided to send her brother Alvise to the USA. He studied finance at the same university as Marina, living in the same house as her for one year. Marina finished her four-year degree in three years, making up for having repeated her final year of school. She returned to Italy, and Alvise stayed on after completing his degree, to take a master's.

Back in Italy, Marina did a few temporary jobs, including one as interpreter at the theatre in Verona. Meanwhile, she was sending applications for permanent business administration roles. In response to one of these, a recruiter invited her to a meeting in Rome. He told her that she couldn't possibly do the role she had applied for, because it was in an all-male agricultural environment. However, her CV was interesting, and he put her forward for a public relations role with fashion designer Valentino. Marina was interviewed, and offered the job in Rome.

She started as the most junior person in Valentino's press office. At that time, Valentino was the world's number one design brand, so there was great demand from the press for pictures and text. Marina worked very hard, often at weekends, for little money.

"It was frenetic. There was drama, tears, laughter, joy, everything. So much energy, from many unique people working together. It was a great learning experience for me. They were four very important years."

When Marina moved to Rome, she lived in an apartment owned by her family. This was bigger than she needed, so she rented some rooms out to American students, to get extra income. After four years, Marina realised that she couldn't progress any further at Valentino, she was no longer developing. She resigned, with the intention of finding another job.

"Of course, that was a mistake. I should have looked for another job while I was still working, not resigned first. My parents, never having been employees, didn't know to give me this advice. Now, I tell my daughter that she should look for another job while she still has a job. Having a job makes you more interesting to a potential employer."

Marina stayed in Rome initially, then returned to the north to seek work. Eventually, she found another public relations role with Golden Lady, a major European ladies stockings business, headquartered at Castiglione delle Stiviere in Lombardy. Golden Lady was founded in 1966, by entrepreneur Nerino Grassi and his wife Erminia. Marina enjoyed working for Nerino and Erminia, who treated her well. She led the press office there and was viewed as their PR expert. This role was calmer and less stressful than the position at Valentino.

During this period, Marina lived at Zambonina, in a few rooms that she kept heated in the winter. She commuted to the Golden Lady office, a 50-minute drive each way.

After four years, she left Golden Lady, to try a completely new venture. Several of Marina's friends had shops, in Rome, Milan and Venice, under franchise from the French children's clothing business, Jacady. Together with a partner, Marina opened her own Jacady shop in Verona. Twice each year, she and her friends travelled to Paris together, to buy their collection for the next season, which was great fun. The shop did well but it involved very long hours. Marina and her partner, together with one employee, covered all the opening hours between them.

"By then, I was in my mid-thirties. I met a man, Massimo, at a party. We became friends, and then we became a couple, and then we got engaged. I had never considered marriage before, perhaps because I was looking for the perfect man, I wanted a marriage like my parents' marriage. Massimo is a psychiatrist. He is very open minded, very relaxed about everything. He never judges. He is the only man I could marry."

They married in 1993, and moved into Massimo's apartment in Rome. This is where we are sitting today. Marina's plan was to split her life between Verona, where she still had the shop, and Rome. She would spend one week working in Verona, then the next week in Rome whilst her partner looked after the shop. However, Marina became pregnant! She realised that this split life simply wasn't going to work. A year or so after her daughter Matilde was born, she and her partner sold the business, and Marina moved completely to Rome.

She wished to continue the tradition, from her mother's family, of employing a German-speaking nanny. To recruit this nanny, Marina compiled a shortlist of Austrian candidates and travelled to Innsbruck, to interview them. She also insisted on meeting their mothers.

"Meeting the mother enabled me to understand their family background, where the girl came from."

"I imagine the mothers would also want to meet you."

"Yes, this is what I think. Sometimes, a girl would tell me that their mother was unable to come. For me, that ruled them out."

With her life now based in Rome, and a nanny in place, Marina started looking for work. In November 1999, when Matilde started at kindergarten, Marina found a position at Christie's, the auction house. She was appointed Operations Manager, with a team of five working directly for her: three permanent staff and two interns. Marina's team was responsible for preparing the catalogue before an auction, ensuring clients had the right documentation, doing background checks and running a bid office to enable each auction. The work was frenetic. During an auctions period, it was common for her and her team to work solidly for two months, every single day, with no time off. At that time, Rome was Christie's headquarters in Italy, employing around 70 people. Almost every operational problem would land on Marina's desk.

Christie's had many departments, including jewellery, silver, art and furniture. Each department had interns, who would rotate through the bid office and spend just a few months there. These interns had to be useful and contribute to the operation. Because Marina's bid office relied so much on the interns, she had overall responsibility for recruiting them. Marina's experience from Valentino, and from recruiting her own nanny, helped her to become a good judge of people, to recruit effectively.

Marina struggled in the early days, because one of the department heads was always in conflict with her. Why, she does not know, but Giovanni seemed unable to trust her, and he was always finding fault. She was determined to win him over. Her experience at Valentino, where there were many difficult personalities, had taught her that relationships can be improved provided you work at them. She knew how to keep quiet and learn from each encounter, and not to react and inflame the situation.

Marina and Giovanni both reported to the same manager, based in Geneva. With this boss being so distant, Giovanni acted as if he were Marina's local manager, although officially he wasn't. The manager in Geneva became aware of this interpersonal conflict, in the Rome office. Marina explains what happened.

"Our manager visited one day, and called me and Giovanni into his office. He said 'Listen. I know that you two aren't getting on, but I don't want to know any of the details. Go and have a drink together, or a meal, whatever you want. Talk to each other and be open about what you are thinking. Just make sure that you clear this up, because I'm fed up . . . with you, and with you!'"

Marina and Giovanni went to have a coffee in Piazza Navona, close to the office. They had a long talk, and cleared the air. From that day onwards, they worked together as if they were the best of friends.

"For instance, after that day, if somebody went to him saying 'Marina says we should do this . . . ', he would reply 'Oh, if Marina said that, then that's fine. No problem.' Everything changed between us. He would trust me, I would trust him, it was amazing."

Marina goes on to tell me about a particular incident that she will never forget. Many of the bidders join the auction by telephone, so Christie's had an enormous telephone bill. Marina found a supplier who installed a new system, that greatly reduced their telephone bills. All their lines were switched over to go through this new provider. Several months later, part way through an important auction, all the telephone lines suddenly went dead. 40 bidders, from all around the world, were cut off from the auction. Giovanni, who was the auctioneer, looked over at Marina in horror and said "Now what?"

Marina remembered that, when the system was installed, the engineer had explained to her that she could switch back to the old telephone system at any time, just by unplugging a particular cable. She ran to the closet, unplugged that cable, and then ran back to the auction room. All the lines came back, and the operatives were able to reconnect with their bidders.

"At the end of the auction, Giovanni said 'You saved my life!' It was his sale, his department."

The years passed, and Marina's parents were getting older. Then, in 2011 Marina's mother died, and her father died in 2012. As so often, for a close married couple, once one of them passes on the other follows soon afterwards. Marina and her brother inherited the Zambonina estate. For simplicity, they kept it all together initially, owned jointly. Later, in 2014, they decided to divide the property.

Alvise suggested they adopt the method used, when they were children, to divide a piece of cake. Marina was to make the cut, then Alvise would choose which piece to take. Marina chose to put the villa, plus one third of the land, into one piece, with two thirds of the land as the other piece. Then Alvise chose to take the piece with two thirds of the land. They continued to run the estate as a single farm, managed by Alvise, because that was more efficient. Marina focused on the villa.

"I have always loved Villa La Zambonina. It's been such an important part of my life. As I walk through it, the walls speak to me. I treasure even the sad memories."

She describes how, when her mother was still alive, Marina received a phone call in Rome. She was told that the farm manager at Zambonina, Carlo, had just died from a stroke, whilst riding his bicycle.

"Immediately, I got in the car and drove for five hours, to the villa. I remember seeing all the men from the village, who knew Carlo, standing in a line by his home at Zambonina. They held their caps in their hands, with heads bowed, as a sign of respect for Carlo, and for the family. Everybody was in shock."

When Marina's mother died, they arranged for her body to lie in the villa for a while. She too had loved Zambonina.

Even I, an occasional visitor, understand how this can happen. Zambonina has an extraordinary beauty, it mesmerises and bewitches in a way few places can. To be brought up there, as a child, and then to be responsible for the place, that must create a bond almost impossible to break.

I have no evidence for this, but I suspect Alvise wanted to

ensure that Marina ended up with her beloved villa, when he proposed that mechanism for splitting the estate.

When Marina took responsibility for her inheritance, it was important that she be recognised by the government as an agricultural entrepreneur: an Imprenditore Agricolo Professionale (IAP). Obtaining IAP certification offers numerous advantages, including tax breaks. To qualify as an IAP, she had to pass an examination, and at least 51% of Marina's income had to come from her agricultural activities.

In the years leading up to 2014, there had been big changes at Christie's. By this time, Marina had risen to become a director. Their HQ in Italy was moved to Milan, where Marina worked for a brief period, and the Rome office became much smaller. In Rome, they only handled modern art and jewellery. Considering all these changes, and the IAP requirement that 51% of her income come from agricultural activities, she told Christie's that she could no longer continue in her role as a director.

"I told them that I could help them out, here and there, but I couldn't continue full time as a director of the company. I was responsible for the villa, for my own business, and these had to come first."

Marina qualified as an IAP in 2014, and finished as a director at Christie's. However, since then, she has occasionally helped out at Christie's, when needed.

I ask Marina whether the villa became a holiday rental for the first time in 2014.

"No, this happened gradually. When my mother was alive, and still using the villa, we rented it out perhaps two weeks each year, just to cover some of the maintenance expenses. As my mother became older, and stopped coming to Zambonina, then we rented it out a little more. In 2014, I started investing more in the house, to make it a viable business. Since then, we have rented it out for most of the summer season, so that it could pay for itself. A house like this requires a lot of work, just to keep it intact. There is always something that requires repair. Everything we earn goes to maintaining the building, and investing in facilities for guests."

"How do you divide your time, between Rome and Zambonina?"

"I spend the winter in Rome, and I am at Zambonina from May to October. I want to be here for the clients, to ensure they have a good experience. I get involved in all sorts of ways. For example, if the cleaning team arrives at the end of the week, but one of them doesn't show up, then I join in to do the cleaning."

Then I ask Marina about her daughter, Matilde, keen to understand whether she might one day take over as owner and manager of the villa.

Matilde went to a high school in the USA, and then studied for three years at Royal Holloway University in England, which she enjoyed very much. After that she did a one-year MA in Arts and Cultural Management, at King's College in London. During the summer holidays, Matilde did voluntary work to bolster her CV, following Marina's advice. When Matilde finished her studies, aged 21, Marina helped her to find her first job, working in Milan's fashion industry. After two years there, the pandemic arrived and almost everybody worked at home. Matilde still went into the office, but she was the only one there, so it was very lonely.

Having learnt from her own experience, Marina had urged Matilde not to leave a job until she had found another one to go to. So, although Matilde hated the work, she stuck it out and stayed in post. Only when Marina visited her one day did she realise that Matilde was unhappy, because she was following her mother's advice. They agreed that Matilde would resign the next day, giving two months' notice. Immediately, the weight was lifted from her shoulders. Matilde finished working her notice period in July, and then took the rest of the summer off to think about her next steps. After a few interviews, she found another job in fashion, which she loves.

"Whenever I visit her apartment, in Milan, it's neat and tidy. However, when she comes to visit us here, within five minutes her luggage, her shoes, her things are all over the place!"

Matilde also loves the villa. As a child, she spent her summer holidays at Zambonina. Even now, she has one week at the villa with her friends, every summer. Marina is hopeful that Matilde will want to continue with Zambonina.

"I want to hand it over to her with everything perfect. Like a piece of jewellery. However, ultimately, it's her life and it's her decision to make."

This feels like a good place for us to finish, so I thank Marina for her time, and say goodbye. Travelling back to my hotel, I reflect on whether having a wealthy family has made Marina's life fundamentally different from the lives of the other Italians I've met. I don't think it has. Marina has embraced the world of work, taking on challenging roles, always learning and always growing. It hasn't been an easy road to travel. Now, as custodian of Zambonina, she carries a huge responsibility with no hint that it is a burden. It's a commitment she embraces with pleasure.

Just like all the others, whose stories I have told, Marina is guided by love. Love for her family. Love for the villa. Love for life itself.

Reflections

Nearing the top of the steep stony path, that leads from the village up to the castle, I'm slightly breathless from the exercise. At least it's not too hot. The sun already feels strong and, later in the day, this would be unpleasant. It's a little before 9am, when the castle opens, so I sit on a wall near the ticket office.

I am in Soave for two days, with the primary objective of doing laundry! Jackie and I are on a one-month road trip, and clothes need to be washed every now and then. She has returned to the UK for treatment, an intravenous infusion administered every three weeks, which reduces the chance of the cancer returning, from 85% down to 50%. Yesterday morning, she flew to London from Milan Malpensa, and tomorrow afternoon I will pick her up at Venice Marco Polo. Soave is conveniently located, near the autostrada, on the way from Malpensa to Marco Polo.

The ticket office opens, I pay the entrance fee, and a guardian lets me into the castle. As the first visitor of the day, I am treated to a guided tour by this affable gentleman, who is about my age. He is a gifted story teller, and takes me through the history of the place as we visit all the key parts of the complex. Restored in the 19th century, this 14th century fortification is in remarkably good condition and well worth a visit. It's a perfect representation of the grand medieval castle that we all have in our imaginations.

The tour finishes at the very top of the castle walls, where he leaves me and descends, to greet the next party of visitors. From these battlements, I can look down on the tiled roofs of the village. I can admire perfectly straight, neat rows of vines, etched across the hillside. I can look south to the distant horizon, the plain of the Adige valley.

What I'm actually doing is looking back, and thinking about the last two years, my conversations with Italians and the research for this book.

What have I learnt?

There is so much I didn't know about Italy, two years ago.

For example, I hadn't realised how different the Italian education system is from that in the UK. From the age of 14, Italians attend a school which is designed to prepare them for a particular type of career. There are several types of liceo, each with a different focus. Every young teenager has to make this life-shaping decision, choosing whether to concentrate on the classics, art, science, accounting, tourism, hotels & restaurants, languages, or something else.

In the UK, all schools teach broadly the same curriculum. Only when they reach the age of 16, do UK students choose three or four particular subjects to study for their final two years.

I'm sure both systems have their advantages and disadvantages, but they are certainly different. This difference reflects, and defines, the national character of each country. In the past, in Italy to a much greater extent than in the UK, the expectation was that a son would follow in the footsteps of the father. The child of a banker would become a banker, the child of a taxi driver would become a taxi driver, and so on. This is changing, and it applies to a lesser extent today, but that attitude is consistent with the idea that most children know what they want to do with their lives, and which type of schooling they need. In this respect, Italian society is fundamentally more conservative. There is a greater respect for tradition, for keeping things the way they have always been.

Also, I get the impression that an Italian is much more likely, than a British person, to meet their future spouse at school. Almost 25% of the Italians I interviewed met their future husband or wife in their schooldays.

When it comes to university, I sense Italians have a healthier attitude. The ambitious British youngster sees a university degree as almost a mandatory rite of passage. In Italy, university is something to explore, an opportunity for enrichment, and certainly not the only option. This is reflected in the statistics. The proportion of students starting a degree, but not qualifying, is 26% in Italy compared with 6% in the UK.

Looking back, at the stories in their entirety, some interesting themes emerge.

For example, migration features more than I might have expected. Many young Italians spend time living abroad, to help them work out what they want to do with their lives. Italians from the south often move to the north, in search of work. Also, immigrants to Italy play a key role in some of these stories.

One phenomenon I expected to encounter, and did, was the traditional family business, handed down from generation to generation. I discovered that the children of restaurant owners, for example, almost always help their parents in the business, from an early age. That seems to be taken for granted. However, it's relatively rare for both parents and child to automatically assume that the child will take over the business. Sometimes, the parents try to encourage their child to explore other opportunities. Sometimes the child goes off, looking for something, and takes a while to finally decide that their parents' lifestyle is really for them. In Italy today, young people have choices.

I also note that several of the stories in this book involve women, in particular, overcoming adversity. Many businesses exist only because strong women fought, against the odds, to make them succeed.

My reverie is interrupted by the arrival of a family with young children on the battlements. The kids run excitedly along the ramparts, delighted with the novelty of their situation, making it difficult for the parents to enjoy the views.

It's time to leave.

Back down in the village, I find a quiet café on the main street. Sitting outside, enjoying the coffee and the view, only one other table is occupied, by a man sitting alone. Based on something he said to the lady who served me, I deduce that he is the owner. By now, dear reader, you know me well enough to realise it is inevitable that I will strike up a conversation.

I'm surprised to learn that he is from Germany. He and his Italian wife have owned this café for almost 40 years.

"You are fortunate to live in such a pleasant village, where the people are so friendly."

"I certainly made the right decision, to move to Italy. The weather and the food are so much better, and here I see smiles on people's faces."

I tell him about my travels, and the research for the book.

"In the beginning, I tried to interview bar and café owners, but they were all so busy it was impossible to book time with them. So, I gave up on that type of establishment."

He clearly has time to sit and chat so, obviously, not all café owners are run off their feet. Immediately after this mental observation, I feel guilty, worried he might think I am implying that he is lazy. He doesn't seem to have taken offence, however.

The important lesson from this encounter, and indeed from everybody I've met, is that each person is different. There is only one thing that all the people in this book have in common, and that is their passion for what they do. In every other respect, they often differ.

Walking back to my accommodation, I start thinking about how the project has affected me. I recall something my friend Claudio said, about the book, when we met in Rome a couple of months ago.

"You know Richard, I wouldn't have the courage to do what you're doing."

I was taken aback. I'd never thought of this as requiring courage. But then I realised that I also, 10 or 15 years ago, would not have been able to do this. By nature, I'm a shy introvert. I hate the embarrassment of getting something wrong, when trying to speak a foreign language for example. I dislike making a fool of myself. Yet, for some reason, now I'm comfortable asking a complete stranger, in a language I speak badly, for an hour or two of their time.

Over the years, I have changed without even noticing.

That's fortunate, because this journey has been amazing.

Each time I start an interview, I feel like a small child unwrapping a mysterious Christmas present. I have no idea what I am about to discover, but I know it will be a pleasure. Even before I speak to them, their life choices have made these people interesting. From every conversation, I learn something new. They always have wisdom to share.

And there's something else, something expressed eloquently by Stefania Martinato: "I like that people share moments . . . that I, however briefly, become a part of their lives."

It's been a joy.

Over the years, my attitude to travel has changed. I still enjoy sightseeing, food & wine, a piazza in the sunshine. But, more and more, pleasure comes from the people I meet. This is something that Antimo Cimino recognises, and vigorously promotes. Antimo was introduced to me by his cousin Maria Giovanna Cimino and, as she predicted, we have a lot in common. His travel business, Voomago, specialises in organising trips to Italy where the emphasis is on meeting local people. That's what brings me to Italy nowadays. The people.

In fact, I would say that the last two years, the time spent developing this book, have been the most rewarding of my life.

Why?

Well, Pasquale Sorrentino summarised it perfectly.

"Friends are worth much more than money."

Printed in Great Britain
by Amazon